Psychology and Law

Psychology and Law: Truthfulness, Accuracy and Credibility

Second Edition

Amina Memon
University of Aberdeen, UK

Aldert Vrij
University of Portsmouth, UK

Ray Bull
University of Portsmouth, UK

WILEY

This publication is designed to provide accurate and authoritative information in regard to the
subject matter covered. It is sold on the understanding that the Publisher is not engaged in
rendering professional services. If professional advice or other expert assistance is required, the
services of a competent professional should be sought.

Other Wiley Editorial Offices

1006180600

John Wiley & Sons Inc., 111 River Street, Hoboken, NJ 07030, USA

Jossey-Bass, 989 Market Street, San Francisco, CA 94103-1741, USA

Wiley-VCH Verlag GmbH, Boschstr. 12, D-69469 Weinheim, Germany

John Wiley & Sons Australia Ltd, 33 Park Road, Milton, Queensland 4064, Australia

John Wiley & Sons (Asia) Pte Ltd, 2 Clementi Loop #02-01, Jin Xing Distripark, Singapore 129809

John Wiley & Sons Canada Ltd, 22 Worcester Road, Etobicoke, Ontario, Canada M9W 1L1

Wiley also publishes its books in a variety of electronic formats. Some content that appears in print
may not be available in electronic books.

Library of Congress Cataloging-in-Publication Data
Memon, Amina.
    Psychology and law : truthfulness, accuracy and credibility / Amina
Memon, Aldert Vrij, Ray Bull. – 2nd ed.
        p.   cm. – (Wiley series in psychology of crime, policing, and
law)
Includes bibliographical references and index.
    ISBN 0-470-85060-4 – ISBN 0-470-85061-2 (pbk. : alk. paper)
   1. Criminal investigation–Psychological aspects.   2. Interviewing
in law enforcement.   3. Lie detectors and detection.   4. Witnesses.   I.
Vrij, Aldert.   II. Bull, Ray.   III. Title.   IV. Series.
   HV8073.M38   2003
   363.25 – dc21

                                                    2003002099
British Library Cataloguing in Publication Data

A catalogue record for this book is available from the British Library

ISBN 0-470-85060-4 (hbk)
ISBN 0-470-85061-2 (pbk)

TABLE OF CONTENTS

ABOUT THE AUTHORS

Dr Amina Memon is a Senior Lecturer in Psychology at the University of Aberdeen. She has a first-class degree in psychology (1982) and a Ph.D. in psychology (1985). Her main areas of expertise are social and cognitive psychology. Dr Memon has published widely on topics such as the investigative interviewing of child witnesses, police interviews, face recognition, eyewitness identification, the performance of elderly witnesses, false memories and jury decision making. Between 1991 and 1997, Dr Memon conducted extensive psychological research on procedures for interviewing child witnesses for the purpose of obtaining complete and accurate witness reports. Dr Memon is co-editor (with R. Bull) of the *Handbook of the Psychology of Interviewing* (Chichester: Wiley, 1999). Her research is international, with collaborations in North America, Italy and Germany. Her current research projects include the memory of elderly witnesses, jury decision making and false memories. Dr Memon has received funds to support her research from the Economic and Social Research Council (ESRC), the National Science Foundation, the British Academy and the Royal Society.

Professor Aldert Vrij is Professor of Applied Social Psychology at the University of Portsmouth. His main area of expertise is deception, mainly the nonverbal and verbal characteristics of deception, and he has published widely on these issues. For conducting this research, he has received grants from the ESRC, the Leverhulme Trust, the Dutch Organisation of Scientific Research (the Dutch equivalent of the ESRC) and the Dutch Ministry of Justice. He gives workshops on deception to police officers in several countries on a regular basis. Other areas of research interest are eyewitness testimony, interviewing children and interviewing suspects. Regarding this latter issue, he sometimes acts as an expert witness in criminal courts. At present, Professor Vrij has published more than 200 articles and book chapters and five books.

Professor Ray Bull is Professor of Forensic Psychology at the University of Portsmouth. His main areas of expertise are police interviewing and the relationship between physical appearance and criminality, topics on which he has published extensively. He is regularly invited to present seminars and lectures to police audiences in many countries. His most recent externally funded research project was from the Innovative Research Challenge Fund of the Home Office for work on improving children's face recognition performance. Professor Bull regularly acts as an expert witness, especially concerning video-recorded interviews with children. From 1998 to 2002, he was President of the Psychology-Law Division of the International Association of Applied Psychology.

PREFACE

The first edition of *Psychology and Law* was published in spring 1998. Much of the text was written in 1995–6, and the last eight years have seen a number of important developments in research and practice in most of the areas covered in the book. The volume of new research in the psychology and law area is reflected in the launch of several new journals, including the British Psychological Society's *Legal and Criminological Psychology* and the *International Journal of Police Science and Management*. This book is based on a detailed analysis of the published research literature as well as on material published in scientific reports, on conference proceedings and on data gathered during the course of our own recent research projects. Not only is our review exhaustive, but it is also up to date so that students and researchers can have access to the latest developments in the field. Our text is directed at students and researchers interested in the forensic issues to do with gathering evidence. We present the experimental and theoretical detail that is required for scientists to be able to evaluate the research and disseminate the findings to relevant professionals.

The emphasis of the current text, like the earlier edition, is on the perceived credibility of participants in the criminal justice system (be they witnesses, suspects or victims) and factors that influence the accuracy of evidence. Chapter 2, for example, examines the nonverbal characteristics and physiological correlates of deception. Chapter 3 reviews work on criminal appearance stereotyping. Throughout the text, there is an emphasis on the usefulness of the research. Thus, in Chapter 3, we ask whether research on stereotyping may help us understand why certain people (such as innocent suspects) may be chosen more often from line-ups than other people, and why the facial appearance of defendants can influence judicial decision making. We also examine how research has influenced practice. For example, Chapter 5 surveys psychology's major contributions to improving the ways that witnesses should be interviewed. The major focus is on children and other vulnerable witnesses (such as adults with learning disabilities). The way that the results from many research studies from several different countries cohere into a set of guidelines (such as those published by the Home Office) is described.

In addition to illustrating the practical relevance of research in the psychology and law area, our text examines the strengths and weaknesses of research methods that have been used to collect data in the laboratory and the field. For example, in Chapter 8, we critically evaluate studies that have used the mock-jury paradigm. Chapter 6 assesses research on factors influencing the quality of witness evidence, and Chapter 9 considers the extent to which there is a consensus among psychologists on the variables influencing eyewitness reliability.

We are grateful to our research collaborators and students for providing us with material for this text and commenting on earlier drafts. The research reported here was supported by grants from the Dutch Organisation of Scientific Research, the Dutch Ministry of Justice, the Economic and Social Research Council, the Home Office, the Leverhulme Trust, the National Science Foundation, the British Academy and the Royal Society.

CHAPTER 1

INTRODUCTION

This text, *Psychology and Law: Truthfulness, Accuracy and Credibility*, provides a comprehensive review of relevant topics as far as determining the accuracy of a witness, victim or suspect is concerned. Each chapter not only focuses on relevant research but also presents readers with a detailed understanding of the research methodology, the theoretical perspectives, the shortcomings of the research/theory and the practical significance of the findings.

Chapter 2 examines the characteristics of liars. Nonverbal, verbal and physiological cues (such as the polygraph) to deception are described together with a discussion of what professional lie catchers believe to be cues to deception and of their ability to detect deceit. We discuss the reasons why professional lie catchers (and people in general) make mistakes while attempting to detect deceit. We also examine the social contexts in which lying occurs and people's reasons for lying. Liars are said to experience three processes during the time that they are engaging in deception (and probably afterwards, too), and much of the research literature is organised around the study of these three processes. The first is an emotional reaction (such as guilt, fear and excitement), and this can independently influence behaviour. For example, guilt may sometimes result in gaze aversion. The second is "cognitive overload" arising from the difficulty of maintaining deceitful behaviour. This can result in disturbances in speech content, gaze aversion and other behaviours. The third process is behavioural control or impression management. This can suppress the behaviours that liars believe may "give away" a lie (for example, a reduction in hand movements). We argue that behavioural cues to deception may become visible only if a liar substantially experiences at least one of these three processes. The bulk of research in this area is laboratory based. However, there are some examples of deception detection in high-stake real-life situations. For example, we describe an analysis of former US President Bill Clinton's behaviour during his testimony before the grand jury in 1998 about his alleged sexual affair with Monica Lewinsky. We also report an in-depth study of the behaviour displayed by 16 suspects who were interviewed by the police in connection with serious crimes such as murder, rape and arson (Mann, Vrij & Bull, 2002).

We end Chapter 2 by concluding that no perfect lie detection test exists, and that lie detection experts make wrong judgements on a regular basis. However, there are detection methods which enable lie detectors to determine whether someone is lying or telling the truth above the level of chance, and these may assist investigators in early stages of their investigation.

Chapter 3 explores the relationship between facial appearance and criminality, a subject that continues to fascinate students and researchers in the psychology and law area. Is there an association between facial characteristics and certain types of crime? Do members of the public hold stereotypes about the facial appearance of criminals? Are attractive people more likely to get away with crime? We divide the review into three parts. The first section of this chapter examines research on the extent to which people assume there to be a relationship between facial appearance and criminality. We review studies which suggest that facial appearance influences ratings of honesty/trustworthiness and may also affect judgements of whether a person is telling the truth (Vine & Bull, 2003).

The second part of Chapter 3 asks whether less attractive faces are thought to be more likely to be associated with crime and what would happen if these faces were made more attractive? What follows is a review of studies on the impact upon prisoners' recidivism rates of surgery designed to improve their facial appearance. These studies suggest that facial surgery is associated with a reduction in recidivism and can aid rehabilitation. There are several problems with these studies, however. First, the details of the prisoners selected for surgery and the attitudes of those who are turned down may say more about recidivism than the changes in facial appearance following surgery. Moreover, it may be that with an improved facial appearance, criminals are less likely to be caught or to be found guilty.

The latter, that is, the effects of facial appearance on "mock" jurors' judgements and in real-life court proceedings, are reviewed in the third part of Chapter 3. The early work suggests that unattractive defendants are treated more harshly, but more recent studies have failed to replicate the findings. More recent work suggests that the effect of facial appearance is likely to be moderated by other factors relevant to the judicial setting such as strength of evidence (Vrij & Firmin, 2001). There is also research to suggest that the jury deliberation process may influence mock jurors' judgements, with evaluations of the attractive defendant becoming more lenient following group discussion (MacCoun, 1990). Finally, as illustrated in the final section of Chapter 3, an examination of the role of attractiveness in real-life cases fails to support the laboratory research suggesting a simple association between attractiveness and trial outcomes. The relationship is much more complex than assumed, and the quality of the methodology and the presence of confounding variables pose problems for researchers in this area.

Chapter 4 reviews relevant theory and research on interviews with suspects, and starts with the premise that the main aim of such interviews is to elicit information that may aid a police investigation. In most of the police literature, it is assumed that suspects are likely to be guilty and uncooperative (Ofshe & Leo, 1997a). The result has been the use of a variety of techniques designed to *force* the suspect to talk (Kalbfleisch, 1994). Perhaps the best illustration is the "nine-steps approach to effective interrogation" (Inbau, Reid & Buckley, 1986), which has proved popular, especially in the USA. This approach, which is described fully in Chapter 4, relies to some extent on the use of trickery and deceit, and it has elicited much controversy about the use of unethical practices. The psychological limitations of this approach are detailed. We question the assumption that suspects are unwilling to talk. Research has shown that most suspects are willing to talk. We review research on the use of the police interview as an information-gathering tool (from cooperative suspects). For example, we review an interview procedure that places emphasis on the preparation/planning of an interview and the rapport-building and social skills of the interviewer (Baldwin, 1992). The advantages of this approach over the nine-steps procedure are described.

The final section of Chapter 4 examines why false confessions may occur with reference to real cases, and presents empirical research and theory on the conditions most likely to result in a false confession. We make a distinction between three psychologically distinct types of false confession: voluntary false confessions, coerced-compliant false confessions, and coerced-internalised false confessions. Voluntary false confessions are false confessions which are given without any external pressure from the police. Coerced-compliant confessions occur when suspects confess to something they know to be untrue as a result of pressure. Coerced-internalised false confessions occur when suspects, typically due to police tricks, are not certain that they did not commit the crime. Police persuasion makes them decide to confess. The conditions under which these different types of confession occur are discussed. The implementation of safeguards to reduce false confessions and ways of identifying vulnerable suspects are also considered.

While Chapter 4 focuses on interviews with suspects, Chapter 5 examines witness interviews with a special emphasis on child witnesses and vulnerable witnesses. Professionals in several important types of cases (such as sexual abuse) may rely heavily on the accounts of children in attempting to determine what happened and deliver justice. The last 25 years have seen a dramatic increase in psychological research on children's strengths and weaknesses as witnesses. The research has focused on children's ability to recall details of events as well as their ability to recognise accurately the faces of perpetrators in identification situations. Researchers have studied whether younger children are more vulnerable to misleading suggestions than older children and adults, and why this may be so. This literature is reviewed together with evidence on the reversed misinformation effect (the provision of misinformation prior to the witnessing of an event). The *Home Office Memorandum of Good Practice* and its successor, *Achieving Best Evidence*, are used to illustrate the impact of this research on policy in England and Wales. Issues to do with training and the conduct of interviews by professionals are also discussed. Chapter 5 also examines the small body of research on the ways in which interviewer manner can influence the conduct of interviews. Finally, there is an exhaustive review of the recent research on the interviewing of vulnerable adults (for example, those with learning disabilities and limited communication).

Chapter 6 continues with the theme of witnesses, focusing on factors influencing the quality of eyewitness evidence. The latter plays a key role in the administration of justice, and identification errors can lead to miscarriages of justice (Scheck, Neufeld & Dwyer, 2000). To address these concerns, researchers have attempted to identify the conditions under which eyewitnesses may be mistaken, and to promote safeguards to reduce the likelihood of eyewitness error. In this chapter, we review the variables that can influence eyewitness performance. We have organised our review around Wells's (1978) distinction between estimator variables (those variables over which the criminal justice system can exert little or no control) and system variables (those factors under the control of the criminal justice system). Both types of variables can be manipulated in research. Estimator variable research includes research on the age of witnesses, their physiological state at the time they witnessed the event, the length of exposure to the crime event and the presence of a weapon at the crime scene. System variable research includes work on the manner in which witnesses are questioned, instructions given to witnesses subject to a line-up or identification parade, the composition of the line-up and investigator biases. The ecological validity of eyewitness research and consensus among experts on the factors which reliably decrease or enhance witness performance are considered briefly in this chapter (a more detailed review on the latter is provided in Chapter 9).

Chapter 7 reviews evidence on the debate about the origin of "recovered memories". It reviews some of the theories about recovered memories and the methods used to study them—for example, studies of infants' memories for childhood events, clinical case studies of repression and experimental studies of retrieval inhibition. We also ask whether memories for traumatic events are any different from memories for non-traumatic events. The conditions under which false memories arise are then discussed with reference to laboratory research on the implantation of entirely "false" memories and to practices that may be used to elicit memories from clients undergoing therapy. It is argued that both the "demand characteristics" inherent in a memory-enhancing interview and the specific techniques (such as guided imagery) may increase a person's beliefs and memory reports about the occurrence of a false event (e.g., Mazzoni & Memon, in press). Moreover, it is argued that the process by which false beliefs and memories are produced may be no different from the processes by which accurate memories are retrieved (Mazzoni & Kirsch, 2003). The final section of the chapter on false memories considers how expert testimony based on scientific research can inform the courts about the reliability of recovered memories (see also Chapter 9).

Chapter 8 introduces the reader to juries as used in parts of Europe, New Zealand and North America. Empirical research on juries has focused largely on the variables that may influence the decisions of individual jurors and juries. Chapter 8 reviews the main research methods used to study jury decision making and examines the advantages and disadvantages of each approach, particularly the mock-jury paradigm. We examine the effect of juror demographics (gender, race and age), juror prejudices (pre-trial and during the trial), jury interaction and other factors on jurors' interpretation of evidence and verdicts. For example, juries are often exposed to information that is not admissible as evidence, and researchers have asked whether instructions to disregard this information can have the neutralising effect intended by the courts (Kassin & Studebaker, 1998).

Several areas of psychological research are relevant here. For instance, the cognitive psychology literature on thought suppression suggests that people find it difficult intentionally to suppress a thought upon instruction, particularly if it is emotionally salient. The harder one tries to suppress, the more difficult it can be (Wegner & Erber, 1992).

The final chapter examines some of the effects of expert witnessing, with a focus on expert testimony on the reliability of eyewitness memory. This chapter also discusses the standards for determining the admissibility of testimony, something that has been an issue for the courts, and ethical issues that may arise when giving expert testimony, particularly on sensitive issues. For example, we examine the effects of expert testimony in child abuse and rape trials. Taking expert testimony on eyewitness issues as an example, we also discuss whether or not an expert has anything useful to add to lay knowledge of variables influencing the reliability of testimony. The results of a recent survey of what experts testify about in court (Kassin et al., 2001) are presented together with a list of issues on which there is consensus among experts. Chapter 9 illustrates how the results of the psychological research reviewed in this text can be applied in legal contexts.

In this book, we have tried to focus in each chapter on how the discipline of psychology can inform the law (including policing) with reference to determining the accuracy of witnesses and suspects. It is our contention that over the last 25 years the contribution of psychology has been considerable in many countries.

CHAPTER 2

TELLING AND DETECTING LIES

This chapter reviews nonverbal, verbal and physiological cues to deception. In particular, we will discuss how liars behave, what they say, how they physiologically react and how good professional lie detectors (police detectives, polygraph examiners and so on) are at detecting truths and lies while paying attention to such cues. The chapter reveals that professional lie catchers, among others, are to some extent able to detect lies by examining behaviour, speech content or physiological reactions. However, as this chapter will also show, no perfect lie detection test exists, and lie detection experts make wrong judgements on a regular basis. We will discuss several problems and pitfalls lie detectors typically face, but we start with some background information, such as a definition of deception, the types of lie people tell, the reasons why people lie and how frequently people tell lies.

SOME CHARACTERISTICS OF DECEPTION

Definition of Deception

Elsewhere we defined deception as "a successful or unsuccessful deliberate attempt, without forewarning, to create in another a belief which the communicator considers to be untrue" (Vrij, 2000a: p. 6). Some elements of this definition are worth mentioning. First, lying (we will use the words "lying" and "deception" interchangeably) is an intentional act. Someone who does not tell the truth by mistake is not lying. A woman who mistakenly believes that she was sexually abused in her childhood and reports this to the police, has given a false report but is not lying (see also Chapter 7). Moreover, sometimes two witnesses give different accounts of the event they have witnessed. This does not necessarily mean that one of the two witnesses is lying. It might well be that (at least) one witness misremembers the event (see also Chapter 6). Second, people are lying only when they do not inform others in advance about their intentions to lie (Ekman, 1992). Magicians are therefore not lying during their performance, as people in the audience expect to be deceived. Third, a lie has been defined solely from the perspective of the deceiver (Vrij, 2002). That is, a statement is a lie if deceivers believe what they say is untrue, regardless of whether the statement is actually false. Strictly speaking, even an actual truth could be a lie. Suppose that a child and his friend have eaten all the biscuits in the open pack and, unknown to the mother, have also eaten those in the pack from the cupboard. When he asks for a new pack to be opened, his mother, in an effort to prevent him from eating too much, tells him that he cannot have more because there are no packs left in the cupboard. This truthful statement is a lie as long as the mother believes that there is a pack left. Fourth, people sometimes fool themselves, a process which is called self-deception. People can ignore or deny the seriousness of several bodily symptoms, such as a severe pain in the chest during physical exertion. According to the definition, deception is an act which involves at least two people. This definition therefore excludes self-deception.

Types of Lie

DePaulo et al. (1996) distinguished between outright lies, exaggerations and subtle lies. Outright lies (also referred to as falsifications) are lies in which the information conveyed is completely different from or contradictory to what the deceiver believes is the truth. A guilty suspect who assures the police that he has not committed the crime is telling an outright lie.

Exaggerations are lies in which the facts are overstated or information is conveyed that exceeds the truth. For example, suspects can embellish their remorse for committing a crime during a police interview.

Subtle lying involves literal truths that are designed to mislead. The former president of the USA, Bill Clinton, was telling such a lie in 1998 when he said to the American people that he "did not have sexual relations with that woman, Miss Lewinsky". The lie was subtle, because the statement implied that nothing of a sexual nature had happened between them, whereas he was relying on the narrower definition by which they did not have sexual intercourse. Another type of subtle lying involves concealing information by evading the question or omitting relevant details. Passengers who tell customs officers what is in their luggage are concealing information if they deliberately fail to mention that they also have illegal drugs in the luggage.

Reasons to Lie

People lie for at least five reasons (Vrij, 2000a, 2002). People lie in order to obtain personal advantage. Sometimes, business people conceal the true financial state of their companies in order not to deter shareholders. People lie in order to avoid punishment. Guilty suspects sometimes lie about their involvement in the crime during police interviews to avoid a possible conviction. People lie to make a positive impression on others or to protect themselves from embarrassment or disapproval. Sometimes people do not wish to admit they have made a stupid mistake.

The lies mentioned so far are self-oriented, and are intended to make the liar appear better or to gain personal advantage (DePaulo et al., 1996). People also lie to make others appear better, or lies are told for another person's benefit. An innocent mother may tell the police that she committed the crime in order to save her guilty son from a conviction (see Chapter 4). Such a lie is other-oriented. Unsurprisingly, many other-oriented lies are told to people to whom the liar feels close and are meant to protect people to whom the liar feels close (Bell & DePaulo, 1996). Finally, people may lie for the sake of social relationships. Goffman (1959) pointed out that life is like a theatre and that people often act as actors and put on a show. Conversations could become awkward and unnecessarily rude, and social interactions could easily become disturbed if people told each other the truth all the time ("I didn't like the food you prepared", "I don't like the present you gave me", and so on). Social relationships may depend upon people paying each other compliments now and again. Most people will probably appreciate it when others make positive comments about their latest haircut. Making deceptive but flattering remarks might therefore benefit mutual relations. Social lies serve both self-interest and the interest of others. For example, liars may be pleased with themselves when they please other people, or might tell a lie to avoid an awkward situation or discussion.

Frequency of Lying

Lying is a fact of everyday life. In an American diary study (DePaulo et al., 1996), 77 college students and 70 community members kept records of all the lies they told during one week. College students reported telling two lies a day, and community members told one lie a day. Most lies were self-serving.

The frequency of lying depends on several factors, such as the personality of the liar, the situation in which the lie is told and the people to whom the lie is told. Regarding personality, extraverts lie more often than introverts (Kashy & DePaulo, 1996). However, instead of labelling introverts as "honest", we often label them as "socially awkward", perhaps because they are honest and tell fewer social lies. Although no gender differences have been found in the frequency of lying, men and women tell different types of lies, women telling more social lies (DePaulo & Bell, 1996; DePaulo et al., 1996). This might be a reason why both men and women appreciate conversations with women more than conversations with men (DePaulo, Epstein & Wyer, 1993; Reis, Senchak & Solomon, 1985). Gender differences also emerged in the types of lies that men and women told during a date (Eyre, Read & Millstein, 1997; Tooke & Camire, 1991). Women more frequently engaged in deceptive acts to improve their physical appearance (for example "sucking in" their stomach when around members of the other sex), whereas men tended to exaggerate their earning potential (that is, they misled members of the opposite sex about their career success).

Regarding this situation, Rowatt, Cunningham and Druen (1998) found that 90% of participants admitted to being willing to tell a lie to a prospective date. DePaulo and Kashy (1998) also found that people lied relatively often to their romantic partners in the early stages of their relationship. One possible explanation is that people wondered whether their "true self" was lovable enough to attract and keep these partners, and they therefore presented themselves as they wished they were instead of how they actually were (DePaulo & Kashy, 1998). Robinson, Shepherd and Heywood (1998) interviewed undergraduate students, 83% of whom said they would lie in order to get a job. These students said that it was wrong to lie to best friends, but they saw nothing wrong in lying if this secured a job. They also thought that employers expected candidates to exaggerate qualities when applying.

Regarding the issue of to whom the lie is told, DePaulo and Kashy (1998) found that the lowest rate of lying occurred in conversations with spouses, while the highest rate occurred with strangers. However, the results demonstrated that deception occurs in all types of close personal relationships. Although participants said they were predominantly honest in social interactions with their spouses, lies still occurred in nearly one out of every ten interactions they had with them. Many of those lies were minor, but interactions with spouses are also the domain of serious lies. When people were asked to describe the most serious lie they had ever told to someone else, they overwhelmingly reported that the targets of these lies were romantic partners (Anderson, Ansfield & DePaulo, 1999). These lies were often told to cover serious issues, such as infidelities, and were told to save the relationship. Sometimes spouses believe that the truth cannot be told without threatening the relationship. In such instances, they may decide that telling a lie is preferable. They perhaps do so reluctantly. They often feel uncomfortable while lying to their spouses (DePaulo & Kashy, 1998), but in their view it is the best option they have in those circumstances.

One reason why people lie less to their romantic partners (and also to friends) than to strangers is that they have a desire to be honest to people they feel close to, but there are also other reasons (Anderson, Ansfield & DePaulo, 1999). The fact that friends and partners know more about us limits the topics that are suitable or "safe" to lie about. We can try to impress strangers at a cocktail party by exaggerating our culinary skills, but this is ineffective with friends who have experienced our cooking. So, we might lie less to people we know well because we may think that we will not get away with deceit.

People tell different lies to their romantic partners than to people they know less well. Metts (1989) found that people are much less likely to tell outright lies to their romantic partners. They believe that the risks are too high and that the partner will eventually find out that they are lying. Moreover, they expect problems as soon as the outright lie is detected, because liars may find it difficult to justify the fact that they lied to their partner, without appearing untrustworthy. Lies told to spouses are therefore usually subtle lies such as concealments (Metts, 1989). These are usually difficult to detect, because the liar does not reveal information that can be checked. The lie is also easier to justify when the truth emerges. The liars could just say that they simply forgot to mention a specific detail, or did not consider it important enough to bring up, and so on.

Although people tend to lie less to those with whom they feel close, there are exceptions. For example, a consistent finding is that college students lie frequently to their mothers (Backbier & Sieswerda, 1997; DePaulo & Kashy, 1998; Lippard, 1988). DePaulo and Kashy (1998) found that students lie in almost half of the conversations they had with their mothers. Perhaps they are still dependent on their mothers (for example, financially) and sometimes have to lie in order to secure monetary resources. Another explanation is that they do not want their mothers to worry or disapprove of them. They therefore tell their mothers that they do not drink much beer, that they attend all lectures, that they study hard for their exams and that they regularly clean their room.

So far, this chapter has demonstrated the complicated role of lying in daily interactions. The conventional view that lying is necessarily bad is not true, and telling the truth all the time is not always desirable. However, some lies are not desirable and may have serious consequences. Lying under oath in court (perjury) is a criminal act which might lead to imprisonment, as Jonathan Aitken and Jeffrey Archer (two former British Conservative politicians) discovered. In many Western European countries, police officers are not allowed to lie to suspects in police interviews. If they do so, they risk that the evidence obtained during the interview will be ruled inadmissible in court (Milne & Bull, 1999; see also Chapter 4).

There are, in principle, three different ways to catch liars. The first is to observe their nonverbal behaviour (body movements, smiling, eye contact, voice pitch, speech rate, stuttering and so on). The second is to analyse the content of what they say. The third is to examine their physiological responses (blood pressure, heart rate, sweating of the fingers and so on). These three aspects will now be reviewed.

NONVERBAL BEHAVIOUR AND DECEPTION

DePaulo et al. (2003) and Vrij (2000a) have reviewed the literature regarding nonverbal indicators of deception. In total, more than 100 studies were reviewed. Both reviews revealed similar findings, one of the most striking of which was that a typical nonverbal response during deception does not exist. In other words, there is no give-away cue such as Pinocchio's growing nose. However, some nonverbal cues are more likely to occur during deception than others, depending on three processes that a liar may experience: emotion, content complexity and attempted behavioural control (DePaulo, Stone & Lassiter, 1985a; Vrij, 2000a; Zuckerman, DePaulo & Rosenthal, 1981). Each of these three processes may elicit specific behavioural responses. The distinction between them is artificial. Lies may well feature in all three, and the three processes should not be considered as opposing camps.

Emotions

Telling a lie might evoke emotions. The three most common types of emotion associated with deceit are guilt, fear and duping delight (Ekman, 1992). Liars might feel guilty because they are lying, might be afraid of getting caught or might be excited about having the opportunity to fool someone. The strength of these emotions depends on the personality of the liar and on the circumstances under which the lie takes place (Ekman, 1992). Guilt, fear and excitement may (independently) influence a liar's behaviour. Guilt might result in gaze aversion because the liar does not feel able to look the deceived person straight in the eye while telling a lie. Fear and excitement might result in signs of arousal, such as an increase in limb movements (movements of arms, hands, fingers, legs and feet), an increase in speech fillers (pauses in speech filled with "ah", "um", "er" and so on), speech errors (word and/or sentence repetition, sentence change, sentence incompletions, slips of the tongue and so on), facial emotional expressions (expressions of fear, anger, disgust, etc.) or a higher pitched voice.

Content Complexity

Sometimes lying can be difficult, as liars have to think of plausible answers, avoid contradicting themselves, tell a lie that is consistent with everything which the observer knows or might find out, and avoid making slips of the tongue. Moreover, liars have to remember what they have said, so that they can be consistent when asked to repeat their story. People engaged in cognitively complex tasks make more speech fillers and speech errors, pause more and wait longer before giving an answer (Goldman-Eisler, 1968). Cognitive complexity also leads to fewer limb movements and to more gaze aversion. The decrease in limb movements is due to the fact that a greater cognitive load results in a neglect of body language, reducing overall animation (Ekman & Friesen, 1972). Gaze aversion (usually to a motionless point) occurs because looking at the conversation partner distracts from thought. It is easy to examine the impact of content complexity on movements and gaze aversion. Ask people what they ate three days ago, and observe their behaviour while they try to remember. Most people will look away and will sit still while thinking about the answer.

Attempted Behavioural Control

Liars may worry that several cues will give their lies away; therefore, they will try to suppress such signs and might engage in "impression management" (Krauss, 1981) in order to avoid getting caught. That is, they may try to give a convincing impression. Most people lie less frequently than they tell the truth. This makes lying a special event which merits special attention. While lying, people may worry about the impression they make on others; they may be keen on making an impression of being honest, perhaps even more so than when they are telling the truth. Someone who smuggles contraband is probably keener to make an honest impression on customs officers than someone who is not smuggling. It will not harm the non-smuggler when a customs officer asks her to open her suitcase. She might be annoyed about the time delay and inconvenience it causes, but other than that, there are no negative consequences. The smuggler, however, will be in trouble when a customs officer wants to check his luggage.

Making an honest and convincing impression is not easy. It requires suppressing nerves effectively, masking evidence of heightened cognitive load, knowledge of how an honest person normally behaves and the ability to show the behaviour that is required. Hocking and Leathers (1980) argued that liars' attempts to control their behaviour focus on the cultural stereotype of deceptive behaviour. For example, if there is a widespread belief that liars look away, increase their movements and stutter, liars will try to maintain eye contact, refrain from making too many movements and speak fluently. When people try to do this, they sometimes tend to overcontrol themselves, resulting in behaviour that looks rehearsed and rigid, and speech that sounds too smooth (with few stutters) as a result (DePaulo & Kirkendol, 1989).

Another effect of inadequate control of behaviour is that performances may look contrived due to a lack of involvement (DePaulo et al., 2003). An artist who applies for a job as salesperson because he needs the money may not look enthusiastic enough about the job opportunity during the selection interview. A mother who punishes her child for wrongdoing might not look sincere enough if she, in fact, was amused by the trick played on her.

The three processes (emotions, content complexity and attempted behavioural control) are hypothetical and are typically introduced post hoc to explain verbal and nonverbal differences between liars and truth tellers (DePaulo et al., 1985a; Miller & Stiff, 1993; Zuckerman et al., 1981). However, there is evidence that liars actually experience the three processes when they lie. In one of our experiments, participants were asked either to lie or to tell the truth (Vrij, Semin & Bull, 1996). Afterwards they were asked to what extent they had experienced the three processes. Results showed that liars experienced all three processes significantly more than truth tellers. We have also found individual differences in the experiencing of these processes (Vrij, Edward & Bull, 2001c). For example, a negative correlation was found between being good at acting and having to think hard while lying. Although these studies were correlational studies, the relationship between the three processes and lying is more likely to be causal: experiencing the processes is the result of being engaged in lying.

The fact that deception in itself does not affect someone's behaviour, but that behavioural indicators of deception are in reality signs of emotion, content complexity and attempted behaviour control, implies that behavioural cues to deception may become visible only if a liar experiences one of these three processes. That is, when liars do not experience any fear, guilt or excitement (or any other emotion), when the lie is not difficult to fabricate and when liars do not attempt to control their behaviour, behavioural cues to deception are unlikely to occur. Most lies in everyday life fall into this category (DePaulo et al., 1996), and are therefore unlikely to reveal any behavioural signs. This may be why false beliefs (e.g., misremembering an event) are difficult to detect because here people are not afraid of getting caught (they do not try to hide something), do not experience cognitive load (they have clear, although mistaken, memories of what happened) and do not try hard to make an honest impression (there is no need to, as they believe that they are telling the truth). This may be one reason why jurors "overbelieve" eyewitnesses (see also Chapter 6).

Nonverbal Cues to Deceit

The literature reviews mentioned above (DePaulo et al., 2003; Vrij, 2000a) have revealed that four behaviours in particular are more likely to occur during deception than while telling the truth (see also Table 2.1): a higher pitched voice,

Table 2.1 Nonverbal and verbal indicators of deception

	During deception
Nonverbal	
High pitch of voice	>
Speech errors	>
Illustrators	<
Hand/finger movements	<
Verbal	
Unstructured production	<
Logical structure	<
Quantity of detail	<
Contextual embeddings	<
Description of interactions	<
Reproduction of speech	<
Unusual details	<
Spontaneous corrections	<
Admitting lack of memory	<

< occurs less often during deception; > occurs more often during deception.
Source: Adapted from Vrij (2000a).

an increase in speech errors (in particular, an increase in word and phrase repetitions), a decrease in illustrators (hand and arm movements designed to modify and/or supplement what is being said verbally) and a decrease in hand/finger movements (movements of hands or fingers without moving the arms). These findings provide support for all three processes. The increase in pitch of voice might be the result of arousal experienced by liars (Ekman, Friesen & Scherer, 1976). However, differences in pitch between liars and truth tellers are usually very small and therefore only detectable with sophisticated equipment. Commercial companies have exploited this idea and brought several voice analysers on the market which, they say, can be used to detect deceit. However, these analysers are not as accurate as many companies claim them to be. Issues such as "the Othello error", "countermeasures" and the failure to make "adequate comparisons" (all discussed below) hamper the accuracy of such analyses. The increase in speech errors might be the result of liars having to think hard about their answer (there is some evidence that the increase in speech errors particularly occurs in complex lies [Vrij, 2000a]) and/or might be caused by nervousness. The decrease in illustrators and hand/finger movements during deception might be the result of lie complexity, in that liars experience cognitive load, resulting in a neglect of body language. Another explanation is that liars, in an effort to make an honest impression, move very deliberately and try to avoid movements that are not strictly essential, resulting in an unusual degree of rigidity and inhibition.

Perhaps a surprising finding is that liars do not seem to show clear signs of nervousness, such as gaze aversion and fidgeting. At least in white, Western cultures, there is a strong stereotypical belief among observers, including professional lie catchers, that liars look away and make grooming gestures (Akehurst et al., 1996; Strömwall & Granhag, 2003; Taylor & Vrij, 2000; Vrij & Semin, 1996; Vrij & Taylor, 2003). Particularly popular in this respect is the claim, derived from neurolinguistic programming, that specific eye movements ("looking up to the left indicates truth telling and looking up and to the right or staring straight ahead indicates lying") are related to deception (Hess, 1997; Leo, 1996a). However, there is no empirical evidence that liars make these types of eye movements (Vrij & Lochun, 1997). In the "incorrect beliefs" section below, we discuss some reasons why people hold incorrect beliefs about nonverbal cues to deception and the consequences of such beliefs on lie detection.

In fact, Table 2.1 suggests that the face does not reveal any information about deception. However, Ekman's (1992) work has shown that this may not be true. Lies may result in fraudulent facial emotional expressions called "microexpressions". Ekman (1992) suggested that observing emotional micro-expressions in the face might reveal valuable information about deception. Strongly felt emotions almost automatically activate muscle actions in the face. Anger, for example, results in a narrowing of the lips and lowering of the eyebrows. Eyebrows which are raised and pulled together, and a raised upper eyelid and tensed lower eyelid typically result from fear, and joy activates muscles which pull the lip corners up, bag the skin below the eyes and produce crow's-feet wrinkles beyond the eye corners. A person that denies an emotional state which is actually being felt will have to suppress these facial expressions. Thus, if a scared person claims not to be afraid, that person has to suppress the facial microexpressions which typically relate to fear. This is difficult, especially because these emotions can arise unexpectedly. For instance, people usually do not deliberately choose to become frightened—this happens automatically as a result of a particular event that takes place, or as the result of a particular thought. The moment fright occurs, a fearful facial expression may be shown that may give the lie away. People are usually able to suppress these expressions within a quarter of a second after they begin to appear (Ekman, 1992). This is fast, and they can easily be missed by an observer (in fact, observers who blink at the moment the expression occurs will miss it).

The opposite can occur as well. Someone can pretend to experience a particular emotion, whereas, in fact, this emotion is not felt. People can pretend to be angry, whereas in reality they are not angry at all. In order to be convincing, liars should produce an angry facial expression; that is, they should try to narrow their lips. However, this muscle action is very difficult for most people to make voluntarily (Ekman, 1992).

It is also difficult to fake an emotion other than the one which is actually felt. For instance, an adulterous husband may become scared during a conversation with his wife when he realises she knows something about his affair, but can decide to mask this emotional state by pretending to be angry with his wife because she apparently does not trust him. In order to be convincing, he therefore has to suppress his fearful facial expression and replace it with an angry facial expression. This is difficult, because he has to lower his eyebrows (sign of anger) whereas his eyebrows naturally tend to raise (sign of fear) (Ekman, 1992).

Reasons for the Absence of Nonverbal Indicators of Deception

Some scholars have provided explanations why nonverbal indicators of deceit are often not found in deception research (Vrij, 2000a), including the following two important reasons. First, truth tellers may show similar behaviour to liars, because they, too, may experience emotions, may have to think hard or may try to control themselves. For example, innocent (truthful) suspects might be anxious during police interviews because they might be worried that they will not be believed by a police detective (Ofshe & Leo, 1997a). They then may show the same nervous behaviours as guilty suspects who are afraid of being caught, because the "fear of not being believed when truth telling" and "fear of getting caught in a lie" will produce the same behaviours (Bond & Fahey, 1987).

Second, the absence of significant findings might be the result of an artefact. Deception research has almost exclusively been conducted in university laboratories, where the participants (mostly college students) tell the truth or lie for the sake of the experiment. Perhaps, in these laboratory studies, the stakes are not high enough for the liar to exhibit clear cues to deception (Miller & Stiff, 1993).

In order to raise the stakes in laboratory experiments, participants have been offered money if they successfully get away with their lies (Feeley & deTurck, 1995; Vrij, 1995a). In other studies, participants are told that they will be observed by a peer who will judge their sincerity (DePaulo, Stone & Lassiter, 1985b). In an attempt to raise the stakes even further, participants in Frank and Ekman's (1997) study were given the opportunity to "steal" $50. If they could convince the interviewer that they had not taken the money, they could keep all of it. If they took the money and the interviewer judged them to be lying, they had to give the $50 back and also lost their $10 per hour participation fee. Moreover, some participants faced an additional punishment if they were found to be lying. They were told that they would have to sit on a cold, metal chair inside a cramped, darkened room labelled ominously XXX, where they would have to endure anything from 10 to 40 randomly sequenced, 110-decibel blasts of white noise over the course of one hour.

Even though no participants actually had to experience this punishment, a study like this should raise ethical concerns. One might also argue that the stakes in such a study are still not comparable with the stakes in some real-life situations, such as police interviews. Laboratory studies are not suitable for examining the responses in high-stake situations, as raising the stakes to a comparable extent is not usually possible for ethical reasons. Therefore, the only way to investigate how liars behave in high-stake, real-life situations is to examine their behavioural responses in such situations. Such research has proved to be very difficult to achieve; as a result, behavioural examinations of real-life, high-stake situations are virtually non-existent. In particular, researchers face three problems.

First, it is difficult to obtain video footage of high-stake situations for research purposes. For example, researchers are rarely given permission to analyse videotaped recordings of police interviews with suspects.

Second, it is often difficult in real-life cases to establish the "ground truth"; that is, to obtain conclusive evidence that the person is lying or telling the truth. President Saddam Hussein of Iraq was interviewed by the journalist Peter Arnett from the Cable News Network (CNN) during the Gulf War (1991). The interview was broadcast on CNN. To avoid their destruction by Allied forces, Iraqi planes were sent to neighbouring Iran. Arnett asked questions about the Iraqi planes landing in Iran and whether they would return to Iraq for use. Hussein replied, "There isn't one single Islamic country that is not on our side in this battle." Davis and Hadiks (1995) believe that at that moment Hussein was fabricating an answer. However, there is no conclusive evidence for this. Hirsch and Wolf (1999) examined how former US President Bill Clinton behaved during his testimony before the grand jury in 1998 about his alleged sexual affair with Monica Lewinsky. Again, there is no conclusive evidence whether and, if so, exactly when Clinton was lying during that testimony.

Third, to examine cues to deception, a useful method might be to compare the response under investigation with a response the lie detector knows to be truthful (the "baseline method"; Vrij, 2001). However, the two situations (the situation under investigation and the responses while telling the truth) should be comparable. For example, Clinton showed specific behaviour when asked about Betty Currie, his personal secretary at that time (Vrij, 2002). For example, he showed rigid behaviour and looked straight into the camera. Why did he do that? Because he was lying? Or did this particular question trigger a specific behavioural response? This latter explanation cannot be ruled out. Davis and Hadiks' (1995) observations revealed that Saddam Hussein used a variety of hand and arm movements, and that he made specific illustrators when discussing certain issues. In summary, certain situations sometimes result in specific behaviours. Lie detectors should be aware of this and should compare situations which are similar to avoid comparing apples with oranges. We shall return to this issue later in the "adequate comparisons" section.

In the most comprehensive study of examinations of behaviour in real-life, high-stake situations to date, Mann, Vrij and Bull (2002) examined the behaviour displayed by 16 suspects during their police interviews. The suspects were all being interviewed in connection with serious crimes such as murder, rape and arson. Regarding the ground truth, video clips were selected where other sources (reliable witness statements and forensic evidence) provided evidence that the suspect lied or told the truth. In addition, for each suspect, truths and lies were chosen which were as comparable as possible in nature (for example, a suspect who gave a detailed description of how he had assisted in killing a person (truth), later denied any involvement in the crime (lie). Forensic evidence indisputably supported his original version). The results revealed that the suspects in these high-stake situations did not clearly show stereotypical nervous behaviours, such as gaze aversion, increased speech disturbances (speech fillers such as "ah", "um", "er" and stutters) or increased movements. In fact, they exhibited an increase in pauses and (male suspects) a decrease in hand and arm movements. This is more in agreement with the content complexity and attempted control approaches than with the emotional approach. The strongest evidence that content complexity affected suspects' behaviour more than nervousness was the finding regarding eye blinks. Suspects made fewer eye blinks when they lied. Research has shown that nervousness results in an increase in eye blinking (Harrigan & O'Connell, 1996), whereas increased cognitive load results in a decrease in eye blinking (Wallbott & Scherer, 1991).

The apparent predominance of cognitive load processes compared to emotional processes in suspect interviews is perhaps not surprising. Many suspects have had regular contact with the police. Therefore, they are probably familiar with police interviews, a fact which might decrease their nervousness during those interviews. However, suspects in police interviews are often less intelligent than the average person (Gudjonsson, 1992). There is evidence that less intelligent people will have particular difficulty in inventing plausible and convincing stories (Ekman & Frank, 1993).

VERBAL BEHAVIOUR AND DECEPTION:
CRITERIA-BASED CONTENT ANALYSIS

Research into verbal cues to deception is less extensive than research on nonverbal indicators. Most research during the last decade has concentrated on testing the validity of criteria-based content analysis (CBCA), a list of 19 verbal criteria expected to be present more often in truthful statements than in deceptive accounts. Trained coders analyse written transcripts and score the strength of presence of each of 19 criteria, typically on rating scales ranging from (0) absent to (2) strongly present. The underlying assumption of CBCA is that the higher the CBCA score, the more likely it is that the statement is truthful. CBCA is the core part of statement validity assessment (SVA), a procedure which consists of three phases: (i) a specific interview procedure to obtain a statement from the interviewee (see Memon & Bull, 1999; Milne & Bull, 1999; and Chapter 5 for information about what constitutes a properly conducted interview), (ii) coding of the transcribed statement using the CBCA procedure, and (iii) an evaluation of the CBCA outcomes.

Unlike analyses of nonverbal behaviour, which, to our knowledge, are never accepted as evidence in criminal courts, SVAs are accepted as evidence in some US criminal courts (Honts, 1994; Ruby & Brigham, 1997) and in criminal courts in several Western European countries, such as Sweden (Gumpert & Lindblad, 1999), Germany (Köhnken, 2002) and the Netherlands (Lamers-Winkelman & Buffing, 1996). Statement analysis originated in Germany and Sweden to determine the credibility of child witnesses' testimonies in trials for sexual offences. Some researchers, however, advocate the additional use of the technique to evaluate the testimonies of adults who talk about issues other than sexual abuse (Köhnken et al., 1995; Porter & Yuille, 1996; Ruby & Brigham, 1997; Steller & Köhnken, 1989). Their view is supported by research findings (Vrij, 2000a). Detailed descriptions of the SVA procedure have been published elsewhere (Köhnken & Steller, 1988; Raskin & Esplin, 1991; Raskin & Steller, 1989; Raskin & Yuille, 1989; Steller, 1989; Steller & Boychuk, 1992; Steller & Köhnken, 1989; Vrij, 2000a; Yuille, 1988). Vrij (2000a) reviewed the CBCA literature and found that several of the 19 criteria do discriminate between liars and truth tellers. These criteria are presented in Table 2.1. However, it should be emphasised that, similar to nonverbal indicators of deception, there is no typical verbal response (Pinocchio's growing nose) to deception either, and the verbal cues listed in Table 2.1 are only less likely to occur in deceptive statements than truthful statements.

The same three theoretical processes which are suggested to be responsible for nonverbal cues to deception (emotion, cognitive load and attempted behavioural control) are thought to underpin these verbal cues as well. Regarding emotion, truth tellers sometimes tell their stories in an unstructured manner (unstructured production), especially when they are upset (Littmann & Szewczyk, 1983; Winkel et al., 1991). For example, someone may start by explaining the core of the event ("My money has been stolen, I've been robbed"), may then start at the beginning

("I was in the shop, and put my purse back in my bag after I had paid"), may then give information about events that happened later ("The guy ran so quickly, I could not follow him"), may go back to the beginning ("I must have left my bag open") and so on.

Several other criteria occur less often in deceptive reports because of cognitive difficulties. As a result, deceptive accounts are sometimes incoherent and inconsistent (logical structure), provided in a chronological time order (structured production) and include fewer details (quantity of detail) than truthful accounts. Regarding details, accounts which are truthful are more likely to include contextual embeddings (references to time and space: "He approached me for the first time in the garden during the summer holidays"), descriptions of interactions ("The moment my mother came into the room, he stopped smiling"), reproduction of speech (speech in its original form: "And then he asked: 'Is that your coat?'") and unusual details (details which are uncommon; for example, a witness who describes that the man she met had a stutter).

Some criteria are more likely to occur in truthful statements for motivational reasons. Truthful persons will not be as much concerned with impression management as deceivers. Deceivers will be more keen than truth tellers to try to construct a report which they believe will make a credible impression on others, and will leave out information which, in their view, will damage their image of being a sincere person (Köhnken, 1999). As a result, a truthful statement is more likely to contain information that is inconsistent with the stereotypes of truthfulness. Two of these "contrary-to-truthfulness-stereotype" criteria (term adapted from Ruby & Brigham, 1998) are spontaneous corrections (corrections made without prompting from the interviewer ("He wore black trousers—no, sorry, they were green") and admitting lack of memory ("I know I saw him but I can't remember the colour of his shirt")).

PHYSIOLOGICAL REACTIONS AND DECEPTION: THE POLYGRAPH

Throughout history, it has been assumed that the act of lying is accompanied by physiological activity within the liar's body. For example, the Chinese used to force suspected liars to chew rice powder and then spit it out. If the resultant powder was dry, the person was judged to have been lying (Kleinmuntz & Szucko, 1984).

The modern way of detecting physiological activity in liars is by using a "polygraph" (the term is derived from two Greek words, "poly", meaning "many", and "grapho", meaning "to write"). This is a scientific measuring device which can display, via ink pens onto charts, or via a computer's visual display unit, a direct and valid representation of various types of bodily activity (Bull, 1988). The most commonly measured activities are sweating of the fingers, blood pressure and respiration (Ben-Shakhar & Furedy, 1990). The polygraph accurately records even very small differences by amplifying signals picked up from sensors attached to different parts of the body. In the typical use of the polygraph, four sensors are attached to the subject. Pneumatic gauges are stretched around the person's chest and stomach in order to measure changes in the depth and rate of breathing. A blood-pressure cuff placed around the bicep measures changes in blood pressure, and metal electrodes attached to the fingers measure sweating.

The polygraph measures physiological activity and can record changes in these activities associated with arousal. It is assumed that liars will be more aroused than truth tellers. This may be the result of feeling guilty, or, in the polygraph context, more likely, because examinees will be afraid that the polygraph will detect their lies.

Polygraph tests are currently used in criminal investigations in countries all over the world, including Canada, Israel, Japan, South Korea, Mexico, Pakistan, the Philippines, Taiwan, Thailand and the USA (Lykken, 1998). In the UK, polygraph trials were recently conducted (with sex offenders) to establish the possible benefits of employing the technique (Wilcox, Sosnowski & Middleton, 2000). In most countries, however, the use of the polygraph is limited, except in the USA, where many polygraph tests take place (Barland, 1988). In the USA polygraph tests are mostly used in criminal and forensic investigation, and security screening (Gale, 1988). The Polygraph Protection Act (introduced in 1988) has limited the use in the USA of polygraph tests for personnel screening. Outcomes of polygraph tests are sometimes used as evidence in court in criminal cases in the USA (Honts & Perry, 1992), although not in all US states (Patrick & Iacono, 1991). (See Faigman et al., 1997, for a review of the history and current legal status of polygraph evidence in the USA.)

The use of the polygraph is the subject of lively debate. Two leading scientific polygraph researchers, David Raskin and David Lykken, have engaged for several decades in prolonged controversy over the reliability and validity of various polygraph tests. They have come into conflict in the scientific literature, and as expert witnesses in court. More recently, others, such as Furedy and Iacono (Lykken camp) and Honts (Raskin camp), have taken over the Lykken–Raskin dispute (Furedy, 1993, 1996a,b; Honts, Kircher & Raskin, 1996; Iacono & Lykken, 1997).

There are several types of polygraph tests. The Control Question Test (CQT) is the test most commonly used in criminal investigations. This is also the test on which supporters and opponents of polygraph testing generally disagree. Some important criticisms are discussed below (see the "Othello Error", "Adequate Comparisons" and "Countermeasures" sections below, and see Vrij, 2000a, for more criticisms). Another test is the Guilty Knowledge Test (GKT). Although Iacono and Lykken's (1997) survey of scientific opinion about CQT and GKT polygraph testing revealed that the GKT is less disputed than the CQT, it is used less often, as it is believed that this test is not always applicable. We will discuss both tests in this chapter, but see Ben-Shakhar and Furedy (1990), Carroll (1991), Lykken (1959, 1960, 1991, 1998), MacLaren (2001), Raskin (1979, 1982, 1986) and Vrij (2000a) for more comprehensive discussion of both test procedures.

People sometimes call a polygraph a "lie detector", but this term is misleading. A polygraph does not detect lies, but only the arousal which may accompany telling a lie. As was the case with nonverbal behaviour and verbal behaviour, Pinocchio's growing nose—in physiological terms, a pattern of physiological activity directly related to lying—does not exist (Saxe, 1991).

The CQT

The CQT compares responses to relevant questions with responses to control questions. Relevant questions are specific questions about the crime. A relevant question in a murder investigation could be this: "On March 12, did you shoot Scott Fisbee?" (Iacono & Patrick, 1997). Control questions deal with acts that are related to the crime under investigation, but do not refer to the crime in question. They are general in nature, deliberately vague, and cover long periods of time. They are meant to embarrass the suspects (both guilty and innocent) and to evoke arousal. This is facilitated by, on the one hand, giving the suspect no choice but to lie when answering the control questions, and, on the other hand, making it clear to the suspect that the polygraph will detect this lie. Examiners formulate a control question for which, in their view, a denial is deceptive. The exact formulation of the question will depend on the examinee's circumstances, but a control question in an examination regarding a murder might be as follows: "Have you ever tried to hurt someone to get revenge?" (Iacono & Patrick, 1997), where the examiner believes that the examinee (that is, the suspect or whoever else is being evaluated) did indeed hurt someone.

Under normal circumstances, some examinees might admit this wrongdoing. However, during a polygraph examination, they will not do this, because the examiner will tell the examinee that admitting this would cause the former to conclude that the examinee is the type of person who would commit the crime in question and may therefore be considered guilty. Therefore, the examinee has no other choice than to deny this earlier wrongdoing and thus to be untruthful in answering the control questions. Obviously, there is no way that an examinee can be found guilty of a crime by answering control questions untruthfully. In this respect, the examiner's statements are deceptive, a fact which makes the test illegal in many European countries, including the UK, where it is forbidden to lie to suspects.

The CQT is based on the assumption that control questions will generate more arousal than the relevant questions in the innocent suspect. This is because, first, the innocent suspect gives deceptive responses to the control questions but honest responses to the relevant questions.

Second, because (i) the examiner puts so much emphasis on the control questions to which examinees will respond deceptively, and because (ii) examinees know they are answering the relevant questions truthfully, they will become more concerned with regard to their answers to the control questions. However, in guilty suspects, the same control questions are expected to elicit less arousal than the relevant questions. A guilty suspect gives deceptive responses to both types of question, a fact which, in principle, should lead to similar physiological responses to both types of question. However, relevant questions represent the most immediate and serious threat to the examinee, and will lead to a stronger physiological response than the control questions.

A typical CQT consists of about ten questions, three of which are relevant questions; three control questions; and four, filler items that are not used when interpreting the outcomes (Iacono & Patrick, 1997). The set of 10 questions is usually repeated three times. The CQT is typically applied in criminal cases in which all other evidence against the suspect is inconclusive. In the USA, if an examiner concludes that the examinee has failed the CQT, a post-test interrogation typically takes place in which the examinee is pressured to confess. Examinees often do confess, thereby resolving a crime that, otherwise, possibly would have been unresolved. Lykken (1998) provides the following example of the confession-inducing aspect of polygraph testing. After making the accusation that the examinee was guilty, the examiner left the room for a while to watch the examinee from another room via a one-way mirror. The examinee, obviously upset, kept looking at the polygraph charts, made his mind up and started to eat the charts, a total of six feet of paper, six inches wide. After he finished this meal, the examiner returned as if nothing had happened, leaned down to the polygraph and said, "What's that? He ate them?" The examinee responded, "My God, you mean the thing can talk, too?" and confessed to having committed the crime. This confession-inducing aspect of the CQT is considered very important. US government agencies justify the use of the CQT by this utility (Iacono & Patrick, 1997).

Guilty Knowledge Test (GKT)

The aim of the GKT is to examine whether examinees possess knowledge which they do not want to reveal about a particular crime. For example, suppose that the examinee killed somebody with a knife, left the knife at the murder scene and tells the police that he is not involved in the crime in any way. The police might then try to find out by the GKT whether the suspect is telling the truth or not when he denies any involvement in the crime. In this test, the examiner will show the suspect several types of knife, including the one used in the murder. For each knife, the examinee will be asked whether he recognises the knife as the one used by him. Both innocent and guilty examinees will deny each time that they have used such a knife. A guilty examinee, however, will recognise the knife he has used. It is assumed that this so-called guilty knowledge will produce a heightened physiological response that will be detected by the polygraph. Lykken (1998) described how the GKT could have been used in the O.J. Simpson murder case. Questions which could have been used in this test immediately after the body of Simpson's wife was found included:

1. You know that Nicole has been found murdered, Mr Simpson. How was she killed? Was she drowned? Was she hit on the head with something? Was she shot? Was she beaten to death? Was she stabbed? Was she strangled?
2. Where did we find her body? Was it in the living room? In the driveway? By the side gate? In the kitchen? In the bedroom? By the pool? (Lykken, 1998: p. 298).

Criticisms of the GKT are all related to its limited applicability. The problem with the GKT is that questions must be asked to which *only the one who designed the test and the guilty examinee* know the answers. The one who designs the test should know the correct answer to ensure that the correct answer is in the set of alternatives. Moreover, the GKT only works when questions are asked about details which are actually known to the culprit; otherwise, there is no guilty knowledge to detect. Culprits may not always know such details. The guilty suspect may not have perceived the details the examiner is asking about, or may have forgotten them by the time the test takes place. For instance, it might be that when the examiner asks a question about the colour of the hat which has been found at the scene of crime, the guilty suspect has simply forgotten the colour. The longer the period between the crime and the polygraph test, the more likely it is that the suspect has forgotten certain details. The problem is that the person who designs the test can never be sure that the culprit knows the answer to the question. For example, one can never be sure that the bank robber actually knows that he lost his hat in the alley. It can only be assumed that the guilty suspect will know this.

Moreover, a suspect may admit having guilty knowledge but nevertheless deny guilt. This happens when the suspect admits being present but denies the specific alleged acts. The most common example is an alleged sexual assault in which the witness claims that force was used and the suspect admits the sexual acts but claims that they were consensual. Similar problems arise in cases where there are several suspects who were involved in the crime and all deny having been the principal actor (Raskin, 1988).

Finally, questions can only be asked about items to which innocent suspects do not know the answer (otherwise, they will have guilty knowledge as well). This is not always the case. In many cases, the salient details of the crime are made available by the news media, investigators or attorneys. In order to minimise this problem, a decision could be made to ask questions about minor details which are not widely known. This, however, increases the likelihood that the guilty suspect does not know the answers either.

The result is that the number of cases in which the GKT can be used is limited. Podlesny (1995) analysed criminal case files of the US Federal Bureau of Investigation (FBI) and found that in only 9 per cent of the cases in which CQTs were used could a GKT have been used as well. Bashore and Rapp (1993) believe that the limited applicability of the test is the principal obstacle to its broader use.

Lykken (1998) rejects the idea that the GKT cannot be used in many cases. He pointed out that, at present, FBI investigators are not trained to search fresh crime scenes for usable GKT items. If they were trained, the test could be used more often. Making a comparison with the search for fingerprints, Lykken stated that "had Podlesny [the one who analysed the FBI case files, just mentioned] been working at Scotland Yard in 1900 at the time of the introduction of the Galton–Henry system of fingerprint identification, it is likely that he would also have found very few cases in the records of the Yard that included fingerprints of suspects" (Lykken, 1998: p. 305).

DETECTING LIES

Field Studies and Laboratory Studies

How good are professional lie catchers, such as police detectives, polygraph examiners and CBCA experts, at detecting deceit? Researchers have attempted to answer this question by conducting field studies and experimental laboratory studies. In field studies, statements made by persons in actual cases of alleged sexual abuse were examined, whereas in experimental laboratory studies the statements of participants who lied or told the truth for the sake of the experiment were assessed. Each paradigm has its advantages, and the one's strength is the other's weakness. The statements assessed in field studies have clear forensic relevance, as these are statements derived from real-life cases. However, as mentioned earlier, it is often difficult to establish the ground truth. In order to establish this, researchers sometimes use medical evidence, material evidence, and/or DNA evidence as the objective "guilt–innocence" criterion, and judge whether these objective criteria match the decision made by the lie detection expert. However, this type of evidence is often not available, and its lack is exactly why lie detection experts have been consulted. If strong evidence is available (such as DNA evidence), no further evidence would be needed for the prosecution, as such evidence is enough to press charges and is likely to result in a conviction. However, in cases where the available evidence is too weak to press charges, prosecutors might be inclined to ask for polygraph tests or SVA assessments in order to strengthen their case. In other words, in cases where polygraph examinations or SVAs take place, the other evidence is typically weak.

Therefore, to evaluate the accuracy of decisions made by lie detection experts, researchers often use confessions as a criterion in attempting to establish ground truth. Suspects are considered "guilty" when they confess and are considered "innocent" when somebody else confesses to the crime they were suspected of. That is where problems arise, as suspects' decisions as to whether or not to confess are sometimes based upon the outcome of the "lie detection test". On the one hand, innocent suspects who failed a lie detection test sometimes see themselves confronted with evidence against them (the lie detection test outcome) and no evidence that they are innocent. This might result in defendants falsely confessing, as they see no opportunity to prove their innocence and obtain an acquittal, and a guilty plea often results in a reduced sentence (Gudjonsson, 1992; Steller & Köhnken, 1989). On the other hand, guilty suspects who passed the lie detection test are unlikely to confess, given the lack of evidence against them. (As discussed in Chapter 4, the main reason for persons confessing to a crime is that they perceive the evidence against them to be strong.) In criminal cases where the evidence is weak, few confessions will be obtained, and such cases will not therefore be included in the field study, as the ground truth criterion (confession) is lacking. Accuracy rates for field studies might therefore be inflated.

In experimental laboratory studies, there is no difficulty in establishing whether a statement is actually true or false. However, they typically differ from real-life situations. Recalling a film one has just seen (a paradigm sometimes used in laboratory CBCA studies) is different from describing a sexual abuse experience. Being subjected to a polygraph test concerning one's participation in a mock crime (a paradigm sometimes used in polygraph studies) is different from being accused of a real crime. Several CBCA and polygraph experts therefore believe that, because of this lack of ecological validity, laboratory studies would be of little use in testing the accuracy of CBCAs and polygraph tests (Kleinmuntz & Szucko, 1982; Lykken, 1988, 1998; Undeutsch, 1984).

Accuracy Rates

The truth-accuracy rates (percentages of correct classifications of truths) and lie-accuracy rates (percentages of correct classifications of lies) of different lie detection techniques are presented in Table 2.2. First, accuracy rates are presented when professional lie catchers judge the accuracy of statements while watching videotapes of people who are telling truths and lies (indicated by "nonverbal behaviour" in Table 2.2). The scores are the average scores of the following nine studies which have been published to date (the professions of the lie detectors are in parentheses); DePaulo and Pfeifer (1986, federal law enforcement), Ekman and O'Sullivan (1991; Secret Service, federal polygraphers and police officers), Ekman, O'Sullivan and Frank (1999; CIA, sheriffs and other law enforcement officers), Köhnken (1987; police officers), Porter, Woodworth and Birt (2000; parole officers), Vrij (1993; police detectives), Vrij and Graham (1997; police officers) and Vrij and Mann (2001a,b; police officers). With the

Table 2.2 Professional lie catchers' ability to detect truths and lies (reported are percentages of correct truth and lie classification) by watching videotapes (nonverbal behaviour), conducting CBCA analyses, and carrying out CQT or GKT polygraph tests

	Truth	Lie
Nonverbal behaviour	55%	55%
CBCA	76%	68%
CQT	72%	87%
GKT	96%	59%

exception of Vrij and Mann (2001a,b), all these studies were laboratory studies in which the truths and lies were detected of people who told such truths and lies for the sake of the experiment. In lie detection studies, an accuracy rate of 50 per cent is expected by chance alone, as simply guessing whether someone is lying or not allows for a 50 per cent chance of being correct. As Table 2.2 shows, the scores were only just above the level of chance with accuracy rates of 55 per cent for both truths and lies. However, some groups of lie detectors seem to be better than others. Ekman and O'Sullivan (1991) and Ekman et al. (1999) found that Secret Service agents (64 per cent total accuracy rate; that is, accuracy rates for detecting truths and lies combined), CIA agents (73 per cent total accuracy rate) and sheriffs (67 per cent total accuracy rate) were better lie detectors than other types of agents or police officers.

The generally low accuracy scores might be an artefact. In laboratory studies, observers are exposed to communicators who tell the truth or lie for the sake of the experiment. For those communicators, the stakes are probably much lower than, for example, for suspects in police interviews. Perhaps lie detection is much more difficult in low-stake situations, as the three processes which might elicit behavioural responses to deceit (emotions, cognitive complexity and attempted behavioural control) will be less profound in low-stake situations. Indeed, a series of experiments in which the stakes were manipulated (although the stakes were never really high) demonstrated that high-stake lies were easier to detect than low-stake lies (DePaulo et al., 1988; DePaulo, Lanier & Davis, 1983; DePaulo, LeMay & Epstein, 1991; DePaulo et al., 1985b; Lane & DePaulo, 1999; Vrij, 2000b; Vrij et al., 2001). In other words, detecting lies in low-stake situations is different from detecting lies in high-stake situations; therefore, police officers' true ability to detect deceit can probably be examined only when they are exposed to truths and lies told in real police interviews.

Mann (2001) was the first researcher to conduct an extensive lie detection experiment using real-life, high-stake materials. She showed 99 police officers a total of 54 video clips in which suspects told truths and lies during their police interviews. None of the sample of police officers belonged to one of the specific groups which have been identified by Ekman and his colleagues as being superior lie detectors. The study revealed accuracy rates which were higher than generally found in previous studies, with a 64 per cent truth accuracy rate and a 66 per cent lie accuracy rate. These accuracy rates were significantly higher than the 50 per cent level of chance and higher than ever found before with ordinary police officers. In other words, ordinary police officers seem to be better at detecting truths and lies than was previously suggested.

The accuracy rates for CBCA experts reported in Table 2.2 are adapted from Vrij's (2000a) review based upon 13 (all laboratory) studies. As can be seen in Table 2.2, the accuracy rates for CBCA experts were 76 per cent for detecting truths and 68 per cent for detecting lies. These scores are higher than for judgements based upon nonverbal behaviour. However, recent research has shown that even higher accuracy rates could be obtained by combining nonverbal and CBCA analyses (Vrij et al., 2000; in press). Typically, such combined analyses do not take place, as lie detectors concentrate on either nonverbal cues or CBCA analyses.

The accuracy rates for polygraph testing reported in Table 2.2 are based upon field studies only. See Vrij (2000a) for accuracy rates for CQT laboratory tests and Vrij (2000a) and MacLaren (2001) for accuracy rates for GKT laboratory tests. Numerous CQT field studies have been carried out, but they are also subject to debate. The main source of concern is whether studies adequately satisfy methodological criteria for inclusion in the literature review. In their review, Iacono and Patrick (1997), opponents of polygraph testing, included three CQT studies. So did Carroll (1991), another opponent, in his review. Honts and Perry (1992), supporters of polygraph testing, also included three CQT studies in their review. However, different researchers have included different studies. Perhaps unsurprisingly, Honts and Perry's (1992) review reported the most favourable outcomes. Saxe, Dougherty and Cross (1985) attempted to provide "an objective description, to the extent that is possible, of current psychological knowledge of polygraph testing" (p. 356). They presented a review which was initiated by the US congressional Office of Technology Assessment (OTA) to advise President Reagan about polygraph testing. They found ten CQT studies that met the OTA standards.

The results regarding CQT tests which are presented in Table 2.2 are based upon a review (Vrij, 2000a) which included more CQT field studies than any previous review (including the 10 OTA studies). This review will not satisfy the polygraph critics, as they will say that it includes some "improper" studies in which the ground truth was not satisfactorily established. It should be noted that the ground truth in most studies which were included was confession based (as was the case in the OTA review). However, given the fact that this is the most comprehensive review to date, it at least gives an accurate review of the results of CQT field studies conducted to date. As can be seen in Table 2.2, the accuracy rates for CQT testing were 72 per cent for truths and 87 per cent for lies. The rates for detecting truths are particularly low. Apparently, many innocent suspects fail CQT polygraph tests (see below for a possible reason). Field studies regarding GKT polygraph testing are rare, and only two studies have been published (Elaad, 1990; Elaad, Ginton & Jungman, 1992). As Table 2.2 reveals, the accuracy rate for truths is high (96 per cent), but the accuracy rate for lies is particularly low (59 per cent). Apparently, guilty suspects often do not know the correct answers to the questions, meaning that they do not have the guilty knowledge to be detected.

DIFFICULTIES AND PITFALLS FOR LIE DETECTORS

There are numerous reasons why professional lie catchers (and people in general) make mistakes while attempting to detect deceit (Vrij, 2000a). Some of the main reasons will now be discussed.

Pinocchio's Nose

Lie detection is a difficult task, as there is no give-away cue like Pinocchio's growing nose. This means that there is nothing the lie detector can rely upon. Despite this, some researchers claim that they have found "Pinocchio's growing nose", and their studies generally attract large media attention. Hirsch and Wolf (2001) took Pinocchio's growing nose literally and claimed that Clinton's nose actually swelled when he lied during his televised testimony in the Monica Lewinsky trial. We have doubts about this claim. Apart from the fact that it is difficult to establish whether and, if so, exactly when Clinton was lying during that testimony (see above), the generalisability of this physiological reaction can be questioned. That is, would the same physiological reaction be found with other liars or even with Clinton himself in another situation? Obviously, consistency between liars and consistency within the same liar is necessary to make an appropriate claim about having found Pinocchio's growing nose.

In a more recent study (Pavlidis, Eberhardt & Levine, 2002) published in the prestigious journal *Nature*, it was claimed that liars could be detected by recording thermal warming around the eyes. The technique, which does not require physical contact with the examinees, has, according to Pavlidis et al., "potential for application in remote and rapid security screening, without the need for skilled staff or physical contact" (p. 35). However, such security checks are likely to cause errors. Thermal warming is more likely to be the result of physiological arousal than deception. In other words, people who are physiologically aroused are likely to get caught, and, as indicated earlier, these people are not necessarily liars. Moreover, not all liars will be aroused, and those who are not will remain undetected (see also the "Othello Error" section below).

Apart from the absence of a typical give-away cue, when differences between liars and truth tellers do appear, these differences are typically small (Vrij, 1994). Freud's (1959: p. 94) view, "He who has eyes to see and ears to hear may convince himself that no mortal can keep a secret. If his lips are silent, he chatters with his finger-tips; betrayal oozes out of him at every pore" is not correct. Obviously, the smaller the differences, the more difficult it will be to detect them.

Othello Error

The fact that truth tellers and liars might experience the same processes (emotions, cognitive load and attempted control) implies that they might respond similarly, hampering lie detection. As mentioned above, both guilty and innocent suspects might be afraid during police interviews: guilty suspects because they are afraid of getting caught, and innocent suspects because they are afraid that they will not be believed. Therefore, because of that fear, guilty and innocent suspects may show the same nervous behaviours. This puts lie detectors in a difficult position. Should the signs of fear be interpreted as a sign of guilt or as a sign of innocence? The behaviour, speech content or physiological response does not provide the answer. Unfortunately, lie detectors seem not to be fully aware of this and are often inclined to interpret signs of nervousness as deceptive even when they are displayed by truth tellers. Ekman (1992) labelled this phenomenon the 'Othello error', after Shakespeare's play. Othello falsely accuses his wife Desdemona of infidelity. He tells her to confess since he is going to kill her for her treachery. Desdemona asks that Cassio (her alleged lover) be called so that he can testify to her innocence. Othello tells her that he has already had Cassio murdered. Realising that she cannot prove her innocence, Desdemona reacts with an emotional outburst. Othello misinterprets this outburst as a sign of her infidelity.

Polygraph examiners are vulnerable to the Othello error. Regarding the innocent suspects, as stated above, polygraph tests are typically carried out when insufficient evidence is available to prosecute a person. The polygraph test is used to obtain further evidence, and in the USA (the country where probably most polygraph tests are carried out), suspects may be convicted on the basis of polygraph test outcomes. For innocent suspects, the lack of evidence implies that there is not enough evidence to prove their innocence. Innocent suspects are also aware that when they fail the polygraph test, they risk being convicted. Given this situation, it is not unreasonable to believe that even innocent suspects will show a strong response when they answer the crucial question: "On March 12, did you shoot Scott Fisbee?" (Ofshe & Leo, 1997a). The literature review concerning CQT field studies (Vrij, 2000a) revealed that 21 per cent of innocent suspects failed the polygraph test and were wrongly accused. (As already mentioned, 72 per cent of innocent suspects were correctly classified, and the outcomes for the remaining 7 per cent were inconclusive.)

Incorrect Beliefs

Observers seem to have incorrect beliefs about how liars behave. Vrij (2000a) reviewed 40 studies examining people's beliefs about deceptive behaviour. These studies were carried out in various countries (although mainly in the West with white participants), including the USA, the UK, Germany and the Netherlands, and with a variety of observers, including laypersons, police officers and customs officers. Despite the variety of locations and observers, the findings were very similar. It appears that there is a common belief, at least among Western, white people, about how liars behave. Results showed that observers associate deception with a high-pitched voice, many speech fillers and speech errors, a slow speech rate, a long latency period (period of silence between question and answer), many pauses, gaze aversion, a lot of smiling and an increase in movements. Many of these behaviours are indicators of nervousness. Apparently, the stereotypical belief is that liars are nervous and will behave accordingly. As we saw earlier, most of these behaviours are not related to deception (such as gaze aversion) or are related to deception in a different way (for example, illustrators and hand/finger movements tend to decrease during deception rather than increase).

People look at the wrong cues for various reasons. Vrij, Edward and Bull (2001a) and Vrij, Semin and Bull (1996) investigated participants' behaviour while lying and truth telling. They also asked the participants afterwards to indicate how they thought they behaved when they lied and when they were telling the truth. The results showed that participants had poor insight into their own behaviour and thought that they responded more stereotypically while lying (showing gaze aversion, an increase in movements and so on) than they in fact did. In other words, it seems that during lie detection, observers look for cues they mistakenly believe they themselves show while lying.

Another reason is that people, including police officers, are taught the wrong cues (Gordon & Fleisher, 2002; Hess, 1997; Inbau, Reid & Buckley, 1986). In their influential manual, *Criminal Interrogation and Confessions*, extensively discussed in Chapter 4, Inbau et al. (1986) describe in detail how, in their view, liars behave. This includes behaviours such as gaze aversion, unnatural posture changes, fidgeting and placing the hand over the mouth or eyes when speaking. They based their view on their extensive experience of interviewing suspects. However, none of these behaviours are found to be reliably related to deception in deception research. Nor do Inbau and his colleagues provide any empirical evidence for their claims. Kassin and Fong (1999), however, tested the validity of Inbau's claims. In their experiment, they taught half of their participants to look at the nonverbal cues mentioned by Inbau and colleagues as indicators of deceit. This group of participants actually performed worse on a subsequent lie detection task than a group of participants who were not informed about these nonverbal cues. This negative finding is a result of the lack of validity in Inbau's claims about behavioural indicators of deception.

Finally, it might be that children do show stereotypical behaviours, such as gaze aversion and fidgeting, when they lie. Perhaps adults form their views about how liars behave by watching (their own) children's responses. However, the (very few) studies published to date concerning children's behaviour when they lie do not suggest that they fidget and look away when they lie (see Vrij, 2002, for a review, and Vrij et al., in press).

These incorrect beliefs have consequences. Nonverbal behaviour is culturally determined. Members of different ethnic groups tend to show different patterns of nonverbal behaviour (Vrij, 1991; Vrij & Winkel, 1991). For example, looking into the eyes of one's conversation partner is regarded as polite in Western cultures but is considered to be rude in several other cultures (Vrij & Winkel, 1991; Vrij, Winkel & Koppelaar, 1991). Therefore, not surprisingly, Afro-American people display more gaze aversion than white American people do (LaFrance & Mayo, 1976), and people from Turkey and Morocco who are living in the Netherlands show more gaze aversion than native Dutch people do (Vrij, 2000a; Vrij, Dragt & Koppelaar, 1992). In the Netherlands, the nonverbal behavioural patterns of white, native Dutch and black Surinamese citizens (citizens originating in Surinam, a former Dutch colony, but now living in the Netherlands) during simulated police interviews were examined (Vrij & Winkel, 1991). Both a Dutch and a Surinamese interviewer were used, but this had no impact on the findings. Surinamese people made more speech disturbances, exhibited more gaze aversion, smiled more often, and made more self-manipulations (scratching the head, wrists and so on) and illustrators, regardless of whether they were lying or not. These behaviours show an overlap with the behaviours Western, white people believe liars display (Vrij, 2000a), suggesting that typical "Surinamese" behaviour in experiments in the Netherlands corresponds with behaviour that makes a suspicious impression on Western, white observers. This gives rise to possible cross-cultural nonverbal communication errors during cross-cultural interactions. That is, nonverbal behavioural patterns that are typical of Surinamese people in these settings may be interpreted by Western, white observers as revealing attempts to hide the truth. This idea was tested in a series of experiments (Vrij & Winkel, 1992, 1994; Vrij et al., 1991). Videotapes were made of simulated police interviews in which native Dutch and Surinamese actors participated. Different versions were made of each interview. The actors demonstrated typical "Dutch" behaviour in one version of the interviews (for example, they showed a moderate amount of gaze aversion) and typical "Surinamese" nonverbal behaviour in another version of the interviews (they showed more gaze aversion). Dutch, white police officers were exposed to one version of each interview and were asked to indicate to what extent the actor made a suspicious impression. The actors (whether Dutch or Surinamese) consistently made a more suspicious impression when they demonstrated "typical Surinamese behaviour" than when they exhibited "typical Dutch behaviour". These findings support the assumption that cross-cultural nonverbal communication errors do occur during cross-cultural interactions, and that nonverbal behavioural patterns that are typical for an ethnic group are often interpreted by Western, white observers as signs of deception.

The incorrect beliefs might also be the reason why people are typically poor at detecting lies when they observe someone's face. A popular belief is that lie detection is easiest when the lie detector has access to the full picture of the potential liar, and that just reading a text or just listening to someone's voice hampers lie detection. However, research has shown that this is not the case. People are generally better lie detectors when they just read a text or listen to a voice, than when they have access to all of a person's communication channels. In fact, they become worse as soon as they are exposed to someone's face (DePaulo, Stone & Lassiter, 1985a; Wiseman, 1995). The reason for this is that lie detectors are inclined to look at someone's eye movements when these are available to them, whereas, as indicated earlier, in fact, eye movements are not related to deception.

One promising method to encourage lie detectors to rely upon more valid cues when attempting to detect deceit is to employ an implicit lie detection method (Vrij, 2001; Vrij, Edward & Bull, 2001b). When police officers were shown video clips of liars and truth tellers, and were asked to indicate either when the person was lying (explicit method) or whether the person was thinking hard (implicit method), they were able to distinguish between liars and truth tellers only when they were allocated to the implicit lie detection condition. Interestingly, only when using this method did they pay attention to the more valid deception cues, such as a decrease in illustrators.

Countermeasures

Polygraph test outcomes might have serious consequences for suspects, as they may eventually lead to their conviction. Examinees might therefore try hard to influence polygraph outcomes and try to produce physiological responses which may lead the examiner to conclude that they are telling the truth. Methods that are used to achieve this are called "countermeasures". It is probably easier for examinees to increase their arousal while answering control questions than to lower their arousal while answering relevant questions. Therefore, countermeasures are generally meant to increase arousal during control questions, and examples of these include foot tensing (by pressing the toes against the shoe sole) or having arousal thoughts while answering the control questions.

Reid and Inbau (1977) do not seem to worry about the effectiveness of countermeasures. They argued that it is highly improbable that countermeasures can succeed, because properly trained examiners would notice that the examinee is trying to fool them. However, several studies, some conducted by polygraph supporters, have shown that the use of countermeasures can be very effective in defeating polygraph tests, and that they sometimes remain unnoticed by polygraph examiners (Honts, Raskin & Kircher, 1994). The most famous countermeasures polygraph test has probably been conducted by Floyd "Buzz" Fay, a man who was falsely convicted of murder on the basis of a failed polygraph examination. He took it on himself to become a polygraph expert during his two and half years of wrongful imprisonment. He coached 27 inmates, who all freely confessed to him that they were guilty, in how to beat the control question polygraph test. After only 20 minutes of instruction, 23 of the 27 inmates were successful in defeating the polygraph examination (Kleinmuntz & Szucko, 1984).

Liars might also seek information about CBCA and train themselves to beat this technique, that is, to produce a false statement which incorporates many of the elements CBCA evaluators typically judged to be truthful. In their experiments, Joffe and Yuille (1992), Vrij, Kneller, and Mann (2000) and Vrij et al. (2002) coached some participants and asked a trained CBCA expert to look at the statements of all participants (truth tellers, coached liars and uncoached liars). The CBCA experts did not notice that some participants were coached, and they could not discriminate between truth tellers and coached liars. Perhaps even more worrying, in Vrij, Kneller & Mann's (2000) study, the CBCA experts could not indicate which statements belonged to the coached liars even after they were informed that some of the participants had been coached.

Adequate Comparisons

As mentioned above, people show different responses in different situations or when answering different questions. This means that lie detectors should only compare responses within a person which are comparable. There is evidence that this does not always happen during police interviews and that apple–orange comparisons are sometimes made (Moston & Engelberg, 1993). In those interviews, suspects' behaviour during small talk at the beginning of the interview is compared with their behaviour during the actual interrogation. Although police officers are advised to establish comparable truths in this way (Inbau et al., 2001; Inbau et al., 1986), this is an invalid comparison. Small talk and the actual investigative part of the police interview are totally different situations. The actual interview matters to suspects and is a high-stake situation. The small talk has no real consequences and is therefore a low-stake situation. People tend to behave differently during low-stake and high-stake situations, and both guilty and innocent people tend to change their behaviour the moment the actual interview starts (Vrij, 1995).

However, it is sometimes possible to make good comparisons. During a videotaped real-life police interview, a man suspected of murder was asked to describe his activities during a particular day (Vrij & Mann, 2001a). The murder suspect gave descriptions of his activities during the morning, afternoon and evening. Detailed analyses of the videotape revealed a sudden change in behaviour as soon as he started to describe his activities during the afternoon and evening. Why did the man suddenly change his behaviour? One reason may have been that he was lying. Evidence supported this view. Police investigations could confirm his story with respect to his morning activities, but revealed that his statement about the afternoon and evening was fabricated. In reality, he met the victim and killed her later that day. Interestingly, the question on which we based this behavioural analysis, "What did you do on that particular day?", could be asked in many interviews.

CQT polygraph examiners face the same comparison problem. It is difficult for them to formulate relevant ("On March 12, did you shoot Scott Fisbee?") and control questions ("Have you ever tried to hurt someone to get revenge?") that are truly comparable, and critics claim that they could never achieve this (Ben-Shakhar & Furedy, 1990; Carroll, 1991; Furedy, 1993, 1996a; Lykken, 1998). Obviously, apple–orange comparisons in polygraph testing will inevitably damage its accuracy.

Validity Checklist

It is known that CBCA scores are affected by factors other than lying. For example, CBCA scores are positively correlated with age; that is, older children and adults typically obtain higher CBCA scores than younger children (Anson, Golding & Gully, 1993; Buck et al., 2002; Craig et al., 1999; Davies, Westcott & Horan, 2000; Hershkowitz et al., 1997; Horowitz et al., 1997; Lamers-Winkelman

& Buffing, 1996; Santtila et al., 2000; Vrij et al., 2002). Research has also shown that CBCA scores are related to verbal and social skills (Santtila et al., 2000; Vrij et al., 2001c, 2002). For example, Santtila et al. (2000) found a positive correlation with verbal ability (assessed with the Wechsler Intelligence Scale for Children–Revised [WISC–R] vocabulary test).

Finally, CBCA scores are also related to the interview style. For example, open-ended questions (Craig et al., 1999; Hershkowitz et al., 1997) and facilitators (non-suggestive words of encouragement; Hershkowitz et al., 1997) yield more CBCA criteria than other, more direct forms of questioning. Davies et al. (2000) found positive correlations between CBCA scores and interviewer verbal affirmations ("Yes, I see", etc.) and confirming comments (interviewer summarised what the child has said). Köhnken et al. (1995) and Steller and Wellershaus (1996) found that statements obtained from interviewees who underwent the cognitive interview technique (see Milne & Bull, 1999, for a description of that technique) received higher CBCA scores than statements obtained with a standard interview technique.

CBCA evaluators therefore look at a range of factors which possibly could have influenced the CBCA scores (they are listed in the "validity checklist", and this evaluation of CBCA outcomes is the third phase of the SVA procedure), and determine whether these external factors have influenced CBCA outcomes. However, there are several problems with this third phase. One might question the justification of some of the factors included in the validity checklist. One factor evaluators look at when a witness gives multiple statements about the same event is whether there are any inconsistencies between the statements. If so, this could indicate that the witness is lying. But this is probably an invalid assumption. Research has shown that contradictory statements by an interviewee do not always mean that one of the statements is fabricated (Moston, 1987; Poole & White, 1991). In fact, Granhag and Strömwall (1999, 2002) found that inconsistency is unrelated to deception. Granhag and Strömwall (2001a,b) also found that assessors often do not agree among themselves as to whether statements are consistent or not.

At least one factor, "susceptibility to suggestion", is difficult to measure. Some witnesses are more prone to suggestions made by interviewers than are others, and might provide information which confirms the interviewer's expectations but which is, in fact, inaccurate. Yuille (1988) therefore recommends asking the witness at the end of the interview a few leading questions in order to assess the witness's susceptibility to suggestion. He recommends asking some questions about peripheral information, and not about central information, as asking leading questions may distort the interviewee's memory (Loftus & Palmer, 1974; see also Chapter 6). The fact that questions can be asked only about peripheral information causes a problem, as children show more resistance to suggestibility for central parts than peripheral parts of the event (Goodman et al., 1990). Moreover, they are probably more resistant to suggestibility for stressful events (likely to be central events) than for events which are less stressful (likely to be peripheral events) (Davies, 1991). Thus, if interviewees yield to a leading question about a peripheral part of the event, this does not imply that they could not resist suggestion when more important aspects are discussed. This factor also seems to assume that suggestion is more the result of individual differences than of circumstances. This may not be a valid assumption (Milne & Bull, 1999).

Finally, some factors which influence CBCA scores, such as the interviewees' social skills, are not present in the validity checklist, and the impact of such factors on CBCA scores will therefore typically be ignored (Vrij et al., 2002).

Research on the validity checklist has hardly been carried out to date, but there is evidence to suggest that SVA experts might use the validity checklist incorrectly (Gumpert & Lindblad, 1999). First, although SVA experts sometimes highlight the influence of external factors on children's statements in general, they do not always discuss how these factors might have influenced the statement of the particular child they were asked to assess. Second, different experts sometimes draw different conclusions about the impact of external factors. Third, although experts sometimes indicate possible external influence on statements, they tend to rely upon the CBCA outcome, and tend to judge high-quality statements as truthful and low-quality statements as fabricated. Gumpert and Lindblad (1999) examined only a limited number of cases, and drawing firm conclusions is perhaps premature, but their findings are worrying because they imply that SVA decisions are not likely to be more accurate than CBCA assessments, as the final decision based upon CBCA outcomes and validity checklist procedure combined will often be the same as the decision based upon CBCA outcomes alone. This also implies that interviewees who naturally produce low-quality statements and therefore are likely to obtain low CBCA scores (young children, interviewees with poor verbal skills and so on) might well be in a disadvantageous position.

SUMMARY AND CONCLUSION

This chapter revealed that some nonverbal, verbal and physiological responses are more likely to occur during deception than others. However, there is not a single give-away cue to deception which lie detectors can rely upon. For this reason, and other reasons discussed in this chapter, lie detection is a very difficult task in which mistakes are almost inevitable. Research has shown that professional lie catchers do frequently make mistakes, a fact which raises serious concerns about allowing lie detectors' judgements as evidence in criminal courts. However, several lie detection methods enable lie detectors to determine whether someone is lying or telling the truth above the level of chance; therefore, these methods could be a useful tool in criminal investigations—for example, in police investigations to eliminate potential suspects or to examine contradictory statements.

CHAPTER 3

FACIAL APPEARANCE AND CRIMINALITY

In 1999, Smith, McIntosh and Bazzini noted (p. 69) that much psychological research had found that

> good looking people are judged less likely to commit criminal acts . . . attractive defendants are more likely to receive lenient verdicts in mock trials . . . mock jurors recommend harsher punishments for defendants who have raped an attractive woman than those who raped an unattractive woman.

Smith et al. (1999) analysed the contents of a large sample of top-grossing Hollywood movies, and they found that film makers have been portraying physically attractive individuals more favourably with regard to their morality and life outcomes. In 1984, Udry and Eckland (p. 47) made the following claims:

> Everyone knows that it is better to be beautiful than to be ugly. There may be some people who would prefer to be bad than good. Some might even prefer to be poor than rich. But we take it on faith that no one prefers to be ugly. The reason for this must be that people expect good things to come to the beautiful. Folklore tells us that beautiful girls marry handsome princes and live happily ever after. Heroes are handsome and villains are ugly.

More specifically, Goldstein, Chance and Gilbert (1984) claimed: "The degree to which a particular individual's face invites facial stereotyping may influence the outcomes of any legal process in which they become involved" (p. 552).

The aim of this chapter is to consider some of the available literature on the question of whether there exists a relationship between facial appearance and criminality. This will include (i) a review of research on the extent to which people assume there to be such a relationship, (ii) an examination of studies on the impact upon prisoners' recidivism rates of surgery designed to improve their facial appearance, and (iii) an overview of the work on the effects on "mock" jurors of defendant and victim facial attractiveness, as well as a description of the very few studies which exist of the effects of facial appearance in real-life court proceedings. The reader of this chapter should consider not only the methodological rigour of the studies but also their ecological validity.

MATCHING FACES TO CRIMES

Psychological research has shown that members of the general public do associate certain crimes with various types of facial appearance. In the USA in 1939, Thornton chose from the Nebraska State Penitentiary files the records of 20 criminals without looking at the file photograph of each criminal. These photographs were shown one at a time to a group of adults who were required to write down which one of four crimes each photographed person had been found guilty of. The adults' decisions were correct more often than could be expected by chance. In Germany, Kozeny (1962) divided several hundred photographs of convicted criminals into 16 crime categories depending on the type of crime committed. For each of these 16 categories, a composite photograph was made from those in the category. When asked to match one of the 16 crimes to each facial composite, members of the public were found to be able to do this more often than would be expected by chance.

A study somewhat similar to those of Kozeny and of Thornton was conducted in London by Bull and Green (1980), with the exception that their photographs were not of criminals (but of the researchers' friends). The photographs all had the same background and the men photographed (aged between 27 and 33 years) had a similar, rather bland, facial expression. Participants were required to say which of the 11 listed crimes the 10 men had committed, more than one face being allowed for each crime. The data demonstrated that for company fraud, gross indecency, illegal possession of drugs, mugging, robbery with violence, soliciting, and taking and driving away, one of the faces was chosen significantly more often than the others, and it was a different face for each of these seven crimes. For the crimes of arson, burglary, rape and theft, no one particular face was chosen more often than would be expected by chance.

In another American study, Goldstein et al. (1984) found participants to agree in their choices of which faces (in an album of actors' faces) looked like an armed robber, a mass murderer, a rapist, a clergyman or a medical doctor. When the chosen "criminal" or "non-criminal" faces were shown to other participants they rated the criminals' faces less positively on the dimensions of calm–excited, cautious–brash, clean–dirty, friendly–unfriendly, good–bad, kind–cruel, refined–vulgar and sane–insane.

ATTRACTIVENESS

In 1988, Saladin, Saper and Breen examined the relationship between criminal facial stereotypes and attractiveness. Participants were asked to say how likely were each of eight male subjects of stimulus photographs (previously rated for attractiveness) to commit each of two crimes: murder and armed robbery. Those with attractive faces were deemed less likely to carry out either act than were those with unattractive faces. (For more on what is an attractive face, see Bull & Rumsey, 1988.)

Yarmey and Kruschenske (1995) reported a study which found that under-graduates indicated that women likely to be battered (that is, those suffering from domestic violence) would be of low facial attractiveness, as would women likely to kill their abuser. They noted that cognitive schemata produce expectations about individuals who fit the schema, and organise information input and output. (For more on forming impressions and stereotypes, see Kunda and Thagard, 1996.) In their study, one group of students rated each of 60 facial photographs of women for attractiveness, with facial expression similar across all photographs. The photographs which were rated as the most and least attractive were then shown to other students, who were asked either to select the two "who best represented a battered woman and the two who least represented a battered woman" (p.343), or to select the ones most and least likely to kill their abuser, although non-selection of any photographs was allowed. From this study, Yarmey and Kruschenke concluded that "students were able to compare their perceptions of women's faces with a conceptual memory schema that represented their personal prototypical battered woman face" (p.347). They suggested that if the results of this study are generalisable to the courtroom, jurors and judges may stereotype women on the basis of their facial attractiveness, a fact which "could have far-reaching effects on due process and impartiality of decisions in the justice system. . . . Battered women do not deserve to be victimized twice—once by their abusive partner and a second time by triers of fact who may be influenced by facial stereotypes" (p. 349). Whether jurors, judges or others within the criminal justice system are actually influenced by stereotypes has barely been researched (see below). Indeed, while Gula and Yarmey (1998) replicated the Yarmey and Kruschenske (1995) study, they found that there was no relationship between the faces chosen as those of battered women and whether, in fact, they were of battered women. That is, among a sample of faces of battered and not battered women, people could not tell which was which.

In 1993, Yarmey noted that the Fourth Amendment to the Constitution of the USA (which is concerned with unreasonable search and seizure) could be interpreted as protecting citizens from being subjected to police harassment on the basis of imprecise stereotypes of what criminals look like. (This was an issue for the US Supreme Court in the 1989 case of *United States* v. *Sokolow*.) In his study, video recordings were made of similarly dressed men reading the same text. These recordings were played to participants (students), some of whom saw and heard the men, some only saw them (the sound being turned off), and others only heard them. These people were then asked to select, if possible, the man who best represented a mass murderer, then a sexual assault felon, an armed robber, a clergyman, a medical doctor, and an engineer (only one man per category). Yarmey found that the participants showed high consensual agreement concerning which men they independently chose for each of these six categories, and that their confidence in their judgements was high. (He noted that his 1993 study did not specifically relate attractiveness to criminality.)

Macrae and Shepherd (1989a) controlled for the possible effects of physical attractiveness in their study of criminal stereotypes. They noted that "the general public possess stereotypical conceptions of the likely appearance of criminals", and that "the selection of a particular individual from an identity parade may be influenced by the degree to which he or she resembles the commonly held stereotype for the incident in question" (p. 189). They pointed out that most prior studies of facial criminal stereotypes had involved faces which probably varied in attractiveness, and that such attractiveness may have mediated the criminality judgements. In their own study, male faces rated similar in attractiveness were used, and students (again!) were asked to select the faces of those most and least likely to commit assault or theft. The faces of those consensually chosen as most and least likely to commit each offence were shown to other students, who, having read an account of the criminal incident, were asked to judge the person as guilty or innocent. Guilt judgements were significantly influenced by whether the persons had been evaluated, by other people, as being likely to commit the offence.

Macrae and Shepherd concluded that their results support the contention that "stereotypes function as schemata" (p. 190) and that with facial attractiveness being kept constant, these stereotypes are different for different crimes. They noted (1989b) that "the psychological laboratory is far removed from the courtroom, and extrapolations and generalisations from experimental data will rightly be viewed skeptically by many legal practitioners" (p. 198). Nevertheless, they suggested that such biases may operate in the judicial process.

For more on identity parades/line-ups, see Chapter 6, but we should note here the interesting study by Lindholm and Christianson (1998), who found that how culpable people were judged to be for a crime and whether they were correctly/ incorrectly identified in a line-up was related to their (ethnic) appearance. We should also note the point made by Van Knippenberg, Dijksterhuis and Vermeulen (1999) that stereotypes may affect memory and judgements concerning guilt/punishment only under high cognitive demand conditions. (See Chapter 8 for more on how cognitive demand/load can affect decision making.)

FACIAL APPEARANCE AND DECEIT

An interesting topic that, rather surprisingly, has received only limited research attention is whether a person's facial attractiveness influences the judgements other people make about whether that person is lying or telling the truth. Anne et al. (1993) found higher female attractiveness to be associated with lower ratings of deception, and we recently found a similar effect (Vine & Bull, 2003). In our study, observers watched video clips of people lying or telling the truth. Those people rated (by other observers) as being lower in attractiveness were significantly more often judged to be lying than were people rated higher in attractiveness, though the actual frequency of lying did not vary with attractiveness. In line with the larger body of previous research (described above), the observers who rated the faces for attractiveness rated the unattractive faces as significantly less trustworthy. Thus, it may well be that facial appearance influences not only ratings of honesty/trustworthiness but also judgements of whether a person is telling the truth.

POLICE OFFICERS

In Bull and Green's (1980) study, only a few of the participants were police officers, and their data did not differ from that of the general public. Thorley (1996) conducted a study similar to Bull and Green's; however, in this study, a larger proportion of the participants were police officers ($n = 46$). These officers and members of the public ($n = 49$) were shown 10 photographs taken against a similar plain background of young men, each with a neutral facial expression. The participants were provided with a list of 10 offences and had to match a different face to each offence. Members of the public chose a particular, different face more often than by chance for the eight offences of robbery/mugging, dealing in drugs, car theft, arson, murder, violence against the person, kidnapping and handling stolen goods. For the two offences of burglary and criminal damage, no one face was particularly chosen. The police officers matched the same faces to the same offences as did the general public for mugging/robbery, violence against the person, and kidnapping, but chose a different face for car theft. For the remaining six offences, the police officers' choice of face did not fall on any one particular face but mostly on two or three faces, one of which was chosen by most members of the general public. Thus, this study found (as did Bull and Green, 1980) that members of the public concur when independently matching a male face to eight of the ten offences. However, the police officers' choices of which offence went with each face were rather more distributed across offences, with strong agreement among them only for four of the ten offences. Nevertheless, the police officers' data do reveal that at least for some offences they concurred on the face most likely to be associated with a crime.

Research has also been conducted on the influence on police officers of a number of other appearance factors (such as skin colour) and of behavioural aspects (such as deference). For more on these topics, see Vrij and Winkel (1992, 1994) and Bull and Horncastle (1989).

CHILDREN

The (above) literature involving adult participants has found that facial stereotyping does take place. It is important to establish whether this also applies to child participants both theoretically (models of cognitive development) and practically (crime witnesses). A study by Price (1996) examined whether children would concur when independently matching faces to crimes. In this study, children aged 8, 12 and 16 years were asked to assign 10 crimes to photographs of 10 young men. They were allowed, if they wished, to assign more than one crime to each photograph, but each crime could be assigned only once. The procedure was then repeated with photographs of 10 young women. It was found for the male photographs that for the crimes of murder, drug dealing and physical assault, the children's choice of face differed significantly from what would be expected by chance. This was also the case for the female photographs for the same three crimes of murder, drug dealing and physical assault, as well as for burglary. For the male photographs, age of child had little effect. However, for the female photographs, the one most frequently chosen for a particular crime varied to a small but noticeable extent across age groups. Twelve adults independently indicated which of the 10 crimes used in the study were the five most serious. They concurred in choosing murder, arson, drug dealing, physical assault and kidnapping (rather than the other five crimes of theft, burglary, mugging, car theft and criminal damage). Thus, children's stereotyping concerning which crimes go with which faces was for crimes considered serious by adults. In this study, other children from the three age groups were asked independently to say how attractive each face was. These children's resultant mean attractiveness ratings were then correlated with the number of times a crime had been assigned to each face by the children in the main study. No relationship for male faces was found, but, for the female faces, there was a strong, significant, negative relationship that emanated largely from the 8- and 12-year-old children in the main study. Thus, this study again found that people, this time children, do associate some crimes with particular faces, and that, for female faces, these were the least attractive ones. (For more on children's stereotyping of faces and on the association between attractiveness and liking, see Bull & Rumsey, 1988.)

In 1982, Yarmey made the point that a main characteristic of stereotypes is the holder's belief in an assumed relationship between psychological attributes and category membership (for example, the view that criminals have a tough appearance). He argued that people "attend to and encode such co-occurrences" and that "these encodings are possible sources of distortion when memory is searched at a later time" (p. 207). Evidence to support this view comes from a variety of studies, including one by Shepherd et al. (1978). In this study, women were asked to construct a photofit of a man's face that they had just seen in a photograph. Half of the women were under the impression that the photograph was that of a murderer, and the other half that of a lifeboatman. In fact, all of them saw the same photograph. The photofits made by these women were shown to other women (who were told nothing about a lifeboatman or murderer). These other participants rated the photofits on a number of evaluative dimensions. The faces in photofits constructed by women who believed the face was that of a murderer were rated by these other women as significantly less attractive than were the faces in the photofits of the (alleged) lifeboatman. Shepherd et al. concluded that differences in the photofit constructors' impressions of the original face affected the photofits they constructed from memory.

If less attractive faces are thought to be more likely to be associated with crime, what would happen if these faces were made more attractive?

FACIAL SURGERY FOR CRIMINALS

In North America in the 1960s, plastic surgery was performed on prison inmates in the hope of reducing their recidivism rates. One of the reasons for this was the belief that appearance and crime are related. For example, the Director of the Texas Department of Corrections was cited by Spira et al. (1966) as stating that facial deformities may contribute to criminality and that reduction of such deformities "enhances the chance of an inmate making a satisfactory adjustment to society after release" (p. 370). In 1965, the *British Medical Journal* stated: "There is no need to justify the correction of cosmetic and other surgical disabilities in offenders" (p. 1449), and, in 1948, Pick argued that juvenile delinquents would benefit from plastic surgery.

Recidivism Rates

Of Texas offenders released from prison, Spira et al. (1966) reported that usually 32 per cent returned to prison within a few years. However, only 17 per cent of those offenders who received plastic surgery while in prison did so. They noted that the within-prison plastic surgery facility was popular, with prisoners actually requesting treatment. They also noted that "Often a prison official will make the convict cognisant of his defect and will suggest the service ... available"! (p. 364). The prisoners who received such surgery exhibited "a most appreciative attitude" (p. 364). Spira et al. pointed out that no definite conclusions could be drawn from their relatively uncontrolled comparison of the effect of plastic surgery on recidivism rates. Indeed, the possible positive effect upon inmates of society doing something for them (that is, improving their physical appearance) may partly have been the reason for the lowered recidivism rate, rather than society's direct reaction to the prisoners' improved appearance. From Spira et al.'s study, it is not possible to be sure why the recidivism rate was lower in the surgery group.

A similar study was reported by Kurtzberg, Safar and Cavior (1968) involving prison inmates (chronic petty offenders) in New York. Over 1500 inmates volunteered for plastic surgery; of these, several dozen (apparently chosen at random) received it prior to being released from prison. Others requesting such surgery were not given it. In each of these two 'surgery' and 'no-surgery' groups, half received social and vocational services preparing them for release from prison and half did not. Thus, in total, there were four groups of participants. During the 12-month post-treatment interval, of the inmates released from prison, the recidivism rates (save for those guilty of heroin offences) were as follows: 33 per cent for the surgery plus services group, 30 per cent for the surgery plus no-services group, 89 per cent for the no-surgery plus services group and 56 per cent for the no-surgery plus no-services group. Thus, surgery, but not the social and vocational services, was related to reduced recidivism. (For those guilty of heroin offences, the overall surgery group recidivism rate was 59 per cent and for the no-surgery group it was 64 per cent.) Kurtzberg et al. concluded that their findings indicated that plastic surgery (much of which was facial) reduces recidivism and aids rehabilitation. They also noted that, while the surgery is not cheap, it costs less than keeping someone in prison for several months. However, as with the study by Spira et al. (1966), one has to ask to what extent the recidivism rate of the no-surgery participants was affected by their request for surgery being turned down. This criticism also applies to a Canadian study, reported by Lewison in 1974, involving several hundred inmates on short sentences that had received plastic surgery in prison for facial disfigurement in the previous 20 years. Those whose requests for such surgery were granted had lower recidivism rates than those whose requests were turned down (again except for drug offenders).

FREQUENCY OF FACIAL ABNORMALITY

In 1967, Masters and Greaves attempted to determine the frequency of facial abnormality in convicted criminals. They used the police files from several large cities in the USA, and chose the crimes of homicide, rape, prostitution, sex deviation and suicide, "since there could be little doubt concerning the personal or social maladjustment of the individual" (p. 204) in such cases. (Now, however, within contemporary society, some people may not agree with this.) Eleven thousand (no fewer!) criminal faces were examined, and 60 per cent of these were judged (their paper does not say how) to have surgically correctable facial defects, compared to 20 per cent from "a control group composed of the general population" (p. 210) (details of whom are not given). This difference of 40 per cent seems striking. However, one should ask whether this study may not have had some major methodological weaknesses (for example, the photographs of the criminals were almost certainly police mugshots whereas those of the comparison group were not). Masters and Greaves's paper was published in the 1960s in a plastic surgery journal rather than in a scientific journal. Nowadays many surgical/medical journals set higher standards for the reporting of investigative methodology.

A critical appraisal of plastic surgery programmes in prisons was published in a criminal justice journal in 1990. In this review, Thompson noted that research has consistently shown that attractive people are perceived more positively within society than are unattractive people, and that disfigured people tend to evoke negative perceptions by others (see Bull & Rumsey, 1988, for an overview). For the disfigured individual, these reactions may become internalised, and feelings of rejection result. One cause of deviance may be individuals' inability to establish themselves within society's conventional groups. This social rejection may lead to status frustration, a process in which (i) the development of a positive self-image is curbed, (ii) employment opportunities decline, (iii) there is an inability to form stable relationships, and (iv) good grades at school are unattainable. Consequently, Thompson suggested social acceptance is sought elsewhere, within a deviant group in which there is a collective disdain of society's rules, expressed in terms of violations of those rules. Plastic (or corrective) surgery was thought to be a solution to this problem for incarcerated inmates, the belief being that if an offender's outward appearance is improved, that person becomes more desirable and employable. Internally, this new feeling of self-worth may subsequently enhance self-esteem. Requests for plastic surgery within institutions were voluntary, but not everyone who requested treatment received it. Good behaviour on the part of the inmate was often a prerequisite for acceptance for surgery. Some inmates regarded corrective surgery as the answer to their problems, that by improving outwardly there would be a corresponding internal (or psychological) improvement also. When surgery failed to remedy an inmate's problems, reactions ranging from aggression to withdrawal may have followed (Thompson, 1990).

WEAK METHODOLOGIES

Thompson (1990) further pointed out that despite the continuing use of plastic surgery in prisons, very little high-quality research has been carried out on this topic, and of those studies which have appeared, the findings are inconclusive, and methodological problems abound: (i) follow-up periods vary from several months to several years, making comparisons between studies difficult; (ii) because surgery is not indiscriminately granted, participants are not really randomly assigned to experimental and control groups; and (iii) recidivism rates in some studies are compared to a baseline recidivism rate for a larger population such as that of the entire prison. Moreover, different studies use different measures to gauge recidivism (such as rearrest, reconviction and return-to-prison rates). Hence, it is extremely difficult to explain differences between control and experimental groups solely in terms of corrective surgery. Age, type and number of prior offences, and length of sentence are all factors which could influence outcomes.

Of the nine studies reviewed by Thompson, the majority failed to rule out alternative explanations of the results. Therefore, more effective research in this area is required before conclusions regarding the efficacy of plastic surgery in reducing offending can be determined. Nevertheless, as already discussed in this chapter, there is accumulating research evidence that people do associate certain types of facial appearance with crime. Furthermore, improved facial appearance could possibly reduce the likelihood of crime perpetrators being apprehended and/or found guilty. Let us now turn to research on the question of whether facial appearance may have an influence in the courtroom.

DOES FACIAL APPEARANCE HAVE AN EFFECT IN THE COURTROOM?

Defendant Appearance

The earliest published study of the possible effects of facial appearance on judgements of guilt was by Efran (1974). In this study, students received a folder containing a fact summary sheet concerning alleged cheating in an examination and were asked to rate the guilt of the accused and the degree of punishment. The facial attractiveness of the accused person (in a photograph) was varied, ratings of facial attractiveness having been gained from other participants. Attractiveness was found to be related significantly to ratings of guilt and punishment, but only for the male raters (for whom all the accused were females). The female raters (for whom all the accused were males) were not affected by facial attractiveness. In fact, the female raters did not rate the accused (male) attractive faces as highly for attractiveness as did other females who had rated the faces but who were not involved in the main study. Efran seemed at a loss to explain the lack of an attractiveness effect upon his female raters in the main study other than to suggest that they may not have looked at the faces. However, one likely explanation of why these participants did not rate the "attractive" (male) faces as highly as did the other female raters is that only the participants in the main study read that the person whose face they saw had been accused of cheating. It may be that the association with cheating made the faces less attractive for these participants. Thus, while this chapter's main focus is on the question of whether facial appearance influences legal/criminality decisions, it is conceivable that 'bad' information about a person (such as conviction for a crime) may influence evaluations of their facial appearance. This reversal of the "what is beautiful is good" notion (that is, "what is ugly is bad" or "what is bad is ugly") has rarely been researched (but see the 1978 study on photofits by Shepherd et al. mentioned above).

Since Efran's study, a number of others have examined the extent to which "mock" jurors' judgements are influenced by the facial appearance of a "defendant" or "victim". Those published prior to 1986 were reviewed by Bull and Rumsey (1988), who pointed out that the vast majority of these studies were ecologically invalid and that many of them were methodologically weak. Since then, a few better studies have been published.

A study by Darby and Jeffers (1988) examined the effect of defendant physical attractiveness and of "mock" jurors' self-perceived levels of attractiveness. In accord with Shaver's (1970) finding that less blame was attributed for an accident to those similar to "jurors" in terms of attitudes, values and feelings, it was hypothesised that the more similar defendant and juror were in terms of attractiveness, the more likely the defendant was to be found innocent or to receive a lighter sentence. Participants in Darby and Jeffers' study were given a written account of one of six crimes, each accompanied by a photograph of either a highly attractive, a moderately attractive or an unattractive young woman. Each of the six cases differed in their degree of ambiguity regarding the guilt or innocence of the defendant. Overall, attractive defendants received fewer guilty verdicts, and lesser sentences (if found guilty). Attractive defendants were also rated as more likeable, trustworthy and happy, and less responsible for the offence than were less attractive defendants. For participants rating themselves as attractive, the more attractive the defendant, the less likely a conviction—an effect which also arose in the sentencing phase. For participants rating themselves as less attractive, guilt was less affected by defendant attractiveness. When sentencing, these participants were most severe on moderately attractive defendants and least severe on very attractive defendants.

In 1991, Wuensch, Castellow and Moore attempted to replicate the oft-cited finding of Sigall and Ostrove (1975) that the effect of defendant attractiveness interacts with the nature of the crime (that is, that if the attractiveness of the perpetrator could in any way have influenced his or her likelihood of success when committing the crime, the tendency of leniency in favour of the attractive defendant is counteracted). Sigall and Ostrove found that whereas an attractive female burglar was sentenced by "mock" jurors to significantly fewer years of imprisonment than an unattractive burglar, no significant effect of attractiveness was found for a female swindler. This was attributed to the fact that the swindler's attractiveness may have been a significant factor in the success of the crime. Wuensch et al., however, found no evidence that the leniency effect of attractiveness disappeared when the crime was attractiveness-related.

In 2001, Abwender and Hough attempted to replicate the now traditional "mock" juror finding that unattractive "defendants" are treated more harshly. However, they found that only their female participants did this. The male participants were rather more harsh on the attractive "defendant", a woman accused of negligent homicide (killing a pedestrian as a drunk driver).

Interestingly, the male participants rated the attractive defendant as more responsible for the incident, this possibly explaining the non-traditional finding for the men. Abwender and Hough (2001) noted Mazzella and Feingold's (1994) suggestion that attractive defendants could be held to higher standards for their conduct/behaviour, and therefore may be treated more harshly when not meeting these standards. The defendant in Abwender and Hough's study was initially stopped by the police for reckless driving. The police did not then arrest her but called a taxi to take her home. However, the woman got out of the taxi, returned to her car, drove off, and then killed a pedestrian. It is possible that the attractiveness-leniency effect is more likely if the defendant has an external justification for the crime. Abwender and Hough make the good point that this effect "is considerably more complex than the 'what is beautiful is good' stereotype indicates" (p. 611).

Victim Appearance

Some studies have examined the effects of the attractiveness of the victim, especially in alleged rape. Again, many of these studies lack ecological validity. Ferguson, Duthie and Graf (1987) noted that a common misconception may exist within the general population regarding motives associated with rape. While most people believe such crimes to be exclusively sexually motivated, in many cases rape may be a show of power or anger, the expression of which is through a sexual act (see Groth, 1981). As such, victim vulnerability rather than victim sexuality may be associated with the rape, yet society, perversely, continues to attribute some of the responsibility for rape to the victims: how provocatively the victims were dressed, their attractiveness, and whether they were known to the rapist have all been posited, and indeed shown empirically, to be factors which displace at least some of the blame on to the victim. This "myth" that rape is primarily sexually motivated is most evident in considering victim attractiveness, and some research has found that attractive victims are deemed less responsible for the rape simply because they are attractive, and therefore more desirable. Conversely, it is sometimes assumed that unattractive women, being less desirable, must in some way have provoked an attack (e.g., Thornton & Ryckman, 1983).

ATTRIBUTIONS OF RESPONSIBILITY

Ferguson et al. (1987) examined the effect of informing male undergraduates of the reasoning behind a rapist's actions on their attribution of responsibility for the rape to attractive and unattractive "victims". As found in previous studies, participants given no rape information attributed less blame to the rapist when the victim was unattractive. In the informed condition, however, blame was attributed regardless of the attractiveness of the victim. Ferguson et al. concluded that educating jurors concerning the motivations which may explain rape may reduce attractiveness bias. In neither condition, however, was full responsibility for the rape attributed to the rapist, a phenomenon which can be explained by just-world theory—the idea that by attributing at least some blame to the victim we subsequently reduce the possibility of our own victimisation. They were victimised, but they did something to deserve it (which we would not do). If no blame could be attributed to the victim, the implication would be that rape can happen to anyone. The topic of victim blame is very relevant to how (alleged) rape victims are cross-examined in trials. In a number of countries (for example, England and Scotland), legislation now restricts the topics that cross-examination can address (for example, prior sexual partners).

Gerdes, Danmann and Heilig (1988) varied not only the attractiveness of the rape victim but also that of the defendant. They also varied whether the alleged perpetrator and victim were acquainted or not. Participants read one of eight versions of a "newspaper article" according to which the defendant was undoubtedly guilty of the rape. This lack of ambiguity allowed a test of Jacobson and Popovich's (1983) hypothesis that attractiveness effects should not be present in situations where the offence is indisputable (there was a rape, and the defendant was the assailant). The blame attributed to the unattractive victim was greater in the acquainted than unacquainted condition (that is, such victims were deemed to have provoked an attack), while it was in the acquainted condition that attractive victims were viewed as most responsible for the rape (perhaps because attractive women are held responsible for their ability to arouse men). At least in the 1980s, victims were thought to be less responsible when raped by an unattractive assailant (but see Vrij & Firmin, 2001).

In 1988, Kanekar and Nazareth found no effect of victim attractiveness on the length of sentence given or the attribution of blame to the victim in a rape case. In their study, attractiveness, physical hurt and emotional distress were manipulated in a passage describing a rape. Longer imprisonment was recommended, particularly by female participants, only when the victim was physically hurt, emotionally disturbed, and attractive, suggesting that punishment largely reflected participants' perceived seriousness of the rape.

Physically attractive people have often been shown (see Bull & Rumsey, 1988, for a review) to be evaluated more positively than less attractive people; in studies of mock jurors' judgements, attractive defendants (even those whom participants were informed were definitely guilty) are commonly treated more leniently. McKelvie and Coley (1993) sought to test whether this effect existed independently of crime severity. Participants read one of two crime descriptions, an armed robbery or an armed robbery plus murder, both of which stated that the person was guilty of the crime. Participants were also assigned to one of three cueing conditions: a low cue, where a picture of the offender (attractive or unattractive) was attached to the case description; a moderate cue, which also included a verbal description of the offender, drawing attention to his attractiveness; and a high cue, which also included another picture of the offender, this one attached to the actual judgement sheet. No effect of offender attractiveness on length of sentence was found for either crime. (Length of sentence, however, did vary as a result of crime seriousness.) However, the less attractive offenders were more likely to receive recommendations for psychiatric care, suggesting the existence of a negative relationship between attractiveness and attribution of mental illness. (For more on this, see Bull & Rumsey, 1988.)

Burke et al. (1990) attempted to evaluate the effect of physical attractiveness in a case of domestic violence. Participants read a hypothetical domestic violence scenario in which pictures of the husband and wife were presented. In the scenario, the husband claims his wife fell onto a table, and the wife claims her husband punched her in the eye. In contrast to Yarmey's studies mentioned above, there was no support for the contention that physical attractiveness affected decision making, whether it be for the victim or the defendant. Burke et al. questioned the validity of using undergraduates as representatives of the general population, a criticism of almost all of the research in this area.

More recently, Vrij & Firmin (2001) also examined the effect of (alleged) victim and defendant physical attractiveness in a "mock" setting. They found no evidence that rape defendant (male) attractiveness had an effect. However, they did find that the more attractive rape victim (female) was rated as more honest and less responsible for the event. Innovatively, they found that the "dependent variable" they entitled "strength of evidence" against the defendant (that is, from the woman's account) had a higher score when the victim was attractive, but since the variable combined the three judgement scales of "How strong was the evidence against this man? Is this case strong enough to bring to court? Do you think the man is guilty?" (p. 250), it is not possible to say whether victim attractiveness significantly affected how strong the (kept constant) evidence was thought to be. This is an important and under-researched question. Vrij & Firmin (2001) also found that victim attractiveness affected only those participants who scored higher in the rape myth acceptance scale ("People who endorse the rape myth tend to attribute more blame to a victim of rape and less to the assailant" [p. 247]). Thus, it seems that the effect of facial appearance is likely to be moderated by other factors relevant to the judicial setting.

GROUP DECISION MAKING

In 1990, MacCoun pointed out that research purporting to examine the possible effects of defendant or victim appearance on jurors had merely studied individuals' decisions, whereas juries deliberate in groups upon their verdict. (For more on this, see Chapter 8.) He noted that some juror deliberation studies (not on appearance) had found individuals' biases to be attenuated by the deliberation process (e.g., Kaplan & Miller, 1978), whereas other studies (e.g., Bray & Noble, 1978; Davis et al., 1978) had not found this. MacCoun attempted to determine whether jury deliberation would attenuate or enhance the effects of the victim and defendant attractiveness. Participants listened to an audiotaped trial simulation of a car theft, with victim and defendant attractiveness, in the form of photographs presented with the tape, being varied. Following the "trial", the participants completed a predeliberation questionnaire and then deliberated in groups of two, three or four; after the "jury" decision, they completed a further questionnaire. "Juries" were found more likely to acquit the physically attractive than the unattractive defendant, and, during deliberation, the participants' evaluations of the attractive defendant became more lenient, while, for unattractive defendants, these ratings did not change. Thus, the deliberation process seemed to exacerbate rather than alleviate the problem. (This is the opposite of what seems to happen with some other types of "inadmissible" evidence—see Chapter 8.)

META-ANALYSIS

This chapter's brief overview of some of the major publications examining the effects of facial appearance on mock jurors has revealed a lack of consistency in the findings. In their 1994 meta-analysis of previously published studies on this topic, Mazzella and Feingold pointed out that "According to law, juridic decisions should be reached exclusively from admissible evidence presented during the course of a trial" (p. 1315). However, their meta-analysis of the 24 studies (involving 4804 participants) resulted in the outcome that "mock jurors were less likely to find physically attractive defendants guilty than physically unattractive defendants although the effect size was small. Mock jurors also recommended less punishment for better-looking defendants, but the mean effect size was trivial" (p. 1325). Thus, overall, the simulation studies they reviewed suggest that in real trials jurors in deciding guilt or innocence could be affected to some extent by defendant attractiveness. The "trivial" effect size regarding punishment need not be generalised to real criminal trials, since in these it is usually the judge, not the jury, who decides upon this. However, while judges have more legal experience than jurors, they are still human and may be influenced by attractiveness. (Mazzella and Feingold also found in their meta-analysis that "The physical attractiveness of the victim had no effects on judgements of mock jurors" [p. 1325]).

In connection with generalising from mock juror research to real-life trials, Mazzella and Feingold made the important point that such research "has often been criticised for being simplistic and lacking ecological validity. A common criticism has been that experimental manipulations are unduly potent because of the brevity of the scenarios, inflating effects of extralegal characteristics" (p. 1336). They also made the crucial point that "the generalisability issue must not be ignored, and the results obtained in this meta-analysis should not be assumed to apply to actual jury outcomes" (p. 1336). (For more on this, see Chapter 8.)

For meta-analytic reviews of research on the effects of physical attractiveness, see Eagly et al. (1991) and Langlois et al. (2000), but also see Feingold (1992), whose meta-analysis found no strong relationship between physical attractiveness and many stereotypically linked qualities.

This being the case, why have researchers used mock jurors rather than real jurors? One reason is that in some countries studying real jurors is legally impossible. Another reason is that psychologists, for various reasons, often take the easy way and study available students' reactions in easily accessible situations (such as the classroom). Only a few researchers have examined real-life court settings.

REAL-LIFE COURT PROCEEDINGS

In 1991, Downs and Lyons noted that what is believed about the possible effect of facial appearance in the courtroom is based upon "mock jury" or simulation studies. However, they pointed out that extrapolation from such studies to the real world "are troublesome" (p. 541) partly because many criminal or civil trial outcomes are decided not by inexperienced laypersons (such as jurors) but by experienced judges, and also because many prior studies had purposely employed high and low levels of facial attractiveness rather than more normally occurring levels. In their own study, Downs and Lyons examined real-life decisions made by 40 judges in Texas concerning the amount of fine those pleading guilty should pay and the amount of bail that would be set for those pleading not guilty. One of the several creative aspects of their study was to ask the police officers who escorted the arrested persons to rate their attractiveness prior to the judges' decisions. (These police officers had not been involved in the arrests and were believed to be naive as to the purpose of the study.) A sample of the arrested persons was also rated for attractiveness by students of Downs and Lyons, and the interrater agreement (that is, police officers/students) was high. The arrested persons were charged with committing minor crimes (misdemeanours) or more serious crimes (felonies). For the misdemeanours, a strong significant relationship between attractiveness and the judges' decisions was found in that those lower in attractiveness received larger fines/higher bail. However, no effect of attractiveness was found for felonies. Downs and Lyons suggest that since more felonies may go to trial the judges knew that for these they were not making the final judicial decision. However, for many misdemeanours, the judge's decision ended the proceedings. Only future research can resolve this issue. Perhaps strength of evidence (in minor versus more serious cases) played a role. In closing, Downs and Lyons made (p. 547) the following important point:

> Over 10 years ago, Wilson and Donnerstein (1977) issued a strong appeal for researchers to move out of the controlled university laboratory setting and into the real-life environment of the legal system. We would echo that appeal even more strongly now. Unless researchers employ innovative means of on-site observation of the litigation process, knowledge in this area will remain confined primarily to the results of an assembly of artificial, perhaps even specious, and typically experimentally-driven findings.

Stewart (1980, 1985) has reported upon criminal trials attended by members of his observational team, who rated the physical attractiveness of defendants. He found that the attractiveness ratings (for which there was significant interrater agreement) correlated significantly, and negatively, not with subsequent judgements of guilt/innocence, but with the sentences received. This appears to be contrary to the outcomes of Mazzella and Feingold's meta-analysis and therefore underlines their point about generalising from simple-minded simulations to the real world. Stewart noted that the less attractive defendants were being tried for more serious crimes, and when crime seriousness was partialled out, the relationship between appearance and sentence severity was weaker. However, it was still significant. We need to ask why the less attractive defendants were being tried for more serious crimes. The psychological research reviewed earlier in this chapter could be used to begin to try to answer this question. We also need to ask why the judges in the real-life trials reported upon by Stewart seemed to be influenced by defendant attractiveness. Perhaps judges are only human! Zebrowitz and McDonald (1991) have also reported upon real-life court outcomes. They studied 506 proceedings in small-claims civil courts. They pointed out:

> A fundamental right guaranteed by the Fourteenth Amendment to the U.S. Constitution is that of a fair trial. This constitutional right rests on the principle that there is a presumption of innocence in favor of the accused and that guilt must be proven beyond a reasonable doubt. ... Because the influence of extralegal factors on judicial decisions poses a significant threat to this fundamental right, it is important to identify those factors that may bias a fact-finder's evaluation of evidence produced at a trial. One source of bias that has received considerable attention is the physical appearance of the litigants. (pp. 603–604)

Zebrowitz and McDonald studied proceedings in the small-claims civil courts for the following reasons: (i) decisions are made by an individual judge (thus group decision making does not occur); (ii) in all cases, each plaintiff is seeking financial damages, and therefore all outcomes will be on a common scale; (iii) such cases usually involve little evidence other than the testimony of the plaintiff and defendant (whereas in many criminal trials, other sources of evidence are common), and thus "the appearance of the defendant and plaintiff should be a more significant variable than in a criminal trial" (p. 606); and (iv) such proceedings involve intentional acts as well as negligent acts, a fact which permits examination of the relationship between facial appearance and judgements of responsibility. They found that the court judgements favoured the more attractive plaintiffs, but this effect was only marginally significant when legal variables were controlled for (such as the extent of legal support and whether responsibility was admitted or denied), and inversed for the most attractive plaintiffs. The attractiveness of the defendants was found to have no effect.

Zebrowitz and McDonald devote several hundred words of their paper to a discussion of why, unlike in published simulation studies, defendant attractiveness had no effect. Perhaps we, and they, should accept that in their study it had no effect precisely because it was irrelevant! However, they did find that as defendants increased in "baby-facedness" (defined as the extent to which a person's facial features resemble those of a prototypical baby), they were more likely to win cases involving intentional actions, but less likely to win cases involving negligent actions.

These real-life court studies of Stewart and of Zebrowitz and McDonald do not concur on the effects of defendant attractiveness. The former found some effect; the latter did not. The types of court cases in each study were different. Perhaps that explains the inconsistency, but, if it does, psychologists cannot generally claim that defendant attractiveness affects court outcomes. Indeed, one wonders how many studies finding null effects of appearance have been rejected for publication.

Other Real-Life Settings

There exists a small amount of research on appearance in other "law" settings. Let us now examine these. In 1973, Cavior and Howard suggested that facial unattractiveness may cause young people to be rejected by society and that this social rejection leads to delinquency. In their study, photographs of male juvenile delinquents and non-delinquents were rated (blind) by students. They found that the delinquents' faces received lower attractiveness scores.

Cavior, Hayes and Cavior (1974) attempted to determine whether the faces of convicted young female offenders (aged 19 years) had any influence within prison. They found that facial attractiveness correlated with (i) frequency of reports of violent aggression within prison (a negative relationship) and (ii) frequency of permitted trips into town (a positive relationship). Cavior et al. adopted a behavioural explanation (common in the early 1970s) of their findings, concluding that "the differing environmental consequences for attractive versus unattractive individuals may shape divergent behavioural repertoires. The relationship between aggression-based behaviour and physical attractiveness is perhaps one such example. If attractive individuals are reacted to more positively they may find less reason for recourse to violent means to achieve their goals" (p. 330).

Agnew (1984) also claimed to have found a relationship between physical attractiveness and juvenile delinquency. He noted that efforts could be made to reduce discrimination against unattractive individuals by making people aware of their own stereotypes and the influences these might have. In his study, male adolescents' self-reported data on delinquency was found to be related to ratings of appearance. However, his raters may not have been blind to the adolescents' delinquency.

More recently, Serketich and Dumas (1997) also investigated whether in real life there is a relationship between appearance and dysfunctional behaviour. They noted (p. 459) that "Despite extensive research on attractiveness and social judgement, we were unable to find a single study that had asked if behaviour-disordered children can be distinguished from nonbehaviour-disordered children on the basis of appearance alone". In their study, adults rated the attractiveness of photographs of young children (whom they did not know) who differed in aggression, anxiety and social competence. They found that the "dysfunctional" children were rated as significantly less attractive. However, this study failed to control for facial expression. (For more on how abnormal facial appearance interacts with negative facial expression, see Dijker, Tacken & van den Borne, 2000.)

A better study was conducted by Zebrowitz et al. (1998a), who found that boys who were "baby-faced" were *more* likely to be delinquent. They noted that Zebrowitz, Collins and Dutta (1998b) had found that baby-faced adolescent boys may be assertive and hostile, and they suggested that this could reflect a compensation mechanism (that is, such boys had to act tough to "survive"). They suggested that if baby-facedness normally elicits positive stereotyping ('What is beautiful is good'), adolescent boys who are good-looking may have to act even more negatively to be seen as tough. They found that among boys from below-average socio-economic status (SES) backgrounds, more of those who were baby-faced were indeed delinquent. However, among boys from above-average backgrounds, fewer of those who were baby-faced were delinquent (in line with the "old" "beautiful is good" stereotype). This appropriately complex study reveals the true nature of psychological effects. That is, many psychological factors impinge upon issues such as criminality often in interactive or opposing ways. To believe otherwise is extremely naive. Zebrowitz et al.'s (1998a) findings could be taken to suggest that higher SES baby-faced boys seek rewards in prosocial ways. Clearly, relationships between facial appearance and criminality will be affected by a variety of psychological phenomena.

SUMMARY AND CONCLUSION

We now need to ask to what extent the studies reviewed above support the notion that facial appearance is related to criminality/wrongdoing. The first main section in this chapter examined research on the extent to which people assume there to be a relationship between facial appearance and criminality. This research collectively seems strongly to suggest that such stereotypes do exist and are shared consensually. However, few studies have examined the accuracy or validity of these stereotypes.

Studies of the apparent effects of facial surgery upon prisoners' recidivism rates were then reviewed. These studies could be taken to suggest that facial appearance and criminality are related. However, the quality of their methodology and the presence of confounding variables need to be considered.

Research on the effects upon "mock" jurors of defendant and victim facial attractiveness was then described. Many of these studies controlled/kept constant the very sources of information thought relevant in court cases (such as the nature of the evidence), and solely as a consequence may have found some effect of an extralegal factor such as facial appearance. Moreover, this type of study seems to lack many other qualities present in the real-life setting (such as the consequences for the defendant of jury decisions). Furthermore, many of the studies used students as participants, who may not be representative of the population of real-life jurors. Nevertheless, the studies of real-life court decision making do claim to find some effect of facial appearance, though the studies do not concur on the nature of this effect or the underlying psychological processes.

We should always keep in mind the complexity of this chapter's topic, and the paper on baby-facedness and delinquency by Zebrowitz et al. (1998b) is an example of what good research should look like. We should also note one of its concluding points (p. 1318): "Clearly, it is important for future research to more definitely establish the mechanism by which facial appearance is related to behaviour. The current literature is too piecemeal to accomplish this important goal."

We will leave it to you, the readers, to decide whether Udry and Eckland (1984) (see the opening paragraphs of this chapter) were correct in stating, "Everyone knows that . . . Heroes are handsome and villains are ugly" (p. 47).

CHAPTER 4

INTERVIEWING SUSPECTS

Most police officers perceive interviewing of suspects to be the critical stage in criminal investigations (Baldwin, 1994). The purpose of a police interview of a suspect is to obtain further information about a crime. The importance of the interview depends on the evidence available in the case. When there is substantial evidence, which might be present in as many as 88 per cent of criminal cases (Wagenaar, van Koppen & Crombag, 1993), the interview would be used to clarify unsolved issues (such as the whereabouts of stolen goods, the motives of the criminal, and so on). The cooperation of a suspect is often necessary to resolve such issues but is not crucial for a conviction. An example is the case of Dr Shipman, the British general practitioner found guilty of murdering 15 women. He received 15 life sentences on 31 January 2000. Shipman denied all 15 charges, and the 57-day trial uncovered no obvious motive for the killings. He was convicted merely on the basis of the evidence against him. (An independent inquiry, carried out after his conviction, revealed that he had murdered at least 215 people, according to the *Independent*, 20 July 2002.)

When there is no evidence, the interview is used to obtain valid information in order to link the suspect or someone else to the crime. The cooperation of a suspect could then be crucial to solve the crime. It is therefore important for the police to induce suspects to talk. The implicit assumptions in most of the police literature are that suspects are very likely to be guilty, are not cooperative during police interviews and prefer to remain silent (Ofshe & Leo, 1997a). As a result of such assumptions, the police officer must *force* the suspect to talk. A comprehensive review of tactics the police use to achieve this is provided by

Kalbfleisch (1994), who reviewed 80 books and articles. However, undoubtedly, the most influential handbook about interrogation techniques, *Criminal Interrogation and Confessions*,[1] was written by Inbau, Reid and Buckley (1986), who, among others, present a "nine-steps approach to effective interrogation". This approach is summarised in the section "How to Get the Suspect to Talk". The nine-steps approach has been heavily criticised by various scholars (Gudjonsson, 1992; Kassin, 1997; Kassin & Fong, 1999; Leo, 1992; Ofshe & Leo, 1997b; Williamson, 1994). We will discuss their criticisms. The technique, in part, relies on trickery and deceit, which, although allowed in the USA (Leo, 1992; Slobogin, 2003), is unlawful in several Western European countries. Therefore, in these countries, interview techniques have been developed to *encourage* suspects to talk. These will be summarised in the section "How to Let the Suspect Talk".

The assumption that suspects are unwilling to talk sounds plausible. Confessing to a crime has negative consequences for a suspect, as it dramatically increases the likelihood of a conviction (Leo, 1996a; Otte, 1998; Wartna, Beijers & Essers, 1999). However, is it true that most suspects are not cooperative and are unwilling to talk? What, then, makes them decide to talk? The second part of this chapter addresses these issues, as well as the quality of police interviewing.

Research has shown that sometimes suspects do confess to crimes which they have not committed. The final part of this chapter deals with the topic of false confessions.

HOW TO GET THE SUSPECT TO TALK

Inbau et al.'s Nine-Steps Approach

Inbau et al. (2001) distinguish between *interviewing* and *interrogating*. Interviews, they argue, are nonaccusatory. The purpose of interviewing is to determine whether the suspect is likely to be guilty—for example, by establishing the suspect's alibi and by observing a suspect's verbal and nonverbal responses. Verbal responses claimed to be typical of untruthful suspects include, according to Inbau et al. (1986/2001), delayed, evasive or vague answers; unusually poor memory; statements against self-interest ("As crazy as it sounds...."; Inbau et al., 2001: p.137); and answering questions with a question ("Why would I do that?"; Inbau et al., 2001; p.133). Assumed behavioural clues to deception include posture changes, retreating posture (crossing arms in a tight fashion, and so on), grooming gestures, placing hand over mouth or eyes when speaking, gaze aversion, and hiding hands (by sitting on them) or feet (by pulling them under

---

[1]Inbau et al. (2001) have published a new edition of *Criminal Interrogation and Confessions*. This new edition is considerably more extensive (640 pages) than the previous version (353 pages). The nine-steps approach, summarised in this chapter, is described in both 1986/2001 editions; therefore, criticisms of the 1986 version, discussed in this chapter, also apply to the 2001 edition. All the quotations from Inbau et al. listed in this chapter appear in both editions, and the page numbers of both editions are added, with the first listed page numbers referring to the 1986 edition.

the chair). Several researchers note that police officers are often encouraged to look for "lie signs" (Baldwin, 1992, 1993; Leo, 1996b; McConville & Hodgson, 1993; Milne & Bull, 1999; Mortimer & Shepherd, 1999; Moston & Engelberg, 1993). It is also part of some local police training (Milne & Bull, 1999).

Interrogations, however, are accusatory, and their purpose is to persuade guilty suspects to confess. They should be conducted only when the investigator is reasonably certain of the suspect's guilt. If the police already believe that someone is guilty prior to the interview, they may be tempted to bypass the interview process and start interrogating. Inbau et al. (2001) state that this is generally not advisable because the interview process can facilitate the interrogation; for example, it creates the opportunity to establish rapport and trust.[2] Inbau et al.'s (1986/2001) interrogation technique consists of nine steps. They based this technique on their extensive interrogation experience and claimed that it has been used successfully by thousands of criminal investigators (Inbau et al., 2001; back cover). Inbau et al. advocate a tough approach, in which interrogation is meant to break the (guilty) suspect's resistance to tell the truth. The nine steps are as follows:

1. positive confrontation
2. theme development
3. handling denials
4. overcoming objections
5. retaining subject's attention
6. handling the suspect's mood
7. creating an opportunity to confess
8. oral confession
9. converting an oral confession into a written one.

Step 1 consists of a direct presentation of real or fictional evidence and the suspect's involvement in the crime; for example, "Our investigation shows that you are the one who...". This accusation is followed by a brief pause in which the suspect's behavioural cues are closely observed. The interrogator then repeats the accusation. Suspects who fail to make a denial after this second direct confrontation are considered to be deceptive. (Inbau et al., 1986/2001, present several assumptions—such as the principle that two denials imply guilt— throughout their book, but most of them have never been empirically tested. The available empirical evidence concerning the nine-steps approach will be discussed throughout this chapter and is mainly related to step 2.)

Step 2 deals with theme development and differs for emotional and non-emotional suspects. In the case of emotional suspects, the interrogator should try to build up rapport, basically by offering them a moral excuse for having committed the offence. This could be achieved by telling them that anyone else in the same situation might have committed the same type of offence, minimising

---

[2]The interview stage is not needed when "the suspect is caught in an incriminating circumstance or clearly evidences a desire to tell the truth during initial questioning" (Inbau et al., 2001; p. 10).

the moral seriousness of the offence, suggesting a more morally acceptable motivation for the offence, condemning others and so on. Suspects who seem to listen attentively to these suggestions are supposed to be guilty. Kassin and McNall (1991) called this the minimisation approach, describing it as a technique in which the police interrogator tries to lull the suspect into a false sense of security by offering sympathy. The following example, given by Inbau et al. (1986/2001) illustrates this technique: "Joe, no woman should be on the street alone at night looking as sexy as she did. . . . It's too much temptation for any normal man. If she hadn't gone around dressed like that you wouldn't be in this room now" (p. 108/257).

Non-emotional suspects perceive an interrogation, according to Inbau et al., as a "contest of endurance", as "pitting their willpower against the interrogator's persistence" (pp. 127–128/281). Effective techniques in interviewing non-emotional suspects include seeking an admission of lying about some incidental aspect of the crime (in that case, the interrogator can say, "You lied to me once, and you will lie to me again"); trying to let suspects associate themselves with the scene of crime, pointing out that all the evidence leads to their guilt and that it is futile to resist telling the truth; and so on. Kassin and McNall (1991) called this the maximisation approach. This is a technique in which the interrogator tries to intimidate the suspect into confessing by exaggerating the seriousness of the offence and the magnitude of the charges, and, if necessary, by making false claims about evidence (as by staging an eyewitness identification or a rigged lie-detector test, by claiming to have fingerprints or other types of forensic evidence, or by citing admissions that were supposedly made by an accomplice [Kassin, 1997]).

Step 3 deals with handling denials of guilt. It involves stopping the suspect's repetition or elaboration of the denial (by using the techniques described in step 2), and is, according to Inbau et al., a crucial step, because the more frequently guilty suspects repeat a lie, the harder it becomes for the interrogator to persuade suspects to tell the truth. It is contended that most innocent suspects will not allow their denials to be cut off, whereas guilty suspects are more likely to allow the interrogator to return to the conversation theme. Innocent suspects are assumed to stick with the denial, but guilty suspects usually change their technique by providing a reason why the accusation is wrong, such as "I couldn't have done that—I don't own a gun".

Step 4 consists of overcoming these objections. It is assumed that an efficient way of doing this is showing understanding and returning to the conversation theme: "That may be true, but the important thing is . . . " (p. 158/336). Once suspects feel that the objections are ineffective, it is assumed they will become uncertain and begin to show signs of withdrawal.

Step 5 requires that the interrogator react to this uncertainty by retaining the suspect's attention. This could be achieved by moving physically closer to the suspect, leaning towards him or her, and maintaining eye contact.

Step 6 deals with handling a suspect's passive mood. When the suspect appears attentive, the interrogator should focus the suspect's mind on possible reasons for committing the crime. The interrogator should exhibit signs of understanding and sympathy, and should urge the suspect to tell the truth. Finally, the interrogator should attempt to create a remorseful mood—for instance, by pointing out the negative consequences the crime has had for the victim.

Step 7 is the use of an alternative question. Suspects are given the opportunity to provide an explanation or excuse for the crime, a step which makes admissions easier to achieve; for example, "Was this your own idea, or did someone talk you into it?" Whichever alternative a suspect chooses, the net effect of an expressed choice is an admission.

After the selection of an alternative, *step 8* consists of the development of the initial admission into a detailed confession that discloses the circumstances, motives and details of the crime. Inbau et al. advise that the questions asked by the interrogator at this stage should be brief, clear and designed so that they can be answered in a few words. Furthermore, questions should not contain harsh or emotionally charged terminology. *Step 9* deals with converting an oral confession into a written one. This step is important because suspects sometimes deny that they made an oral confession.

An Adaptation of the Inbau Technique: A Case Study

In 1996, a Dutch solicitor consulted one of the authors (Aldert Vrij) about a police interview with a man (a hash dealer) suspected of kidnapping and murdering in the Netherlands. The suspect had been extensively interviewed before, but had remained silent throughout these interviews. He was therefore exposed to a special technique apparently successful in dealing with reluctant suspects. At the beginning of the interview, the detectives (several were involved throughout the interviews, which lasted nearly 30 hours in total) told the suspect that he could expect a jail sentence up to 12 years if he did not talk.[3] Although the police detectives did not present any real or fictional evidence at this stage, they made clear to the suspect that it was pointless for him to remain silent (step 1 of Inbau et al.'s approach). They then introduced several minimisation and maximisation techniques. Regarding minimisation techniques, the suspect was told, "We know you did not intend to kill this person—you are just an honest hash dealer, and there is nothing wrong with that [whilst selling and dealing hash are illegal in the Netherlands, prosecution for small amounts has been abolished]. We know that

---

[3]Informing suspects about the sentence they might expect could be seen as a threat. Confessions as a result of explicit threats (and promises) typically lead to dismissal in court, even in the USA (Kassin, 1997). Inbau et al. (1986/2001) are also against explicit threats and promises, as they believe that these may elicit false confessions. However, they do believe that implicit threats and promises (the minimisation and maximisation approaches discussed above, as well as presenting fictitious evidence) do not entail this risk, nor are such tactics illegal in the USA (Kassin, 1997). Kassin and McNall (1991) argue that explicit threats and promises have the same effect on suspects as implicit threats and promises.

you are not the type of person to kill somebody. Killing someone sometimes happens even to the best of characters"; and "I am sure you will get a lower sentence if you confess." He was also shown photographs of his wife and daughter (whom he had not seen or spoken to for the last two months), and was told that he would be allowed to telephone them after making his confession. Regarding maximisation techniques, he was told, "If you don't confess, your wife will also end up in prison for complicity", "If your wife goes to prison, your daughter will have to go to an orphanage, and you know what happens to girls sent to orphanages: they all end up as prostitutes." He was also told, "Your wife received several telephone calls from a person threatening to kill her and your daughter. We will protect them, but only if you confess." (In fact, no threatening telephone calls were made.) The suspect confessed to both kidnapping and murder, and informed the police where the victim's body could be found. However, his confession was later thrown out in court, and several elements of the interview technique were banned by the Dutch government. The police detectives who conducted this interview did not appear to think that anything was wrong with the technique; the team leader defended the method in court. This is perhaps not surprising because police officers tend to view several interrogation tactics as more acceptable than do civilians (Skolnick & Leo, 1992).

A Social-Psychological Explanation of the Nine-Steps Approach

Attitude Change in the Interview Room

Theoretically, the effectiveness of Inbau et al.'s nine-steps model may be explained in terms of social-psychological theories of attitude change (Ajzen & Madden, 1986). Attitudes are an individual's evaluations of particular persons, groups, objects, actions or ideas, and are important in predicting behaviour. Simply stated, somebody's attitude towards an attitude-object (for instance, confessions) is based upon the perceived positive and negative aspects of that attitude-object. The more positive and/or the fewer negative aspects that are perceived, the more positive the attitude will be; the more negative and/or the fewer positive aspects that are perceived, the more negative the attitude will be. An attitude will become more positive when positive aspects are emphasised and negative aspects diminished. In police interviews, a more positive attitude towards confession and, consequently, an increased likelihood of a confession, can be obtained in the following manner. First, one must eliminate the negative consequences of admitting guilt. The major disadvantage of confession compared to a denial is that a confession will lead to a conviction while denial possibly may not. An effective way of eliminating this negative aspect is by giving the suspect the impression that denial will also lead to a conviction. This can be done by telling the suspect that there is already enough evidence for a conviction (step 1 of Inbau et al.'s approach: "If you remain silent, you will end up in prison for 12 years"). Subsequently, one emphasises the positive aspects of admitting guilt (minimisation approach, step 2 and step 6): "I am sure you will get a lower sentence if you confess"; "If you confess, we will protect your wife and daughter"; and so on), and one emphasises the negative aspects of not making a confession (maximisation approach, step 2: "If you don't confess, your wife will also end up in prison for complicity, and your daughter will become a prostitute") in order to create a more positive attitude towards confession. The more positive the attitude towards confession, the more likely that the suspect will finally confess.

Nine Concerns with the Nine-Steps Model

Despite its popularity among practitioners in some countries[4] (Gudjonsson, 1992), numerous problems arise with Inbau et al.'s nine-steps approach, as summarised in the following nine points.

1. Trickery and deceit (providing fictional evidence, creating a false sense of security, exaggerating the seriousness of the offence and so on) are unlawful in several countries (Gudjonsson, 1992), a fact which implies that evidence obtained via trickery and deceit will not be allowed in court. This happened in the Dutch case already described. Pearse and Gudjonsson (1999) describe several British cases in which the evidence obtained in police interviews was disallowed in court.

   Apart from being illegal, trickery and deceit may be considered unethical too. Inbau et al. themselves do not deny this, but they believe that such practice is justified when dealing with criminals. Referring to the case of a man who confessed to murdering his sister-in-law, they say:

   > It involved the taking of a human life by one who abided by no code of fair play toward his fellow human beings. The killer would not have been moved one bit toward a confession by being subjected to a reading or lecture regarding the morality of his conduct. It would have been futile merely to give him a pencil and paper and trust that his conscience would impel him to confess. Something more was required—something that was in its essence an "unethical" practice on the part of the interrogator; but, under the circumstances involved in this case, how else would the murderer's guilt have been established? (pp. xvii/xv).

   Inbau et al.'s view is shared by some American scholars (Slobogin, 2003). However, Williamson (1994), now a retired British deputy chief constable, pointed out that unethical behaviour may undermine public confidence and trust in the police (and other agencies).
2. The nine-steps approach of psychologically manipulating people via trickery and deceit may lead to false confessions (Gudjonsson, 2001). The problem with tricks and deceit is that they make both guilty and innocent suspects more willing to confess. There is no trick that makes only guilty suspects more willing to talk. As a result, the more successful a trick is in eliciting confessions from guilty suspects, the more likely it is that this trick will result in false

---

[4]McKenzie (1994) refers to Inbau et al.'s book as "the bible of the American interrogator" (p. 249). In the UK, Walkley (1987) followed the Inbau model in his *Police Interrogation: A Handbook for Investigators*, and more recent manuals (Gordon, Fleisher & Weinberg, 2002; Hess, 1997) also rely heavily on the Inbau model.

confessions as well. Inbau et al. acknowledge the problem of false confessions and give the following solution: "A guideline that an interrogator may use in any case situation where he may be in doubt as to the permissibility of any particular type of trickery and deceit, is to ask himself the following question: 'Is what I am about to do, or say, apt to make an innocent person confess?' If the answer is 'no', the interrogator should go ahead and do or say what was contemplated. On the other hand, if the answer is 'yes', the interrogator should refrain from doing or saying what he had in mind" (pp. 217/486–487). The obvious problem, not addressed by Inbau et al., is that the police can never know for sure whether they are making a correct judgement. In the false confessions section of this chapter, more valid methods to determine the veracity of confessions will be discussed.

3. Pressing suspects to confess may result in the opposite effects to those intended by the police; that is, suspects who would normally confess may not confess at all if they feel they are being rushed or unfairly treated by the police (the "boomerang effect": Gudjonsson, 1994a).

4. When suspects feel that they have been induced to confess by unfair means, they retain strong feelings of resentment towards the police, even many years afterwards (Gudjonsson, 1992).

5. Moston and Stephenson (1992) illustrated that bluffing is a poor interview technique: "Suppose an interviewer lies and tells a burglar that his fingerprints have been found at the scene of crime. If that burglar had been wearing gloves then he would know this statement is a lie and he will probably view anything the interviewer says from that moment on with either contempt, or at least with a high degree of cynicism" (p. 214). Inbau et al. (2001) acknowledge this problem and recommend that this tactic be used only as a "last resort effort" (p. 429). Ofshe and Leo (1997a) have demonstrated that American police detectives can be very creative in introducing examples of bluffing, such as non-existent technology: "The Cobalt Blue test has proven that the fingerprints on the body of the victim belonged to you"; "The Neutron Proton Neglicence Intelligence Test has indicated that you are the person who shot the man." These sorts of tricks are allowed in the USA, but are illegal in several Western European countries.

6. Use of trickery and deceit may encourage the police to lie in other contexts as well (Leo, 1992).

7. In vulnerable individuals, oppressive police interviewing may result in post-traumatic stress disorder (Gudjonsson, 1994a).

8. By asking in the confession phase (step 8) questions which can be answered by suspects in a few words, the police risk that the confession reflects more what they believe has happened than what actually has happened. (See Moston and Engelberg, 1993, for examples.)

9. Inbau et al. mention nonverbal cues of deception (postural shifts, grooming gestures and placing a hand over mouth and eyes) that are not identified as such in the literature on nonverbal indicators of deception (Vrij, 2000; see also Chapter 2). Inbau et al. rely heavily on such nonverbal cues to detect deceit, probably more than is justified. Very few people are skilled at detecting

deception on the basis of nonverbal behaviour (Ekman, O'Sullivan & Frank, 1999; Vrij, 2000a; Vrij & Mann, 2001).

HOW TO LET THE SUSPECT TALK

The Situation in England, Wales and the Netherlands

Baldwin (1992) described a less oppressive approach to interviewing suspects. The use of trickery, deceit, and other methods to build up psychological pressure is no longer included, and nonverbal cues to deception are disregarded. Preparation/planning, rapport building and the social skills of the interviewer are accentuated instead. Baldwin gives the following description of a good interviewer:

> The best interviewers appear to bring to interviews some natural social skills which they adapt as the circumstances demand . . . they had generally prepared carefully beforehand, they put the allegations clearly and calmly and made no assumptions about what the response to the allegations should be . . . they listened to what the suspects had to say, challenging denials that were made when they did not square with the available evidence and, without harrying or bullying, retained a firm control of what was taking place. A good interviewer therefore has well-developed communicative and social skills, a calm disposition and temperament, patience, subtlety, and ability to respond quickly and flexibly, legal knowledge and some imagination. (p. 13)

The three major elements in Baldwin's definition, planning, rapport building and social skills, were emphasised more recently by other researchers. Cherryman and Bull (1996) and Williamson (1993) pointed out that preparation and planning are of considerable importance for the quality of investigative interviews (see Chapter 5). Soukara, Bull and Vrij (2002) interviewed 40 police detectives working in the south of England, who reported that they considered preparation of the interview to be the most important aspect of interviewing suspects. Cherryman and Bull (2001), who interviewed 81 police officers, also found that police officers considered preparation (together with listening) to be very important. Köhnken (1995) also stressed the importance of planning. He considered planning as a method to reduce cognitive load on the interviewer during the interview, resulting in more cognitive capacity being available for information processing during the interview. Moreover, Köhnken believes that rapport building is an important factor in the success of an interview, because it creates a more relaxing atmosphere, in which people are more willing to talk. After listening to 69 taped police interviews with suspects, Bull and Cherryman (1996) concluded that differences between "skilled" and "not skilled" interviews could be attributed to the communication skills of the interviewer, particularly the ability to show flexibility, empathy and compassion. Stockdale (1993) mentioned that fairness, an open mind, listening skills and maintaining integrity are important elements of a good interview style.

Williamson described a new ethical framework of police interviewing in the UK (Sear & Williamson, 1999; Williamson, 1994), which is based upon three principles: (i) to shift the police service from its traditional reliance on getting a suspect to confess to seeing its task as a search for the truth; (ii) to encourage officers to approach an investigation with an open mind; (iii) to encourage officers to be fair.[5] There are reasons to believe that these principles have not been achieved yet. Securing a confession remains an important objective in a police interview; the majority of police detectives continue to believe that a suspect is guilty, and the police still use illegal tricks to obtain a confession, particularly when they interview suspects who are suspected of serious crimes and are reluctant to talk. We will return to these issues in the "quality of a police interview" section.

Blaauw, now a retired Dutch police chief constable, published in 1971 his 99 guidelines for police interviewing. Like Baldwin and Williamson, who published their ideas more than 20 years later, he believed that a good police interviewer is flexible, has an analytic style of thinking and is socially skilled. Back in 1971, Blaauw strongly opposed the use of trickery and deceit.

Van den Adel (1997), a former employee at the Dutch training institute for police investigations, has published the most detailed manual for police interviewing written in Dutch to date. In 1999, Brian Ord, a retired British detective superintendent and Gary Shaw, a detective inspector, published their detailed police manual in English. Although the manuals are written by different authors working in different countries, they are remarkably similar. Both manuals emphasise the importance of detailed information-gathering at the beginning of the police investigation. Both manuals argue that, before the interview starts, the detectives should have been to the scene of crime and know its description; should know all available facts relating to the crime (evidence obtained at the scene of the crime, statements of witnesses and any peculiarities); and should know the suspect (background characteristics, family circumstances, possible addictions, possible diseases and so on).

Both manuals further describe how to use open and closed questions in police interviews. They both advocate an information-gathering strategy at the beginning of the interview, as this increases the possibility of eliciting an account from the suspect. The use of open questions is generally preferable (see also Bull, 1999; Shuy, 1998; and Chapter 5). These usually elicit longer answers and therefore more information. They are an invitation to suspects to present their point of view and will increase the likelihood that suspects believe that the interviewer takes them seriously. Open questions encourage suspects to talk and therefore facilitate the desired format of a police interview: the suspect talks and

---

[5]In England and Wales, several books and booklets have been published that list guidelines for ethical police interviewing, including *A Practical Guide to Investigative Interviewing* (NCF, 1998). Among other things, this book recommends a specific interview structure (PEACE) which consists of the following five steps: Planning and preparation, Engage and explain, Account, Closure and Evaluation. See Milne and Bull (1999) for a discussion of the five PEACE steps.

the interviewer listens and asks for clarifications (Van den Adel, 1997). An interviewer who is prepared to listen has more chance of being liked by suspects, and this, in turn, might make them more willing to talk. According to Ord and Shaw (1999), closed questions are also useful in interviews, particularly to obtain short, factual answers on specific points. However, these questions should be used sparingly at other times, and rarely in the early stages of the interview (Ord & Shaw, 1999).

Differences Between Inbau et al. and Baldwin/Williamson

Inbau's technique is aimed at impressing the suspect and breaking down the resistance of the suspect. In Baldwin's and Williamson's views, interviewing is essentially an information-gathering exercise, and certain skills are needed to elicit relevant and accurate information. In fact, their police interviews do not differ substantially from interviews in other contexts, such as interviews with patients or selection interviews (Buckwalter, 1980; Stephenson, 1992). Patients may sometimes lie to their doctors about their symptoms or behaviour, and candidates for a job may have an incentive to be economical with the truth. In all these situations, the interviewer must try to find out the truth and must create an atmosphere in which the interviewee is willing to talk. Needless to say, Inbau's interrogation technique differs strongly from doctor–patient interviews and job interviews.

The different styles of police interviewing are, at least partly, influenced by cultural differences. Inbau et al. are Americans and Baldwin and Williamson are British, and, as already mentioned, some tactics, apparently used in the USA (such as trickery and deceit), are not allowed in England and Wales. Since the introduction of the Police and Criminal Evidence Act (PACE) in 1986 (Baldwin, 1993; Moston & Stephenson, 1993b), the use of these tactics to obtain a confession may well render the confession inadmissible in court.[6] PACE included new legislation governing the way in which suspects are arrested, detained and interviewed by police officers. The Act was intended to provide safeguards for suspects (and also for police officers). For example, a special code ensured that suspects are not subjected to undue police pressure, tricks or oppression (Moston & Stephenson, 1993a). In the case of vulnerable suspects, an independent and responsible third party (the "appropriate adult") has to be called in by the police to provide special assistance to the suspect during the police interview. Moreover, PACE prescribes that all police interviews with suspects in police stations are audiotaped. These audiotapes are accessible to solicitors, judges, juries and experts, making the use of unacceptable tactics easy to check in principle. However, Pearse and Gudjonsson (1996c) pointed out that, in the first decade after the introduction of PACE, only a handful of tapes have actually been

---

[6]We do not suggest that all Americans are in favour of Inbau et al.'s approach. On the contrary, American scholars such as Kassin, Leo and Ofshe are among the fiercest opponents.

listened to in court so far. The tapes are mostly used for research. We will return to the audiotaping and appropriate adult issues later.

Gudjonsson (1992) believes that the British outcry for, and subsequent legislation regarding, less oppressive police interview techniques is heavily influenced by cases such as "the Guildford Four" and "the Birmingham Six", well-known British miscarriages of justice. Both cases are described in detail by Gudjonsson (1992). McKenzie (1994) and Leo (1992) provide detailed information about the background, history and development of police interviewing in England/Wales and the USA, respectively.

At first sight, Baldwin's and Williamson's approaches look "softer" than Inbau et al.'s technique; however, this is not necessarily the case. Moreover, in Baldwin's and Williamson's approaches a "tough" interview is allowed, but the use of tricks is forbidden. It might be that suspects who decided not to talk during the interview will remain silent without the use of tricks. If this is true, Baldwin's and Williamson's approaches will not be successful in interviewing uncooperative suspects. Whether this is a real disadvantage depends, of course, on the percentage of suspects that are unwilling to talk during police interviews. The higher this percentage is, the bigger the disadvantage will be. We will now discuss suspects' willingness to talk.

HOW MANY SUSPECTS CONFESS AND WHY?

Percentage of Suspects That Confess

Several studies have been published which provide estimates of confessions occurring at police stations during police interviews. Most of these studies have been carried out in England and Wales, and they all provide similar confession/admission rates, ranging from 49 per cent to 61 per cent (Baldwin, 1993; Evans, 1993; Moston & Stephenson, 1994; Moston, Stephenson & Williamson, 1992; Pearse & Gudjonsson, 1996c; Pearse et al., 1998; Softley, 1980). The comparison between the Softley (1980) study and the other studies is interesting because Softley's study was conducted before PACE was introduced in 1986. One might therefore conclude that the "softening" of the interview technique, the result of PACE, did not result in a strong decrease in confessions. This conclusion is further supported by findings of Irving and McKenzie (1989). They concluded that, while the number of manipulative and persuasive tactics has declined in England and Wales as a result of PACE, the number of admissions has remained relatively constant at 62 per cent in 1979 and 65 per cent in 1986. However, the conclusion is premature for at least three reasons: (i) many suspects are willing to talk without much encouragement, so coercive interview techniques were often not necessary even when they were still allowed; (ii) there is evidence to suggest that PACE has resulted in "off-the-record interviews" (interviews which are not audiotaped and not registered) in which unallowed coercion still takes place; and (iii) there is also evidence that, despite being illegal, coercive interviews still take place in England and Wales in certain circumstances. We will return to these three issues below.

Thomas (1996) and Slobogin (2003) reviewed studies examining the confession rates of American suspects. The average rates varied from 50 per cent to 55 per cent and are thus similar to the rates in England and Wales. In another American study, Leo (1996a) reported a 65 per cent confession/admission rate.

The confession studies further reveal that most interviews are short (typically 20–30 minutes [Vrij, 2003]). Longer interviews are typically concerned with serious offences (Robertson, Pearson & Gibb, 1996), and most suspects are cooperative during police interviews. Baldwin (1993) examined 600 taped police interviews of suspects in England and reported that in the majority of these cases (80 per cent) suspects were thoroughly cooperative and answered police questions of any significance. Baldwin gave the example of a suspect who gave full details of a very serious assault on his girlfriend. The suspect said he had been "insane with jealousy" and was completely open about what happened. He was more concerned about the future of the relationship with his girlfriend than the legal consequences of the assault. Moston, Stephenson and Williamson (1993) examined 1067 police interviews (fully reported in Moston et al., 1992), and found that only 5 per cent of the suspects remained completely silent. In Moston and Stephenson's (1994) study, nobody remained silent and in a study of Dutch suspects (Wartna et al., 1999), hardly anyone (0.3 per cent) remained silent. The stereotypical belief that suspects tend to deny involvement in crimes or prefer to remain silent, and that interviewing is a tough and lengthy process, is thus simply untrue.[7]

It is not surprising that research findings contradict the common beliefs. First, a refusal to talk might not be in the suspect's own interest. Baldwin (1994) pointed out that about a third of all cases end as police cautions. However, this option is available only to suspects who admit involvement in a crime. Second, being interrogated is often a very stressful experience, even for some experienced criminals (Gudjonsson, 1993; Sear & Stephenson, 1997). Cooperation reduces the period of interviewing. Third, being detained in a police station is a stressful experience, too (Gudjonsson, 1993). Once arrested, suspects are regularly detained in police cells for up to four hours, and in some instances for considerably longer periods (Evans, 1994). Suspects who are initially unwilling to talk may be much more cooperative after a few hours in a police cell (Foppes, 2000, personal communication). Fourth, it is difficult for people to keep information entirely private. For example, a study regarding the role of secrets in people's lives (Vrij et al., 2002) revealed that the vast majority of people confide a secret to somebody else, even when they believe that there are serious negative consequences if these secrets come out.

---

[7]Baldwin (1993) pointed out that the fact that suspects can be cooperative is usually overlooked in popular police culture, where attention is typically paid to the awkward individuals.

Reasons to Confess

Numerous studies have examined why suspects confess (Baldwin, 1993, 1994; Bordens & Bassett, 1985; Evans, 1993; Gudjonsson & Petursson, 1991; Gudjonsson & Sigurdsson, 1999; Holmberg & Christianson, in press; Lowenstein, 1999; McConville & Hodgson, 1993; Moston & Stephenson, 1994; Moston et al., 1992; Pearse & Gudjonsson, 1996c; Pearse et al., 1998; Pearse & Gudjonsson, 1999; Sigurdsson & Gudjonsson, 1994, 1996; Wartna et al., 1999). Many of these studies, including several comprehensive ones, have been conducted in England and Wales. For example, Moston et al. (1992) examined a random sample of 1067 interviews conducted in England and tried to find out which factors led to a confession. They proposed four main sets of factors that may influence confessions, namely, background characteristics of the suspect (age, sex, criminal history), characteristics of the offence (type of offence and offence severity), contextual characteristics (strength of evidence and legal advice) and the interviewer's questioning techniques. Elsewhere we describe most of these studies (all the English studies) in more detail (Milne & Bull, 1999; Vrij, 2003). Here we restrict ourselves to the main findings of these studies.

Different studies reveal somewhat different outcomes to explain why suspects confess, but the following factors were significant predictors in more than one study: (i) strength of evidence, (ii) perceived seriousness of the crime, (iii) the presence of a legal adviser and (iv) the criminal history of the suspect.

As was predicted by the theoretical framework regarding attitude change, the stronger the suspects perceive the evidence against them to be and the less serious the offence, the more inclined they are to confess. Moston et al. (1992) found that 67 per cent of the suspects confessed when they perceived that the evidence against them was strong, whereas only 10 per cent confessed when the evidence was weak. Evans (1993) also found that only 9 per cent of (juvenile) suspects confessed when the evidence against them was weak.

Suspects are also less likely to confess when there is a legal adviser present during the interview, for at least two reasons. It might be that legal advisers advise suspects not to confess. Alternatively, as conformity studies have revealed, people are less likely to give in in the presence of an ally (Allen & Levine, 1971; Asch, 1956). It may therefore be that the mere presence of a legal adviser strengthens the suspect's resistance.

Suspects with previous convictions were least likely to confess. Several explanations are possible. More experience with police interview tactics may make suspects better able to resist such tactics. Alternatively, people with previous convictions are more likely to be questioned on a routine basis for subsequent offences. They therefore run a higher risk of being interviewed for offences which they have not committed. It may also be that for offenders with previous convictions the consequences of confessing are more serious than for those without convictions, as previous convictions may contribute to harsher sentencing in case of conviction.

Finally, the studies revealed that only a small minority of suspects changed "position" throughout the interview. The great majority of suspects (more than 95 per cent) stick to their starting position (admission, denial or somewhere between), regardless of how the interviews were conducted. These findings inspired Moston et al. (1992; p. 38) to write: "Police officers would probably like to think that suspects make admissions because of skilled questioning techniques. The reality, however, is in all probability quite different." Although this conclusion probably makes good newspaper headlines, it is somewhat misleading. In many cases which were analysed, the offences were minor, the evidence was substantial and the suspects were (therefore) willing to talk. In such cases, interviewing is simple and straightforward, and no enhanced questioning techniques are required. Such techniques, however, are required with reluctant suspects, especially if they are suspected of serious offences. There are numerous examples of reluctant suspects who are suspected of serious crimes and who do start talking as a result of interview tactics used by the police (for example, see the Dutch case described above). The problem is that such tactics are often unprofessional, as will be outlined below.

QUALITY OF THE INTERVIEW

As mentioned before, the new ethical framework of police interviewing in England and Wales (after the introduction of PACE) is based upon three principles: to shift the police service from its traditional reliance on getting a suspect to confess to seeing its task as a search for the truth; to encourage officers to approach an investigation with an open mind; and to encourage officers to be fair. There are reasons to believe that these principles have not been achieved yet, perhaps because police officers are not taught how to conduct such interviews, as it seems to have been assumed that this would happen automatically (Sear & Stephenson, 1997). Another explanation is that the spirit of the guidelines is in direct conflict with the police culture (Stephens & Becker, 1994).

Search for the Truth

Both Moston et al. (1992) and McConville and Hodgson (1993) found that in the great majority of cases (in both studies, 80 per cent) the objective of the police was to secure a confession. More recently, Plimmer (1997) reported that experienced British police officers believe that obtaining confessions is the main aim of interviews with suspects, and Mortimer and Shepherd (1999) concluded that the confession culture still lives on. There are several reasons why obtaining a confession seems attractive to police officers. First, there is often pressure on the police (from the general public, media and political agenda) to solve crimes quickly. Clear-up rates are an important measure of police performance, and obtaining a confession is one of the quickest routes to clearing up a crime

(Baldwin, 1993; Evans, 1994; Maguire, 1994; McKenzie, 1994; Milne & Bull, 1999; Stephenson, 1992). For example, Baldwin (1993) noted that a confession would result in praise from colleagues and considerable saving of time spent interviewing witnesses, preparing lengthy files, and appearing in court. McKenzie (1994) quotes a police officer: "It is far easier to sit comfortably in the shade rubbing pepper into a poor devil's eyes, than to go out in the sun hunting up evidence" (p. 245).

Second, suspects who confess are much more likely to plead guilty (Stephenson, 1992). Third, confession evidence is often seen as a prosecutor's most potent weapon (Baldwin & McConville, 1980; Kassin, 1997; Kassin & Neumann, 1997; McCann, 1998a; Ofshe & Leo, 1997a; Wakefield & Underwager, 1998). If a defendant's confession is admitted at trial, it may have considerable value, and many other aspects of the trial will be viewed as less important (Kassin & Neumann, 1997; McCann, 1998a; Otte, 1998; Stephenson & Moston, 1994; Underwager & Wakefield, 1992). Underwager and Wakefield (1992) pointed out that confessions have a compelling influence on jurors, who are more likely to vote guilty on the basis of a confession than almost anything else, including eyewitness identification. Indeed, few confessions are challenged in court; fewer still are challenged successfully (Baldwin, 1993). Experimental studies have revealed that jurors rely on confessions even after they know that they have been obtained with coercive interview techniques, and even after they have been told to dismiss the confession evidence in their decisions (Kassin & McNall, 1991; Kassin & Sukel, 1997; Kassin & Wrightsman, 1980, 1981; see also Chapter 8). These findings reveal an error of judgement frequently found in psychology research called the "fundamental attribution error" (Jones, 1990; Ross, 1977), the tendency to neglect the influence of external factors on people's actions. Wagenaar et al. (1993) provide explanations of why confessions are so convincing. Among others, they argue that confessions are by definition plausible because they fit the prosecution's story of what has happened (see also Chapter 8). Denials and retractions are less plausible, because they do not usually provide a strong alternative story of what has happened.

Fourth, confessions are seen by police detectives as a mark of personal and professional prowess if obtained from an initially resistant suspect (Mortimer, 1994). Fifth, police officers readily assume that a suspect is guilty (Bull, 2002b; Evans, 1994; Mortimer & Shepherd, 1999; Moston et al., 1992; Stephenson & Moston, 1994). For example, Stephenson and Moston (1994) found that in cases where the evidence was moderate, 74 per cent of the officers were "sure" of the suspect's guilt before they interviewed that suspect, and in cases where the evidence was weak, 31 per cent still assumed guilt. Not surprisingly, the tendency to seek a confession increases when police are sure of the guilt of a suspect (Stephenson & Moston, 1994).

Sixth, the UK legal system might encourage police officers to obtain confessions (Stephenson & Moston, 1994). In the UK, defendants can be, and sometimes are, convicted merely on the basis of their confessions, even when the confession is disputed at trial (Gudjonsson, 1999a).[8] In many other countries, such as the Netherlands and the USA, a confession has to be corroborated by some other evidence, although in practice the corroboration criteria allowed by judges are sometimes weak (Wagenaar et al., 1993).

Open-mindedness

Moston et al. (1992) noted two interview styles used by the police. An accusatorial strategy (whereby suspects were confronted with the accusation against them at the very outset of the questioning) and an information-gathering strategy ("open" questioning style intended to let suspects describe their actions in their own words, without an overt accusation being made). Although the latter corresponds with the desired open-mindedness of police officers, the usual form of interviewing was accusatorial (Stephenson & Moston, 1994). Moston et al. (1992) found that the choice of style did depend on the perceived strength of evidence and offence severity. An accusatorial strategy was used in cases when the officers perceived the evidence against the suspect to be strong, whereas the information-gathering style was used when the evidence was perceived to be weak. The latter strategy was also commonly observed with serious offences, particularly those sex-related. However, Holmberg and Christianson (in press), who investigated the views of convicted murderers and sexual offenders about their own police interviews, found that sexual offenders more often reported a high degree of coercion than did murderers.

Lack of open-mindedness might also have to do with police officers' personality. Sear and Stephenson (1997) investigated personality measures among police detectives, finding that many of them had "a cold, calculating and dominant approach to others" (p. 32). Obviously, such an interpersonal style goes well with accusatorial interview strategies.

Assuming a suspect's guilt makes it difficult for a police officer to be open-minded (see also Hargie & Tourish, 1999; Mortimer & Shepherd, 1999), as can be explained with the concepts of "confirmation bias" and "belief perseverance" (Brehm, Kassin & Fein, 2002). The confirmation bias refers to people's tendency to seek, interpret, and create information that verifies their existing beliefs. People want to support their own "theories" and are therefore eager to verify their beliefs but less inclined to seek evidence that might disprove them. In fact, people tend to maintain beliefs even after they have been discredited (belief perseverance). The reason is that once early impressions are formed it is difficult to "see straight" when presented with improved evidence (Bruner & Potter, 1964).

---

[8]Although in England and Wales a suspect might be convicted on the basis of a confession alone, the judge should give a strong warning to the jury that care is needed before convicting on the basis of a confession only (Sear & Williamson, 1999).

Although police officers typically praise their own interview skills (Bull & Cherryman, 1995), researchers in England and Wales who listened to audiotaped police interviews disagree with this point of view and generally criticise the interview skills of police officers (Vrij, 2003). For example, Baldwin (1993) criticised the communication skills of the interviewers. He found most attempts to build rapport highly artificial. Some interviewers tried an approach on the lines of "Tell me something about yourself"—an invitation that was usually received with confusion and unease. Moreover, most officers appeared nervous, ill at ease, and lacking in confidence throughout the interview. Several interview styles were questionable and unprofessional (such as misleading the suspect, interrupting the suspect, terminating the interview as quickly as possible after an admission, and losing control of an interview—for example, overreacting to provocations by the suspects). Similar findings were obtained by Moston et al. (1992): interviewers appeared to be very nervous, often more nervous than the suspects. Police interviewing skills were, as Moston (1996: p. 92) described in another study, "almost non-existent".

Several authors (Baldwin, 1993; Moston et al., 1992; Pearse & Gudjonsson, 1996c; Stephenson & Moston, 1994) noticed that police detectives had a somewhat limited repertoire of interview techniques and limited strategic flexibility. Baldwin (1993) pointed out that even when the suspects denied an allegation, no challenge was made by the interviewer in almost 40 per cent of cases. Stephenson and Moston (1994) came across several strategies, but they noticed that each officer tried only one strategy, and tended to stick to it even when it clearly did not work.

However, the question, "what is a good interview?", is difficult to answer, as it is a subjective judgement. There is no guarantee that different people would reach the same assessments of the quality of any particular interview. Cherryman (2000) looked at this issue. She found that four experts did agree in their assessments of the quality of the interviews they were asked to listen to. However, none of these raters were police officers (nor were the raters in Baldwin's and Stephenson and Moston's studies mentioned above). Cherryman therefore invited police officers (both police detectives and police supervisors) to assess the interviews, which were also rated by the experts. Perhaps the most interesting finding was the presence of a "confession effect" among police detectives. They evaluated interviews that contained a confession more positively than interviews that did not contain a confession. No confession effect was found among the four experts nor among police supervisors.

Fair Interviewing and the Use of Tactics

Pearse et al. (1998) noticed that the police generally placed very little pressure on suspects. However, their sample included many straightforward cases in which the evidence was strong and the suspect willing to talk. In these interviews, pressure is not necessary. More insight into the use of police tactics would be obtained by looking at interviews with reluctant suspects, particularly when they are suspected of serious crimes.

Evans (1993) found that persuasive tactics were most frequently used in these cases. McConville and Hodgson (1993) observed several persuasive techniques used in interviewing reluctant suspects, including downgrading (trying to get the suspect to talk about anything—for example, lifestyle or relationships—if the suspect does not want to talk about the offence; once a dialogue is established, the conversation can be led back to the offence in question), upgrading (providing information which tends to implicate the suspect) and direct accusation (suggesting that silence implies guilt). They concluded that sometimes these strategies are effective in persuading reluctant suspects to talk, but they also believed that sometimes these tactics soured the atmosphere and alienated suspects who might otherwise have been persuaded to cooperate. Moston and Engelberg (1993) and Stephenson and Moston (1994) observed police tactics in 133 cases where right of silence was exercised. Upgrading (explained above) was used most often, followed by persistence (merely repeating the same or a similar question), which was found to be a highly unproductive and sometimes embarrassing strategy that revealed that the officers were at a loss. Perhaps the most detailed analysis of police methods in interviews with reluctant suspects was published by Pearse and Gudjonsson (1999). They examined the techniques used in 18 serious criminal cases. To overcome resistance and secure a confession, the police relied heavily on tactics such as intimidation (manipulating details, manipulating self-esteem, maximising anxiety, threats and so on) and manipulation (minimising seriousness and responsibility). In three cases, the interview style resulted in a guilty plea and conviction. Several times, however, the police resorted to tactics which were unprofessional, unethical and illegal. As a result, in four cases, the interviews were classified as inadmissible, and two cases were withdrawn because the interview was found to be unreliable.

Leo (1996a) probably carried out the most detailed study of tricks used by the police in the USA (for descriptions of more tricks, see also Leo, 1992, 1996b; Ofshe and Leo, 1997a,b). As mentioned above, more tactics are allowed in the USA than in many European countries. Leo concluded that in his sample of 182 custodial interrogations, police questioning methods in only four (2 per cent) of the cases could be labelled as "coercive". In 30 per cent of the cases, detectives began the interview session by confronting the suspect with false evidence suggesting the suspect's guilt. (Providing false evidence is allowed in the USA but is illegal in many Western European countries.) Leo's (1996a) results further revealed that most tactics were used when the crime was serious and the evidence weak. In particular, appealing to the suspect's conscience, identifying contradictions in the suspect's story and minimisation (the use of praise or flattery, and offering moral justifications) were the tactics most likely to yield incriminating information. On average, 5.62 tactics were employed per interview.

In summary, the police in some countries use tricks which lead to confessions. However, the use of tricks has two disadvantages. First, the police run the risk that the confession will be dismissed as evidence in court. Second, these tricks may result in false confessions. The problem with tricks is that they make both guilty and innocent suspects more likely to confess. The next section deals with false confessions.

FALSE CONFESSIONS

How Often Do False Confessions Occur?

How often false confessions occur is unknown. Kassin (1997) reported that estimates range from 35 per year to 600 per year in the USA alone. It is often difficult to establish whether a confession is false. One might look at police coercion during the interview; however, a confession which is obtained with an oppressive interview style could be truthful. One might look at the retraction of the confession; however, a confession could be truthful, even when the suspect retracts it after the interview, and suspects who are convicted on the basis of their confession and do not appeal against their conviction could nevertheless have made false confessions. Finally, one might look at the accuracy of the confession; however, a confession the accuracy of which cannot be established beyond doubt (for example, because independent case facts are not available) is not necessarily false, and innocent suspects may give accurate "incriminating" accounts of what has happened—for example, because police detectives provide case information to suspects, who subsequently incorporate this into their statements. We return to the issue of how to check the veracity of confessions later.

Some researchers classify confessions as "proven false confessions" and "disputed confessions" (Gudjonsson, 1999c), as "unsafe confessions" (Gudjonsson, Kopelman & MacKeith, 1999), or as "proven", "highly probable" and "probable" false confessions (Leo & Ofshe, 1998). However, this does not prevent disagreement in the literature about the actual falsity of false confessions (Olio & Cornell, 1998; Perr, 1990).

Among others, Kassin (1997), Leo (1996a), Underwager and Wakefield (1992) and Wakefield and Underwager (1998) all pointed out that enough cases have been documented to suggest that a concern with the risk of false confessions is justified. Leo and Ofshe (1998) documented 60 cases in which false confessions were certainly or very likely made; Gudjonsson, sometimes in cooperation with others, has described numerous cases (Gudjonsson, 1992, 1999b,c; Gudjonsson & MacKeith, 1990, 1994; Gudjonsson, Kopelman & MacKeith, 1999), and others have reported cases as well (Brinded, 1998; Huff, Rattner & Sagarin, 1986; Kassin, 1997; Ofshe & Leo, 1997a; Santtila et al., 1999; Wagenaar et al., 1993; Wright, 1994).

The problem is that police officers themselves (and also laypersons and judges; McKenzie, 1994) are generally reluctant to accept that false confessions occur (Gudjonsson, 1992; McConville, 1992; Perske, 1994), as the following statement by a police interviewer (American) shows: "There is a principle in interrogation. A person will not admit to something they haven't done, short of torture or extreme duress. No matter how long you are grilled, no matter how much you are yelled at, you are not going to admit to something you have not done" (Perske, 1994: p. 159). Unfortunately, this police officer was involved in interviewing Johnny Lee Wilson, a mentally disabled man who falsely confessed to having murdered a woman. Perske (1994), who had access to the audiotapes of that interrogation, gives a detailed description of this case. The interrogation was tough; Wilson initially denied guilt but finally confessed. The police themselves helped Wilson to make his confession. For example, Wilson was asked what he used to bind the victim's ankles. "'I'm thinking. . . . Handcuffs, I think,' Wilson said. 'No. No. Wrong guess,' responded the officer. 'The victim's ankles had been bound with duct tape'" (pp. 157–158). A couple of years later, Wilson explained why he confessed. He became frightened when the officers grabbed his face and turned it toward them. "A cop said: 'Well, if you confess—we can all go home.' At that point I thought he meant me too" (p. 158).

Inbau et al. (1986/2001) acknowledge the danger of false confessions. In their view, three interview techniques lead to false confessions: (i) inflicting physical force, (ii) the threat of physical harm, and (iii) an interrogator's promise to suspects that if they confess they will go free or receive only a lenient penalty. They therefore reject such techniques. However, regarding their nine-steps approach, Inbau et al. (1986/2001) state that "it must be remembered that none of the steps is apt to make an innocent suspect confess" (p. 78/212). Gudjonsson described this point of view as "naive" (Gudjonsson, 1992: p. 323) and "misguided" (Gudjonsson, 1994a: p. 241).[9] The problem is that Inbau et al. look at each trick separately. For example, about presenting fictitious evidence, they (Inbau et al., 2001: p. 428) say: "Consider an innocent rape suspect who is falsely told that DNA evidence positively identifies him as the rapist. Would this false statement cause an innocent person to suddenly shrink in the chair and decide that it would be in his best interest to confess? . . . Of course not!" However, they ignore the notion that it is a *combination of issues* that may result in false confessions (Gudjonsson, 1992, 1994a). For example, it is probably the combination of several tricks employed by the police, a susceptible suspect, and interviewers determined to secure a confession (Milne & Bull, 1999) that makes false confessions possible. Moreover, in apparent contrast with Inbau et al.'s views, Leo (1992) noticed that police officers believe that psychological tactics are far more effective at eliciting confessions than the use of physical force. McKenzie (1994), a psychologist but once a police officer, shares this point of view.

Different Types of False Confessions

Several authors distinguish between three psychologically distinct types of false confession: *voluntary false confessions*, *coerced-compliant false confessions*, and

---

[9]Later in their book, Inbau et al. (2001: p. 446) take a position which is somewhat less extreme when they state that their interview technique "greatly reduces the risk of an innocent suspect confessing".

coerced-internalised false confessions (Gudjonsson, 1992; Kassin, 1997, 1998; Kassin & Wrightsman, 1985; Stephenson, 1992).

Voluntary False Confessions

Voluntary false confessions are false confessions which are given without any external pressure from the police. Commonly, people go voluntarily to the police station and inform the police that they have committed a crime they learned about from television or the newspaper. There are several reasons why people give voluntary false confessions. First, people may falsely confess because of a "morbid desire for notoriety", that is, a pathological need to become infamous and to enhance self-esteem, even if it means the prospect of imprisonment. For example, Huff, Rattner and Sagarin (1986) mentioned a case in which a man confessed to murder in order to impress his girlfriend. Gudjonsson (1999c) conducted a psychological evaluation of the "serial false confessor", Henry Lee Lucas, a man who is estimated to have confessed to over 600 murders in the early 1980s. When asked why he had made all these confessions, Lucas answered that, prior to his arrest, he had no friends and nobody listened to him or took an interest in him, but that once he began to make false confessions, all that changed, and that he now had many friends and enjoyed his celebrity status.

Second, people may falsely confess in an attempt to relieve guilt. Gudjonsson (1992) stated that this type of false confession is most likely in depressive people, and he described the case of a depressive man who had a disturbed and turbulent childhood. As a result, he tended to confess to murders which had taken place in a part of the country where he had been at some point in his life. Third, people may falsely confess because they are unable to distinguish fact from fantasy. According to Gudjonsson (1992), schizophrenic people especially are prone to this type of confession. He described the case of a schizophrenic woman who heard a conversation in a hospital ward about a murdered woman, and who subsequently thought that she was the murderer. Fourth, people may falsely confess because they want to protect the real criminal. For example, a father might falsely confess to a crime he knows his son has committed. Fifth, people may confess because they see no possible way of proving their innocence (after failing a polygraph test or after being accused by a psychological expert as being guilty), and confess in order to get a reduced punishment. Sixth, suspects may falsely confess to pre-empt further investigation of a more serious offence (Milne & Bull, 1999; Shepherd, 1996). Finally, suspects may confess to hide other, non-criminal facts. Huff et al. (1986) mentioned the case of an adulterous woman who falsely confessed to a murder in an attempt to hide the fact that she was with her secret lover at the time of the murder.

Coerced-Compliant False Confessions

Coerced-compliant false confessions occur when suspects make a confession they know to be untrue as a result of the police interview. Compliance refers to a change in one's public behaviour for instrumental purposes (Kassin, 1997), and this phenomenon was demonstrated in the classic conformity experiments of Asch (1956) and the obedience experiments of Milgram (1974). This type of confession results from the pressures of police interviews and from the tricks used by the police in these interviews. As a result, suspects believe that the benefits of confessing outweigh the costs. People confess in order to escape from the police interview, which they consider to be stressful and intolerable (Paddy Armstrong, one of the Guildford Four, said he confessed for this reason); they confess because of police tricks in which they have been promised a reward to confess; or they confess because of a combination of the two. The Dutchman suspected of murder (case is described above) may have made a confession due to a combination of pressure and tricks (although we do not say that his confession was false). He was told that a confession would lead to a reduced sentence, and that his wife and daughter would be protected by the police (the police gave him the false impression that their lives were in danger). A confession would also result in the termination of an interview in which he was severely humiliated for over 20 hours.

As an example of a coerced-compliant false confession, Santtila et al. (1999) describe the Finnish case of Ms A., who falsely confessed to having been an accomplice in a bank robbery. When she was later asked why she had made this confession, she said that she was confused and not feeling well (at the time of the confession, she had withdrawal symptoms due to the abrupt cutting off of her consumption of alcohol and medication), so she thought there was no point in resisting the questioning and gave in.

On the other side of the world, in New Zealand, it is believed that R.S., a 17-year-old man with a sensory motor deficit and poor reading and writing skills, falsely confessed to arson. Although the fire brigade and insurance company were both under the impression that the fire was accidental, the police suspected arson and interviewed R.S. Tearful and greatly distressed, he falsely confessed during the interview because the police told him that he would be in more trouble if he continued to deny setting the fire than if he admitted that he had set the fire deliberately. R.S. retracted his confession and was acquitted by the jury.

Coerced-Internalised False Confessions

Coerced-internalised false confessions occur when people come to believe, during police interviewing, that they have committed the crime they are accused of even though they have no actual memory of having committed the crime. Internalisation refers to a private acceptance of the beliefs espoused by others (Kassin, 1997), a phenomenon observed in Sherif's (1936) autokinetic studies and Moscovici's (1985) minority influence work. Carole Richardson (one of the Guildford Four) reported such an experience.

Moreover, Ofshe (1989) gives a detailed description of the case of Tom Sawyer, a socially anxious man and former alcoholic, who finally came to believe he had committed a murder of which, in fact, he was innocent. In trying to engage

Sawyer in conversation about the crime, the detectives asked him to help them create a scenario of how the murder might have happened. Sawyer, who loved to watch detective shows on television, was eager to help and joined in. The police let Sawyer explain several scenarios and accused him at the end of having committed the murder. The police claimed that Sawyer knew nine facts that only the killer could have known. Analysis of the interrogation transcripts afterwards showed that all the crucial information had been introduced into the interrogation by the police. After the accusation, Sawyer strongly denied his guilt. The police obtained fingerprints and hair samples from Sawyer and suggested a polygraph examination. Sawyer believed that the polygraph examination would prove his innocence and agreed to the examination (see Chapter 2 for more on polygraphs). After the test, the examiner told Sawyer that the test proved he was lying (subsequent rescoring of the test by a polygraph expert revealed that the test outcome was inconclusive).

Once told that the polygraph showed him to be lying, Sawyer's confidence began to erode. He was no longer able to express firm denials of guilt; he could only say that he still did not believe he had done it. His main defence against the police demands to confess was his lack of memory of having committed the crime. The police replied that he was blocking out his memory of the crime, that he had a blackout, just as he often had when he had been drinking. At this point, Sawyer still refused to accept that he had committed the crime, hoping that the other tests (fingerprints and hair test) would prove his innocence. The detectives decided to lie to him and told him that his hair samples matched hairs found on the victim's body. With receipt of this information, Sawyer's resistance collapsed, and he agreed that "all the evidence was in" and that he must have committed the crime.[10]

Kassin and Kiechel (1996) have demonstrated in the laboratory that false incriminating evidence can lead people to accept guilt for a crime they did not commit. Participants were accused of damaging a computer by pressing the ALT key that terminated the program. All were truly innocent and initially denied the charge. Half of the participants were then confronted with a witness (in fact, a confederate) who told the experimenter that she had seen the participant pressing the ALT key. Of those participants, 65 per cent falsely confessed to having pressed the key. The remaining participants were confronted with a witness who told the confederate that she had not seen what happened. Of those participants, only 12 per cent made a false confession.

Internalised false confessions do not imply that suspects become convinced that they have committed a crime. According to Ofshe and Leo (1997a,b), internalised false confessions occur because suspects have formed the opinion that it is *more*

---

[10]The fact that these tricks lead to false confessions might appear surprising. However, one should realise that police suspects are often not average people. For example, their IQ is typically low (Gudjonsson, 1990). A sample of 160 suspects in England had an average IQ of 82 (Gudjonsson et al., 1993), and people with low IQ are more suggestible (Gudjonsson, 1999a). Sawyer was also a socially anxious man and a former alcoholic, and it might have been the combination of police tricks and the personality of the suspect that created the false confession.

likely than not that they are guilty. They typically have no memory of having committed the crime, but the tactics used by the police aiming to diminish suspects' confidence in their memory make them less certain of their innocence and make them wonder whether it might be possible that they did commit the crime.

Ofshe and Leo (1997a) distinguish between five types of false confessions:

1. *Voluntary false confessions*, which were also identified by Kassin (1997).
2. *Coerced-compliant false confessions*, which are the result of coercive police interview tactics (also identified by Kassin, 1997).
3. *Stress-compliant false confessions*, which are not caused by the interview techniques, but by the interview situation. Being confined in an unfamiliar setting, isolated from social support; having little or no control over the timing, duration or emotional intensity of the interview; and the uncertainty of the interview and outcome may all induce significant distress that results in suspects trying to escape the situation—if necessary, by making a false confession.
4. *Non-coerced persuaded false confessions*, which are elicited when the police shatter suspects' confidence in their memory, with the result that they become convinced that it is more likely than not that they have committed the crime (identical to Kassin's coerced-internalised confessions).
5. *Coerced-persuaded false confessions*, which occur when suspects, despite having doubts about their own memory, are still reluctant to confess. Persuasive police tactics are then used, eventually resulting in a confession.

McCann (1998a,b) makes a distinction between four types of false confessions by adding one more category to Kassin's (1997) typology: *coerced-reactive false confessions*. These confessions are the result of coercion from sources other than police. McCann (1998a) describes the case of a woman who had confessed to the murder of one of her children after her husband physically assaulted her and intimidated her into taking the blame for the child's death.

How to Detect False Confessions

The best way to distinguish between false and true confessions is to look for intimate knowledge and impossibilities (Wagenaar et al., 1993). Intimate knowledge is present when the suspect provides information which only the guilty suspect could know (for example, information about where the victim's body is located). Impossibilities refer to providing evidence which conclusively demonstrates that the person could not have committed the crime. Gudjonsson (1999c), for example, pointed out that Lucas's confession could not be true because on the day of the murder he was over 1300 miles away from the scene of crime. The problem, however, is that courts tend to attribute such impossibilities to errors in the confession rather than as evidence of a false confession (Wagenaar et al., 1993). Gudjonsson (1999c) concludes that the uncritical willingness to accept Lucas's confession was the most fundamental mistake made by the police. However, Milne and Bull (1999) cite a police officer who claims that it is the responsibility of the court, and not the police, to check the veracity of a confession.

Gudjonsson (1992) suggested analysing the language structure used by false confessors and genuine confessors during interrogations to find out whether these two types of confessions differ linguistically from each other. Although, at least to our knowledge, such analyses have not yet taken place, employing techniques to assess the veracity of speech content, such as statement validity assessment (Köhnken & Steller, 1988; Raskin & Yuille, 1989; Steller, 1989; Steller & Köhnken, 1989) or reality monitoring (Johnson & Raye, 1981, 1998), might be a way of doing this. See Vrij (2000) for a discussion of these techniques.

Suspects are likely to retract or withdraw their coerced-compliant and coerced-internalised false confessions as soon as the immediate pressures are removed (Kassin & Wrightsman, 1985). Retracted confessions should therefore be treated with prudence because they may indicate false confessions. However, voluntary false confessions are unlikely to be withdrawn; therefore, confessions which are not withdrawn could be false too.

How to Prevent False Confessions

Several ways can be suggested to prevent false confessions. However, one should keep in mind that none of the suggested methods are perfect and that, despite these measures, false confessions could still occur. Therefore, carefully checking the veracity of each confession remains necessary.

1. Both coerced-compliant and coerced-internalised confessions are the result of police pressure and police tricks during interviews. Hence, an obvious way to prevent false confessions is to reduce such pressure and tricks. This could be established by utilising more information-gathering techniques rather than techniques used solely to obtain confessions.
2. It might be fruitful to audiotape or videotape all interviews. These recordings could then be checked for any illegal coercive tactics. Moreover, knowing that the interviews will be audiotaped and videotaped might prevent police detectives from using oppressive tactics. As stated above, as a result of PACE legislation, all interviews with suspects are currently audiotaped in England and Wales. However, audiotaping and videotaping have disadvantages too (Vrij, 2003). For example, in videotaping, the behaviour of the suspect might have an impact on the impression judges and jurors form about the suspect's potential guilt. This could be problematic. People have strong beliefs about how liars behave, and these beliefs are often inaccurate (Vrij, 2000; see also Chapter 2). As a result, by watching videotapes, observers may well come to an inaccurate impression about a suspect's alleged guilt or innocence.
   Kassin (1997) mentioned additional problems with using videotaped interviews in the courtroom, such as the "point-of-view bias" (if the camera

focuses on the suspect during the interview, this camera perspective may lead observers to underestimate the amount of pressure exerted by the "hidden detective"; Lassiter & Irvine, 1986), and the "recap bias" (observers are unlikely to see the whole interview, but only part of it). This is potentially very manipulative, as the prosecution or defence may show only those parts of the interview which support their view.

McConville (1992) pointed out that the standard audiotaping of police interviews in England and Wales (a PACE requirement) has resulted in "off-the-record interviews" in which pressure still occurs. He gave examples of off-the-record exchanges between the police and suspects in which unallowed coercion (threats) or unallowed deals (promises) took place. These off-the-record interviews were held before the formal, audiotaped interviews, and led to confessions during the latter. This practice led McConville to conclude that "tape recorders provide no protection for suspects against police wrong-doing" (p. 962). Evans (1993, 1994), Gudjonsson (1994a, 1995) and Moston and Stephenson (1993b, 1994) acknowledge that pressure on suspects outside the formal interview setting is a serious problem in England and Wales. Moston and Stephenson (1994) compared the outcomes of interviews conducted in the police stations of two groups of suspects: those who were, prior to these interviews, interviewed outside the police station and those who were not interviewed outside the police station. They found that suspects who had been interviewed outside the station were more likely to make an admission in the station and less likely to deny an accusation. They further found a positive link between "non-offence-related conversations" (conversations about topics other than the offence) held outside the station and subsequent admissions during police interviews. Moston and Stephenson (1994) give several explanations for this. It may be that some suspects, for reasons of personality, are more likely to chat with police officers, and these "friendly" suspects might also be more inclined to confess. Alternatively, something said by the officers during the non-offence-related conversations (perhaps comments about the possibility of bail) might have an effect on subsequent interviews.

3. Solicitors should be present during the interviews. They could act as a safeguard and protect the interests of their clients by preventing detectives from unfair questioning. However, experiences with legal advisers present during interviews are not entirely satisfactory in England and Wales. A main concern is the passivity among legal advisers (Baldwin, 1993; Pearse & Gudjonsson, 1996a, 1997a,b). Baldwin (1993) observed several cases where legal advisers sat in silence throughout the interview when one would have expected some intervention from them. Pearse and Gudjonsson (1996a, 1997a,b) noticed that the interventions of legal advisers were mostly related to administrative matters rather than improper tactics. The presence of a passive legal adviser during an improper interview is worrying, as it can give that interview an unjustified legitimate and credible status. In other words, an interview style which could be classified as illegitimate when the solicitor was not present is unlikely to be challenged if a passive solicitor was present.

4. Individuals who are more likely to give false confessions should be identified. PACE introduced the concept of "appropriate adult", an independent and

responsible third party, called in by the police to provide special assistance to a vulnerable suspect during a police interview. The role of appropriate adults is to advise the person being questioned and to observe whether or not the interview is being conducted fairly. It is also their role to facilitate communication with the person being interviewed (Sear & Williamson, 1999).

The introduction of appropriate adults is not yet entirely successful in England and Wales. It is still unclear what their exact role is in a police interview, and there are instances where their role has been devalued. The latter was illustrated by a police officer's explanation of an appropriate adult's expected role: "You are wallpaper, pal" (Pearse & Gudjonsson, 1996b: p. 573). Moreover, appropriate adults do not always act in their client's interest. Pearse and Gudjonsson (1996b) described the case of a 14-year-old who was suspected of kidnapping and robbery. His uncle was present as an appropriate adult. At the very beginning of the interview, the uncle launched a series of 15 challenging and sometimes hostile questions, before he was stopped by the police officer. Finally, like the presence of legal advisers, the presence of an appropriate adult in an interview gives the interview legitimacy and credibility (Pearse & Gudjonsson, 1996b; Robertson et al., 1996).

Gudjonsson's research deals with identifying vulnerable people. He claims that people with mental disorders (schizophrenia, depression or learning disabilities), abnormal mental state (phobias, high anxiety or recent bereavement), low intellectual abilities (low IQ), and personality characteristics, such as suggestibility and compliance, are more likely to give unreliable confessions (Gudjonsson, 1994b, 1999a). The problem is that it is difficult for the police and even for trained clinicians to identify such vulnerable subjects (Gudjonsson, 1993; Milne & Bull, 1999; Pearse, 1995). This problem is partly caused by the fact that no operational definition exists in relevant UK laws of "mental disorder" (Pearse & Gudjonsson, 1996d).

Gudjonsson (1984, 1987, 1989, 1997) developed scales to measure interrogation suggestibility and compliance.[11] He claims that his scales are highly accurate in identifying interrogative suggestibility and compliance. For example, in the Birmingham Six case, the four people who confessed had higher scores on the suggestibility and compliance scales than the two who did not confess. However, as Gudjonsson (1992: p. 312) admits, suspects' mood (anger, for example) influences their susceptibility to suggestion (see also Chapter 7). This creates a problem. A suspect's mood during the interview that led to a confession can differ from his or her mood during completion of the test, leading to different scores of susceptibility to suggestion between the two occasions (Vrij, 1995). Moreover, Milne and Bull (1999) pointed out that in this approach suggestibility is seen as a personality factor; in contrast, they argue that suggestibility might be more the result of situational factors, such as inappropriate interviewing.

---

[11]According to Gudjonsson (1992), in suggestibility there is personal acceptance of the proposition offered by the interrogator, whereas a compliant response does not require personal acceptance of the proposition; people may disagree with the proposition or request made, but they nevertheless react in a compliant way.

An alternative way of identifying vulnerable suspects is asking suspects about their own vulnerability. Singh and Gudjonsson (1984) found that individuals' opinions of their own competence and intelligence are related to their suggestibility, and Gudjonsson and Lister (1984) demonstrated that people who perceived themselves as lacking competence and control during the interview, and who judged the interviewers to be strong and powerful, were more suggestible. Clare and Gudjonsson (1992) asked suspects who had already been independently established as vulnerable or not whether they found themselves vulnerable. Results showed that 80 per cent of the suspects classified themselves correctly; that is, they identified themselves as vulnerable. Unfortunately, they did not ask suspects who were objectively not vulnerable to estimate their own vulnerability. It is therefore unknown to what extent these suspects find themselves vulnerable. The method of identifying vulnerable people will work only if a high percentage of non-vulnerable people classify themselves as not vulnerable.

5. Finally, perhaps the most convincing safeguard against false confessions is the requirement of additional, corroborative evidence (apart from the confession evidence) that the confession was not false (Wagenaar et al., 1993).

SUMMARY AND CONCLUSION

Some police tactics have been claimed to be effective in persuading even reluctant suspects to talk. However, many of these tactics are illegal in several Western European countries; if they use them, the police risk that the obtained confession will be dismissed as evidence in court. Additionally, such tactics can result in false confessions.

The use of persuasive techniques will probably be necessary to get reluctant suspects to talk, and in serious cases this is in the public interest. Guidance should therefore be given to the police about which persuasive techniques are effective and legitimate. It is probably the role of researchers to design such appropriate techniques.

However, one should not concentrate just on reluctant suspects. They are in the minority; most suspects are willing to cooperate during police interviews. Many researchers have criticised police interview skills in such interviews, and guidance should be given to the police on how to conduct these interviews more skilfully and more effectively (McGurk, Carr & McGurk, 1993; Milne & Bull, 1999; Soukara et al., 2002). Psychologists give such advice already, although in some countries (such as England and Wales) more than in others (the USA) (Milne & Bull, 1999).

Research has further indicated that suspects are most likely to talk when they perceive the evidence against them to be strong. This finding contains the ultimate method to get reluctant suspects to talk: obtain evidence which links them to the crime.

CHAPTER 5

INTERVIEWING WITNESSES

Just 20 years ago, there had been published very few quality psychological studies on the interviewing of child witnesses (see Loftus & Davies, 1984, for a review). In the next 10 years, the situation improved a little so that the body of such research (plus useful ideas derived from developmental, cognitive and other "core areas" of psychology) was sufficient to enable the government in England and Wales to produce an official guidance document entitled *Memorandum of Good Practice on Video Recorded Interviews with Children for Criminal Proceedings* (Home Office and Department of Health 1992), which the third author of the present book and a professor of law (Diane Birch) were commissioned to draft (Bull, 1992, 1996). However, in the last 10 years, the number of high-quality psychological studies on this topic has grown to several thousand (for a comprehensive review, see Westcott, Davies & Bull, 2002; for a series of seminal papers see Bull, 2001).

In this chapter, space permits us to provide only an overview of a few of the major current research topics on interviewing children (for a wider view of child witnesses, see also Poole & Lindsay, 1998; Schaaf et al., 2002). Readers interested in the developmental underpinning of children's testimony, children's memory for repeated events, the use of toys, dolls and props, and the effects of various types of questions in interviews should consult Westcott et al. (2002), and those interested in the effects of the cross-examination style of questioning should see Zajac & Hayne (2000).

In this section on children, we will look in some detail at the topics of the effects of long delays on their recall, attempts to improve child witnesses' facial identifications, the effects of individual differences, and suggestibility.

THE EFFECTS OF LONG DELAYS

On 13 July 1994, at Newcastle Crown Court, the Hon. Mr Justice Holland made a ruling concerning the admissibility in a criminal trial of six young children's allegations of sexual abuse against two co-defendants (in *Regina* v. *C. Lillie and D. Reed*). He noted that with regard to young children's testimony there had been made a "relatively new provision of the criminal law", namely, the Criminal Justice Act 1991. In England and Wales until 1990, criminal courts had interpreted the competency requirement as making it impossible to admit testimony from any child under the age of 6 years. In 1990, the Court of Appeal then ruled that a child of *any* age *could* give evidence so long as the judge deemed the child competent. The Criminal Justice Act 1991 (and the subsequent 1993 Act) attempted to abolish altogether any special competency requirement regarding young children. The 1991 Act also made provision for video-recorded interviews with children routinely to be admissible as their evidence in chief so long as the judge deemed the interviewing of the child to be appropriate.

Judge Holland pointed out that in the case before him all of the six children were very young (that is, aged 5 or 4 years at that time), and they were the only direct sources of evidence. They had been interviewed (on video) about a year prior (when aged 5, 4 and 3) about alleged events at a nursery when they were aged 3 or 2 years. The oldest of these children was nearly 6 when Judge Holland made his ruling. With regard to her video-recorded interview, he made no criticisms of the interviewing. His major focus was firstly on her age and secondly on the delay between her interviews and the trial. He ruled that this child, when video interviewed at the age of 4 years and 10 months, "did not have the capacity to give an intelligible account of material events". The judge added that her incapacity was no criticism of her but "merely a reflection of her age, of the subject matter, of its emotional impact upon her and, perhaps, above all, of the delay between the events under investigation and the interview itself".

The judge also ruled that this oldest child also did not have the capacity to be cross-examined about events very distant in time. He noted that had she been interviewed "about a very recent event which she had witnessed, and which was well within her capacity to remember, it may be I should be in a position to make a totally different ruling". The judge's ruling accepted the defence's objection to the admissibility of the children's evidence. It having been ruled that the oldest child's evidence was not admissible, the prosecution withdrew the evidence of the younger children. The parents of these children and those of other children who had been at the nursery were very angry about this. They complained, in part, about delays in the investigation.

In October 1995, the local authority set up an independent inquiry, which, in 1998, asked the third author of the present book for "your views on the issue of children's evidence in a case such as this, when the children who are the subject of the alleged abuse are under five years, especially in view of the time lag between the alleged events and the court case". In the reply, the point was made that what seemed reasonably clear from the published literature was that a child's testimony should not be dismissed merely on the basis of the child's age and/or the time lags/delays involved.

Let us now look at some of the research on this topic. Fivush and Schwarzmueller (1998) noted that 100 years of research has found that adults have difficulty recalling events that occurred in the first few years of life, but research has also demonstrated that 2–3-year-old children are able to recall verbally accurate details of their past. Fivush and Schwarzmueller also stated that we now know that 2-, 3- and 4-year-old children can recall distinctive events that occurred up to a year or two in the past. The report emphasised that the extent to which children can do this depends, of course, on many factors, and they may need the assistance of a skilful interviewer to do so. However, Fivush and Schwarzmueller would contend that it would be entirely inappropriate to dismiss the testimony of very young children merely on the basis of their young age, or on the basis of a time lag of months between the event in question and children's recall of it. One important factor seems to be whether, at the time of the event, the child was old enough to verbalise about an event when it is experienced; that is, old enough to store the event in memory in a verbal form. (See Chapter 7 for more on this.)

In New Zealand in 1997, Salmon and Pipe looked at the effect of a 1-year delay/time lag between children (aged 3 and 5 years) experiencing an event and later being interviewed about it. In their review of the previous literature, they pointed out that "Studies of children's recall of events suggest that even quite young children are capable of accurately recalling information about personally experienced events over extended periods of time" (p. 262); "Over time delays of several months or years, however, there is generally a decrease in the amount of correct information reported by children. . . . This decrease over long delays tends to be more marked for younger than for older children" (p. 262).

In their own experiment, Salmon and Pipe found that young children's recall of an event (a medical examination of a large teddy bear by a doctor) was reduced by the passage of time between the event and the interview (that is, 3 days versus 1 year). The time lag resulted in significantly less correct information being recalled by the 4- and 6-year-old children. However, even though the time lag was associated with more errors in the recall of the youngest children, these were not sufficient to result in a statistically significant delay effect for errors. Overall, the recall accuracy of the 6-year-olds was not affected by the 1-year time lag, but that of the 4-year-olds dropped from 87 per cent to 69 per cent (a statistically significant effect). Even so, most of what the 4-year-old children recalled after 1 year was accurate (see also Bruck et al., 1995; Ornstein et al., 1995). However, see Goodman et al. (2002) for poor recall after a 4-year delay.

In connection with whole events that *never* took place, research has shown that, in certain circumstances, some people will provide "recall" of events from the past which they never experienced (Ost et al., 2001). However, little research, save for that by Ceci and colleagues (e.g., Bruck, Ceci & Hembrooke, 1998), has been published on the effects of age and delay on children's reports of whole events that never, in fact, took place.

Ceci and colleagues have examined the effects of various manipulations on children's willingness to go along with manipulative suggestions made to them by others about events that never happened or about incorrect aspects of experienced events. Their research generally finds that younger children (for example, aged 3) are more affected by these manipulations than are older children (for example, aged 6). However, by no means all of the children are affected. For example, Ceci et al. (1994) found that only a small proportion of children falsely reported (that is, 26 per cent of 6-year-olds and 18 per cent of 3-year-olds), and that 2 years later, fewer still falsely reported (14 per cent and 11 per cent, respectively). (For more on suggestibility, see below.)

Studies typically, for ethical reasons, involve children's recall of events (real or fictitious) that were not unpleasant for them. Some psychologists have been creative enough to study, in an ethical way, young children's recall of unpleasant events. In 1991, in a study by Goodman et al., 3–7-year-old children were re-interviewed a year after a visit to a clinic to have an inoculation. The children's free recall of the event, even a year after, was very accurate. Their responses to specific questions were largely accurate but they were misled by half of the misleading questions.

Quas et al. (1999) noted that most previous studies of young children's long-term memory had not involved events of emotional, personal significance to the children and that studies of children's reporting of fictitious events had rarely examined emotionally negative, non-experienced events. In their own study, the recall of children (aged from 41 months) for VCUG tests was examined. The VCUG test is a doctor-ordered, intimate and distressing procedure. The children had experienced these tests between 2 and 7 years ago, the average time lag being 3 years. It was found that children who were only 2 years old at the time of the VCUG test could later provide "no clear evidence of remembering it" (p. 32), but that children who were 3 years old at the time later demonstrated memory of it. Although age at VCUG predicted whether or not children remembered it and how much information they provided when "minimally prompted" (p. 25), it did not relate to the accuracy of children's answers to direct questions about it. Age did relate to how negatively affected were children's responses by misleading questions about the VCUG event. Length of time interval (that is, less or more than 3 years) did not have a significant effect on free recall, but only on recall using dolls and props. Errors were not strongly related to delay. In fact, "longer delays were not associated with greater inaccuracies in children's memory or to heightened suggestibility" (p. 26). The children were also interviewed about a fictitious medical test involving the nose. Thirteen of the 40 children provided information about the nose test not provided by the interviewer's initial mention of it. Age of child at interview related to "their willingness to assent to the non-experienced event and the extent of their false reports" (p. 31). Three-quarters of 3–5-year-olds, half of 6–8-year-olds, but only one of 9–14-year-olds assented that the nose test had taken place. The 3–5-year-olds' extent of false report was greater than that of the 6–8-year-olds. However, we should note that all the children were told, "I want to ask you about another test that you had a while ago at the hospital. It was a medical test you had because you had problems with your nose. Tell me everything you remember about that test" (pp. 15 and 16). Thus, the children's false reporting was not spontaneous but the result of suggestion from the adult interviewer. This would be poor practice in investigative interviews (Bull, 1996; Milne & Bull, 1999). After having tried to recall the nose test, all the children were read a description of it and were asked whether they had indeed experienced it. Only five of the 40 children then said that they had. (For a somewhat similar study, see Peterson, 1999.)

In their 1995 paper on the competency of child witnesses, Lamb and Sternberg note that while "most developmentalists would agree that there is a gradual increase with age in the likelihood that young children can be found competent to testify" (p. 4), "disagreement might well emerge concerning the age at which most children could be presumed competent. We have yet to see convincing evidence that children of or under the age of 3 have the communicative and memorial capacity to be competent witnesses, although competence rapidly increases over the remaining preschool years. . . . Extensive variability in competence and performance thus characterizes children between 3 and 5 years of age" (p. 4). Lamb and Sternberg conclude that "courts, like mental health professionals and children's advocates, need to recognize that most 3-year-olds and many 4-year-olds will prove to be incompetent witnesses" (p. 19), but they acknowledge that some children of this age may be able to produce reliable evidence if interviewed appropriately. This could especially be the case if methods could be designed to assist young children to recall effectively after long delays.

One possible method, to date only used with relatively short delays (such as 2 weeks), involves training in and the use of cue cards designed to remind young children of the general categories that their verbal recall should focus on (such as participants, actions and settings). Camparo, Wagner and Saywitz (2001) found this to assist most children.

Another possible method involves using photographs to assist children's recall. Paterson and Bull (1999) have found that young children's verbal recall of a magic show seen 1 year before was very much enhanced if they were shown a few photographs of objects used in the event. In fact, the children's recall with photographs after the 12-month delay was better than without photographs after only a 7-day delay (see also Salmon & Irvine, 2002).

FACIAL IDENTIFICATION

Another area of recent research and development focuses not on children's verbal recall but on their facial identifications. In 2001, Bull et al. pointed out that a great deal of psychological knowledge and possible improvements in professional practice had now accumulated concerning how to obtain verbal information from child witnesses/victims about what they had experienced. However, the authors said that hardly any similar developments had yet taken place regarding their attempts visually to identify perpetrators. This was a particular cause for concern because laboratory-based studies from around the world have usually found that children, more so than adults, will pick out a face from an array or "line-up" when the perpetrator's face is absent (see Pozzulo & Lindsay, 1998, for a review).

This inability to "reject" a target-absent array has been put down to a combination of cognitive and social factors. The memory/cognitive factors include the possibility that when the target is absent children have to retrieve sufficient details of that person from memory to make the decision that none of the other similar faces in the line-up/array is the target. The social factors include the child's being under the (false) impression that the line-up must always contain the target/perpetrator and thus feeling pressure to choose one of the faces (see also Chapter 6 for similar issues with adults).

Bull's research project (Bull, 2002a) involved a series of three experiments designed around these cognitive and social factors. Study 1 sought to determine the descriptors (words) children use to describe faces. A list of such descriptors was used in study 2 to prompt half of the children to provide fuller description of a face than they (and the other half of the children) provided spontaneously. While this prompting was successful in assisting children to provide a more of the kinds of descriptors thought to assist face processing, it did not have an overall effect on improving their performance on a target-absent array.

Study 3 examined the effects of enhanced line-up instructions as well as those of prompting children for more descriptors. It, like study 2, found no simple positive effect of prompting. It also found that the enhanced instructions that emphasised the appropriateness of responding "not there" or "don't know", that involved a practice line-up from which the target (the child's head teacher) was absent, and that asked the child to look at the whole face, were not generally effective.

In 1996, Schwartz-Kenney, Bottoms and Goodman stated: "We are confident that future investigations will culminate in the development of a line-up interview technique that will effectively facilitate children's person identification. . . . It is up to empirical researchers to help ensure the attainment of this goal so that children's actual abilities are not underestimated . . . so that questions o₁ ᵇ innocence are answered" (p. 131).

Unfortunately, we are not there yet. However, one promising idea developed with adult witnesses (Dysart & Lindsay, 2001) involves asking witnesses before the identification attempt "if they believe they would be able to correctly reject a target-absent line-up" (p. 155), by saying to them, "How confident are you that you will realise that the guilty person is *not* in the line-up with only innocent people in it?" (p. 157) (but see Memon & Gabbert, in press, for non-replication). Another promising idea comes from Pozzulo & Lindsay (1999), who noted that "To date, attempts to find training tasks or instructions that reduce children's false-positive line-up decisions have fared poorly" (p. 168). They found that their "elimination procedure resulted in children making fewer false-positives" (p. 174). This promising procedure essentially involves requiring witnesses to eliminate all but one of the faces in the presented array before they are asked whether the remaining face is the target, but the instructions on this need to be in a form suitable for children.

INDIVIDUAL DIFFERENCES

Another recently evolving research topic relates to the fact that dozens of previous studies have found that some child witnesses' event and person recall is much better than others of the same age. Some children also seem to benefit much more than others from procedures designed by psychologists to assist them. Therefore, an important question is whether this variability relates to any known psychological individual differences among children (Bruck & Ceci, 1999). As yet, relatively few studies have been published on this topic. Vrij and Bush (2000) found a relationship with self-esteem; Greenhoot et al. (1999) with temperament; and Eisen et al. (1998) with some cognitive measures. It was recently found that a variety of cognitive and social individual difference measures significantly related not only to child witnesses' responses to questions but also to their amount of correct free recall, where the variance accounted for was around 40 per cent (Paterson, Bull & Vrij, 2000, 2001). (For more on individual differences, see the following section on suggestibility.)

SUGGESTIBILITY

It is not unusual for children to give evidence in criminal matters involving abuse or domestic violence, and in family law disputes. Evidence from actual cases in the UK (for example, the Orkney investigation into suspected child abuse—see Clyde, 1992) and the USA (Ceci & Bruck, 1995) indicates that children can sometimes be exposed to repeated and/or suggestive questioning on multiple occasions during the course of a criminal investigation. In their broad definition of the "suggestibility" or "misinformation" effect, Ceci and Bruck (1993) acknowledge that suggestibility effects in children reflect a combination of memory-based changes to children's memories for the original event and social demand factors (see Bruck & Ceci, 1999; Holliday, Reyna & Hayes, 2002, for reviews).

Studies of suggestibility typically rely on the misinformation paradigm (described in Chapters 6 and 8 of this text). The fate of the memories for the witnessed event is still debated, some people arguing that misinformation replaces the memory of the witnessed event, and others proposing partial degradation of memory and a less accessible trace that can lead to source confusion errors (see Chapter 6). Of most concern here is whether children's memories are more malleable than adults' when they are exposed to misinformation. The evidence suggests that this is the case. For example, younger children (5-6-year-olds) are more likely to make errors after exposure to misinformation than older children (9–12-year-olds) and adults (Ackil & Zaragoza, 1995; Sutherland & Hayne, 2001). Trace-strength accounts allow the most useful predictions to be made here. According to trace theorists (e.g., Brainerd & Reyna, 1998; Reyna, Holliday & Marche, 2002), a memory trace is a record of the event made at encoding. Whether or not misinformation occurs is a function of the strength of the memory traces for the original event and of the misleading suggestions (Holliday & Hayes, 2002). Several lines of research point to weaker memory traces and storage failures as a viable account of age differences in suggestibility (Holliday, Douglas & Hayes, 1999; Marche, 1999; Warren, Hulse-Trotter & Tubbs, 1991). For example, Warren et al. (1991) report that children subjected to multiple interviews are more likely to be misled if they have not reported their memory for the original event in an earlier interview.

Trace-strength accounts of misinformation effects are broadly compatible with source-monitoring accounts of suggestibility. Source monitoring involves identifying the origins of our memories to elucidate or validate them (Johnson, Hashtroudi & Lindsay, 1993)—for example, the time and place that an event occurred, the speaker of an utterance and who said what (see Chapters 6 and 8 for more examples). Under some conditions (such as degraded memory traces), participants misattribute the source of their memories to misinformation instead of to the original event (see Bruck, Ceci & Melnyk, 1997, for a review of relevant research on memory strength and suggestibility). The significance of accurate source monitoring in determining suggestibility effects in children has also been subject to empirical research. For example, Roberts and Blades (1998) asked 4-year-olds, 10-year-olds and adults to watch a live event. They were then shown some similar events by video and asked about the source (live or video) associated with each event. For example, they were asked: "Did I eat some cornflakes in real life?" (the cornflakes were eaten on the video, but a cake was eaten in real life). Four-year-olds made more incorrect answers to questions than did 10-year-olds.

Thierry, Spence and Memon (2001) were interested in whether children could benefit from instructions designed to orient them to the source of events (live or video). In their study, 3- and 4-year-olds and 5- and 6-year-olds watched a woman (Mrs Science) perform science demonstrations live and on video. Half of the children were given a source-monitoring (SM) test using pictures that corresponded to three response options. One picture was a photograph of Mrs Science on television, one was a snapshot of Mrs Science in real life and the third was a photograph of a distracter item (something she did not do at all). A control group received the same recognition questions without source cues. All children were then asked for a free recall of the live event and received questions that misled them about the source of the details in the experiments. For younger children, those in the SM group produced a higher percentage of correct responses to misleading details than did those in the control group. For older children, the SM and control groups did not differ in the accuracy of their responses to misleading questions. Thierry et al. (2001) suggest this is because the details they generate in the free recall test provide them with sufficient cues to identify the correct source. In line with this, in a second study, omitting the free recall test, the SM group of 5–6-year-olds gave more accurate responses to misleading questions than a control group (Thierry et al., 2001). As pointed out by Roberts (2002; p. 403), "Sensitivity to the nature and development of children's source monitoring skills can inform interviewing practices."

Research on young children's memories as affected by suggestive practices such as misleading questions has been conducted with forensically relevant scenarios. For example, it has been shown how source confusion errors can arise through subtle interventions such as parents or teachers reading a story to a child (Leichtman & Ceci, 1995; Poole & Lindsay, 2001), as well as through more explicit techniques such as asking a child to think repeatedly about and image an event (Ceci et al., 1994). These errors appear to reflect genuine confusions about what was seen. Even when participants are warned before their final recall not to believe things that were said to them after the original event, they continue to recall these (Lindsay et al., 1995). Ceci and colleagues based their 1994 study on the procedures used in some real child abuse investigations in the USA (Ceci & Bruck, 1995). In several of the cases, trial testimony and therapy records documented repeated imagery instructions and repeated encouragement to recreate events with props (for example, dressing a doll as a witch to represent the defendant). Parents also read books with abuse themes to their children. These books depicted situations where the fantasy character had a "bad" secret that he was afraid to tell, but once he told he felt better (Ceci & Bruck, 1995). That these factors are even more powerful than the use of suggestive questions was illustrated by Garven et al.'s (1998) experimental simulation of the child-interviewing techniques that were used in the McMartin Preschool case. In this child abuse investigation, seven teachers were accused of abusing several hundred children over a 10-year period. None of the accused were convicted, and the charges against most were dropped prior to trial. Several problematic techniques were identified by psychologists in the original taped interviews, such as reinforcement (approval or disapproval), invitations to speculate and repetitive questioning. Garven et al. (1998) found these techniques were more powerful than simple suggestive questions in encouraging 3–6-year-olds to make false allegations about a teacher.

In research studies, one can check for accuracy of the memory, but in the real world it is difficult to determine whether a child is lying or truth-telling (Chapter 2). There is evidence to suggest that once a child has been subjected to a suggestive interview it is virtually impossible to distinguish accurate from inaccurate reports (Bruck, Ceci & Hembrooke, 2002). Moreover, cross-examination of witnesses in court cannot distinguish accurate reports from those arising from suggestive questioning (Rosenthal, 2002).

Not all researchers, however, have found younger children to be more suggestible. For example, Flin et al. (1992) exposed 6-year-olds, 10-year-olds and adults to a realistically staged argument during a presentation on foot hygiene. Few participants accepted erroneous suggestions. Rudy and Goodman (1991) asked 4–7-year-olds about an encounter with a stranger in a caravan during which they played "dressing-up" games and the stranger took their photograph. The older children were more accurate on the non-suggestive questions, but the accuracy rate on abuse-relevant misleading questions ("Did he take your clothes off?") was similar for younger and older children. Only one child (a 4-year-old) gave a false report.

In a study of 5–7-year-old girls' memories for medical examinations (Saywitz et al., 1989), the older children were more accurate regarding non-suggestive questions, but there was no difference in their resistance to suggestive, abuse-relevant questions (for example, "How many times did the doctor kiss you?"). As Ceci and Bruck (1993) point out in their review of the literature, numerous factors may account for the discrepancy in the research findings, such as the use of relatively small sample sizes that neglects individual differences, the number and complexity of the misleading questions, the delay between event and testing, the timing of the misinformation, the nature of the event and so on. The credibility and authority of the source providing the misinformation may also influence how much weight participants assign to the source and how they respond to discrepant information (Lampinen & Smith, 1995). The current view of misinformation effects is that they may be the end result of more than one processing mechanism (see Holliday & Hayes, 2002), and that both cognitive and social factors may be important in understanding suggestibility (Bruck et al., 2002; Milne & Bull, in press).

SUGGESTION FROM STEREOTYPES

The research reviewed so far has examined the effect of various post-event suggestions on memory. An alternative to this is the "reversed misinformation paradigm", which examines the effect of suggestions acquired *prior* to an event. An example of this type of suggestion is stereotype induction. Interviewers may adopt this method with children who are reluctant to disclose sexual or physical abuse. It is a subtle but potentially powerful method of communicating a negative characterisation of a person or situation. In the forensic context, the impact of negative stereotypes on children's reports of an event can be seen in

allegations of sexual abuse made by preschool children in the Litt
Care and the McMartin Preschool cases, and in the 1987 dea
Frederico Macias in Texas (see Ceci & Bruck, 1995, for a review). I
6 months after Macias was charged with two counts of first-degree muraei, .
year-old girl told police that she had seen the defendant on the day of the
murders with a rifle and blood on his clothing. During interviews with police, it
became evident that for many years the girl's mother had warned her to keep
away from this "bad" man. Hence, the child possessed a negative stereotype of
Macias *before* she allegedly witnessed the event (Leichtman & Ceci, 1995). Several
years later, and 2 weeks before Macias's execution, the child recanted her
testimony. Her reasons for the earlier testimony were that she knew Macias was a
bad man and she wanted to comply with the adult interviewers. In another case,
a preschooler told the interviewer that he was glad the defendant was in jail
because he was bad. When asked why he thought he was bad, the child replied,
"because my mother told me" (Bruck et al., 2002). This form of misinformation is
likely to arise during the course of an investigation in which a child may be
interviewed about a particular person on several occasions by numerous people
(parents, teachers, social workers, police and lawyers); it is one of the more
blatant signs of interviewer bias (Ceci & Bruck, 1995).

Leichtman and Ceci (1995) were the first to demonstrate the effects of negative
stereotypes (see Chapter 3) on children's eyewitness memory. They studied 3–4-
and 5–6-year-old children's memory for the actions of a man called Sam Stone.
Children were told, once a week (in the month prior to Sam's visiting their
nursery school), during story reading, that Sam was "clumsy". Then they were
interviewed repeatedly after Sam's visit. Children who were given pre-visit
expectations about Sam and interviews which contained incorrect suggestions
about his misdeeds (for example, ripping a book) made high levels of false
reports up to 10 weeks after Sam's visit. In a somewhat similar manner, Holliday
and Hayes (2002) employed a reversed misinformation design, in which 5-year-
olds were given misleading suggestions prior to a picture story, and they found
evidence of a suggestibility effect. Finally, Greenhoot (2000) examined the effect
of presenting prior knowledge (stereotypes) of fictional children before the
presentation of stories about them on 5–6-year-old children's story recall. The
children heard three stories about the same two child characters across several
sessions, and there were three different prior knowledge/stereotype conditions:
positive, negative and neutral. The knowledge manipulations included only very
general information about the characters and no descriptions of specific
behaviours, and only open-ended questions were used throughout the memory
interviews. Thus, Greenhoot reasoned that any memory errors had been
"constructed" by the children themselves, rather than suggested by the
experimenters. In line with predictions, children given positive information
developed positive impressions of the fictional character in the stories, and those
given negative information developed negative impressions. Finally, a critical
issue in the Greenhoot study was what would happen to the children's memories
if their opinions/knowledge about the characters changed after hearing the
stories (for example, initially believe that the character is a bully, but later become

convinced that he or she is a nice child). In other words, do stereotypes change memories retroactively? Greenhoot's findings suggested that they do.

In recent years, there has been a great deal of interest in individual differences in suggestibility and how they may contribute to suggestibility in different situations (see also Chapter 8). Researchers have begun to ask whether there are internal factors, such as cognitive, social, and personality characteristics, that can distinguish children who readily report false information from those who are resistant to doing so (e.g., Eisen, Winograd & Qin, 2002). Suggestibility as a "personality trait" is one such factor that may assist in competency and accuracy determinations in a legal context. The best-known scales of suggestibility are the Gudjonsson scales (GSS-1 and GSS-2), which measure suggestibility in an interrogative context along two dimensions. The first is yield or the degree to which a person initially responds to suggestive questions. Participants are then given negative feedback and asked to attempt the question again. This gives a measure of shift or the number of answers that are changed. Between the ages of 6 and young adulthood, there is a decline in shift and yield scores (Gudjonsson, 1996). More recently, Scullin and Ceci (2001) tested a scale of suggestibility for young children: the video suggestibility scale for children (VSSC). This scale was able to predict which children complied with a suggestion that they experienced events that they were repeatedly asked to think about (Scullin & Hembrooke, 1998).

In addition to individual differences in suggestibility, a variety of other factors such as intelligence, personality and temperament may affect children's responses to misleading questions (see Bruck et al., 1997; Pipe & Salmon, 2002). For example, children who are shy are more likely to comply with an interviewer's suggestions (Endres, Poggenpohl & Erben, 1999). However, the relative influence of these factors may vary depending on the population sampled. Much of the research reviewed in this section has focused on mainstream samples. To what extent will these results generalise to other samples? The research is limited, but one recent study suggests that IQ and age have a significantly greater influence on the shift scores on the GSS-2 of intellectually disabled children than it does on mainstream children (Young, Powell & Dudgeon, 2003). This is an area where more research would be valuable.

Much psychological research on interviewing child witnesses has, perhaps understandably, focused on the additional human frailties that young children present. However, parallel research on how best to assist children to provide reliable evidence has resulted in legislative changes and the strengthening of the training of relevant professionals such as social workers and police officers (Milne & Bull, 2003), though the effectiveness of such training is not yet as strong as one would wish (Warren et al., 1999). Nevertheless, in a recent pioneering American study, Faller et al. (2001) examined which aspects of the interviews with adults alleged to have sexually abused children had an influence on whether the adults confessed. (See Chapter 4 for other studies concerned with the interviewing of suspects.) They found that confessions (complete or partial) were more likely to occur when the interviews were conducted by the state police (who, the authors suggest, had better training) than by the local police, and they concluded: "These findings highlight the value of having skilled, experienced law enforcement officers who work collaboratively and follow a protocol" (p. 46). Faller et al. end their paper with the important point that "Justice can be done by eliciting accounts of abuse from perpetrators, rather than placing the onus and responsibility for successful outcomes on children" (p. 47).

In 1999, Milne & Bull emphasised that the majority of incorrect information obtained from (alleged) child witnesses/victims was not the fault of children but of interviewers. It is on such interviewing that psychology can make one of its greatest impacts. Recently, in a number of countries (for example, Norway [Melinder, 2001; Myklebust & Alison, 2000] and Israel and the USA [Lamb et al., 2002]), steps are being taken to improve such interviewing through psychological knowledge.

INTERVIEWING VULNERABLE WITNESSES

In their book on investigative interviewing, Milne and Bull (1999) noted that justice systems rarely received evidence from particularly vulnerable (alleged) witnesses/victims such as those with physical/communicative disabilities or those with learning disabilities (which used to be referred to as "mental retardation" or "mental handicap"). Such a state of affairs is very reprehensible, especially since there is slowly accumulating research evidence that such vulnerable people are targeted by criminals (Brown, Stein & Turk, 1995; Kebbell & Hatton, 1999; Westcott & Jones, 1999), sad as this makes us feel.

In England and Wales, the government was made ever more aware that such vulnerable members of society were being excluded from seeking justice (e.g., Bull, 1995), and eventually new legislation was introduced in the Youth Justice and Criminal Evidence Act 1999, which came into effect in 2002. This very innovative legislation was, in part, created to assist particularly vulnerable witnesses/victims to testify. Cooke and Davies (2001) review the relevant aspects of this legislation. One key aspect focuses on the use of "special measures" that may improve the information provided by such witnesses. These measures include the use of video-recorded interviews, live television links to the courtroom and the use of communication aids. One crucial aspect of the Act makes it clear that it should no longer simply be assumed that certain types of vulnerable people are not competent to give evidence in criminal trials, but that their competence should be assessed only when they have had the benefit of relevant special measures. The communication aids aspect of the measures include anything that enables people to communicate with a vulnerable person and that person to communicate with others such as the police and courts. Thus, these aids involve not only devices such as computers and communication boards but also appropriate interviewing.

To increase the likelihood that vulnerable witnesses would be interviewed appropriately, the UK government invited a small team of experts to write the document *Achieving Best Evidence in Criminal Proceedings: Guidance for Vulnerable or Intimidated Witnesses Including Children* (Home Office, 2002). The third author of the present book wrote the section on interviewing vulnerable people, and some other members of the team wrote the section on interviewing children, which updated the relevant part of the government's 1992 Memorandum of Good Practice.

The section on vulnerable people emphasises, as have many guidance documents on investigative interviewing (e.g., Milne & Bull, 1999), the importance of the "phased approach" of (i) establishing rapport, (ii) seeking "free recall", (iii) questioning/question types and (iv) closure. Such a phased approach is based on what is now a wealth of research from largely cognitive psychology (Bull & Barnes, 1995), but the section goes beyond this by bringing in relevant ideas from social psychology. Each of these two main sources of relevant research will now briefly be summarised.

CONTRIBUTIONS FROM COGNITIVE PSYCHOLOGY

Over 20 years ago, Sigelman and colleagues (e.g., Sigelman et al., 1981) emphasised that people with handicaps have a right to be involved in decisions affecting them, but that almost no research had been conducted on how best to pose questions to them. This is especially important, since they found that many vulnerable people experience difficulty when asked to provide free recall or to respond to open questions, but very often reply "yes" to yes/no questions (see also Heal & Sigelman, 1995).

Milne, Clare & Bull (2002) found that witnesses with mild intellectual disabilities were more negatively affected by misleading questions, and that verbal recall of the witnessed incident correlated (negatively) with the extent to which they were affected by misleading questions.

Similarly, Ericson, Perlman and Isaacs (1994) noted that many people with "developmental handicap" went along with suggestive questions, and also had problems understanding questions if they contained pronouns. Isaacs, Schuller and Turtle (1998) found somewhat similar effects, but they noted that with appropriate interviewing, while vulnerable witnesses may provide less information than ordinary witnesses, this information may be no less accurate. Porter, Yuille and Bent (1995) found the same with deaf children.

Much of Milne and Bull's research has focused on whether the "cognitive interview", originally developed in the USA for ordinary adult witnesses (Fisher & Geiselman, 1992), would also be of assistance to vulnerable witnesses. This interview procedure has a structure similar to the phased approach but additionally incorporates a number of techniques derived from cognitive psychology (for more on this, see Milne & Bull, 1999, 2002). Milne and Bull have found that witnesses provide more correct information if they experience an appropriate cognitive interview compared to just a good, phased interview. This is the case not only for "ordinary children" (Memon et al., 1996, 1997; Milne & Bull, in press) but also for children with learning disabilities (Milne & Bull, 1996) and adults with learning disabilities (Milne, Clare & Bull, 1999). However, more research on this topic is needed. Only a few years ago, Cardone and Dent (1996) stated: "At present there is no experimental literature examining the most effective ways of eliciting recall of an event from memory of adults who have learning disabilities" (p. 175).

CONTRIBUTIONS FROM SOCIAL PSYCHOLOGY

The *Achieving Best Evidence* document points out that many interviewers will not as yet be familiar with the various types of vulnerable witnesses, and that research from social psychology has made it clear that when people meet others with whom they are not familiar, their own behaviour becomes abnormal. For example, Heinemann (1990) stated that "Feelings of insecurity, tension, uneasiness, embarrassment, distress and anxiety" (p. 324) often occur, and that a possible interpretation of such results is that some vulnerable people "elicit potentially conflicting tendencies in others. People respond to their deviance, but at the same time they regard them as victims deserving help and compassion" (p. 325). People who receive "such contradictory messages will perceive that somehow, something is wrong" (p. 328).

In contrast to this is another finding concerning behaviour and vulnerable people, which is that many vulnerable people not only wish to be treated as if they were ordinary, "normal" people, but that many of them (such as those with mild learning disabilities) have become skilled at behaving in a way that masks their disabilities (this is sometimes referred to as "passing as normal"). Thus, in such circumstances, interviewers may initially be unaware that such interviewees require special skills/special measures (Perske, 1994).

Another relevant contribution from social psychology is that the "yea-saying" or acquiescence tendency noted by researchers such as Sigelman et al. (1981) may be heightened in certain social settings (Mattika & Vesala, 1997), as when the vulnerable interviewee feels disempowered in the interview setting or "sees" the interviewer as an authority figure. (For more on the effects of interviewer authority, see a later section of this chapter.) A similar point was made by Henry and Gudjonsson (1999), who suggested "that social factors account for the increase in suggestibility for closed misleading questions in children with mental retardation" (p. 502).

The document *Achieving Best Evidence* also mentions that some vulnerable people may adopt or prefer greater or smaller interpersonal distance than interviewers are used to, and that their forms of facial or bodily expression may easily be misunderstood. Thus, the more "mainstream" social psychology topics of personal space and facial expression are relevant to this fairly new area of research. We feel sure that other "mainstream" topics can, with a leap of imagination, be made relevant, and we invite the reader to think of some. In this way, vulnerable witnesses can be assisted to play a full role in our justice systems, though some recent research (Stobbs & Kebbell, in press) suggests that a new challenge for vulnerable witnesses, now that they are at last becoming more likely to give evidence, is jurors' willingness to rely on the evidence provided by such witnesses. Here again, we hope that psychology can start to make a positive contribution.

INTERVIEWER MANNER

Should police officers experienced at interviewing adults suspected of committing crimes adopt the same behavioural style they employ for this setting when "transferred" to a "vulnerable witness unit"? This important issue has hardly been addressed in psychological research, in police training or in relevant guidance documents. However, there is a slowly accumulating body of research which suggests that this is an important issue.

In England and Wales, the government's *Memorandum of Good Practice for Video-recorded Interviews with Child Witnesses for Criminal Proceedings* (Home Office and Department of Health, 1992) recommends that "the interviewer should be careful . . . throughout the interview not to overemphasise his or her authority in relation to the child" (p. 16). While this recommendation may well make sense from a psychological and professional point of view, there was, at the time of the drafting of that document (Bull, 1992, 1996), very little published on the role of interviewer authority in investigative interviews. Avoiding too much authority was recommended not solely to better enable the child to feel at ease but also to reduce the chances of the child's going along with suggestions, wittingly or unwittingly, made by the interviewer (Milne & Bull, 1999). Milne and Bull's recent update of that document (that is, *Achieving Best Evidence in Criminal Proceedings: Guidance for Vulnerable or Intimidated Witnesses, Including Children—* Home Office, 2002) was again not able to offer much guidance on this particular topic.

Prior to 1992, almost no research had been published directly on the effects in investigative interviews with witnesses of the interviewer's manner of behaving. Quite a lot of relevant research had been published, for example, about the phases such interviews should go through and about the effects of various types of questions (Milne & Bull, 1999). However, all that was available to guide the 1992 guidance about interviewer manner was psychological research on social influence. For example, Latené's (1981) account of social impact noted that the strength of social influence is largely determined by the status and ability of the influencers and the nature of their relationship with the subject. Investigative interviews with young children or vulnerable adults would seem a ripe setting for social influence to occur. However, comprehensive accounts of work on social influence (e.g., Cialdini, 1995, 2001) make no mention of such a setting. It is possible that witnesses, especially vulnerable ones, are more likely to respond incorrectly to misleading questions about a witnessed event when they are interviewed in an authoritative manner. In his seminal work on adults' false confessions, Gudjonsson (e.g., 1988, 1992, 1999, 2002) has noted that authority may be a factor causing compliance, and that compliance may relate to an eagerness to please and/or to a desire to avoid conflict.

Work concerning the interviewing of children that has relevance includes a study by Ceci, Ross and Toglia (1987), who found that young children's accounts were more biased by misleading information when this was presented by an adult than by a child. Goodman et al. (1991) found that the provision of social support to children in the form of smiles and verbal encouragements (and a snack) by the interviewer reduced incorrect free recall and (for the younger ones) errors in response to misleading questions. In a study by Tobey and Goodman (1992), young children participated in an event and were later interviewed by someone dressed as a police officer or as a layperson. The recall of the children in the former condition was less accurate. However, the effect of the interviewer being a police officer was confounded by only the children in this condition being earlier told by another police officer, "I am very concerned that something bad might have happened. . . . My partner is going to come in now and ask you some questions about what happened" (p. 783).

In their comprehensive overview of research on children's testimony, Ceci and Bruck (1995) briefly described the limited published research which had examined the possible effects of interviewer status. They mentioned the above studies by Ceci et al. (1987) and by Tobey and Goodman (1992), and noted that the latter study's findings suggest "that interviews by high status adults . . . may have negative effects on the accuracy of children's reports" (p. 153). They also referred to their 1993 overview, which mentioned the study by Goodman et al. (1991), when stating that "Young children are sensitive to the status and power of their interviewers and as a result are especially likely to comply with the implicit and explicit agenda of such interviewers. If their account is questioned, for example, children may defer to the challenges of the more senior interviewer. To some extent, the children's recognition of this power differential may be one of the most important causes of their suggestibility" (p. 152). While such a claim may seem reasonable, very few previously published studies have directly examined the effects on witnesses' accounts of variation in interviewer's authoritative manner.

Excellent guidance to professionals who conduct investigative interviews with children, published by the American Psychological Association (Poole & Lamb, 1998), includes a bullet list of nine points concerning interviewer behaviour and demeanour (p. 121). However, only two of these points explicitly mention interviewer social behaviour ("appear relaxed" and "avoid touching"). This book very briefly mentions the above studies by Goodman et al. (1991) and by Tobey and Goodman (1992). However, it made no mention of studies which had directly investigated the possible effects of the interviewer's social behaviour.

In 1996, Meyer and Jesilow noted that the literature on children's testimony says little about the effect upon interviewees of obedience to authority. However, children's, especially younger ones', obedience to authority may be one of the reasons why they appear to be more suggestible. Using the procedure Milgram (1974) developed to investigate the effects of authority on adults, Shanab and Yahya (1977) found children willing to deliver electric shocks to others. Meyer and Jesilow suggested that children's desire to be obedient could be stronger than their desire to report only that which they remember and that "being helpful to the interrogators outweighs any consequences due to filling in forgotten details" (p. 92). They also noted: "Through lowering the authority factor in interviews, we may be able to increase the measure of truth in children's reports" (p. 93).

More recently, a few research studies have been conducted to examine whether interviewer authority does affect children directly. In 1997, Ricci, Pacifico and Katz reported that 5-year-olds interviewed in an authoritative and professional atmosphere in an office setting by an interviewer who wore professional attire more readily changed their answers to repeated questions than those who received an informal interview that involved adapting the setting for children and a friendly atmosphere, the interviewer wearing casual dress. However, authority had no effect on the recall which occurred prior to the repeated questions. Templeton and Hunt (1997) reported that 3–6-year-old children correctly answered more questions when interviewed by the low-authority interviewer than when interviewed by the high-authority interviewer. However, we should note that in their study the low-authority interviewer was a puppet. They did not suggest that adult interviewers be replaced by puppets, but only that the authority of the interviewer may well be an important issue.

Another way of beginning to examine the possible effects of interviewer authority was studied by Ricci, Beal and Dekle (1996). They compared the effects of having as the interviewer an unfamiliar adult or their parent on 5-year-old children's memory of an event. Few differences were found. This could have occurred because, while children may be more comfortable with their parents, they may also be more obedient to them. Studies of authority need to avoid confounding these two possible effects.

Carter, Bottoms and Levine (1996) linked the social and cognitive approaches regarding witness testimony by suggesting that in interviews "social support might enable children to perform at their optimal level of cognitive ability" (p. 338). In their study, interviews with children aged 5–7 years were conducted either in a supportive manner or in an intimidating manner. In the supportive condition, the interviewer frequently smiled, sat in a relaxed manner with an open body position, used supportive eye contact, employed warm intonation and introduced himself at the beginning of the interview to establish rapport. In the intimidating condition, the interviewer did not attempt to establish rapport, did not use warm intonation, made minimal eye contact, smiled infrequently, and sat in a formal body posture. Carter et al. (1996) found that this social support had no effect upon children's free recall of a witnessed event. However, it did have an effect on responses to certain types of questions. When the interview was conducted in a supportive manner, children demonstrated increased resistance to misleading questions. However, social support had no effect on the accuracy of responses to questions that were not purposely misleading, nor on the number of "don't know" responses, nor on the answers to control questions that "were intentionally written in simple language" (p. 348). Carter et al. (1996) commented that the specific effect of social support regarding misleading questions could suggest that the supportive style of interviewing "led children . . . to feel less anxious, more empowered, and, in turn, less intimidated and better able to resist misleading suggestions from the interviewer. Were this not the case, a more generalised effect would have been found across all question types" (p. 351). However, they noted that replication of their results would enhance confidence in their interpretations.

Replication has recently been attempted by a few researchers. Imhoff and Baker-Ward (1999) examined the effects of interviewer style on very young children (aged 3–4 years). They found no effects on the children's responses to misleading or specific questions. However, this lack of effect may have been because their "non-supportive" interview involved the interviewers smiling at the children.

Quas, Eisen and Rivers (2000), like Imhoff and Baker-Ward, found no positive effects of interviewer style; in fact, they found only one significant effect, that for their youngest children (aged 3–4 years) a supportive style was associated with more inaccurate responses to misleading and to specific questions.

However, Davis and Bottoms (2002) recently replicated some of the findings of Carter et al. (1996). They found that children (aged 6 and 7 years) interviewed in a supportive manner were more resistant to misleading suggestions. Bull and Corran (2002) found a similar effect. Thus, there is now some accumulating evidence that interviewer manner may affect witness recall. However, one criticism of some of the previous studies is that the interviews largely consisted of only closed questions. This does not permit examination of the possible effects of interviewer style on the major parts of good investigative interviews with witnesses (that is, those that request free recall and then use open questions before closed questions). Such a study was conducted by Paterson, Bull and Vrij (2002), who found that a supportive style (smiling, eye contact and casual clothes) resulted in more correct recall than a formal style in the free recall and open question phases of a "Memorandum of Good Practice" interview, but in no more errors.

Thus, the limited amount of directly relevant research does seem to suggest that in future greater attention be paid to interviewer manner/style/behaviour when interviewing witnesses. While what are now a large number of research studies on memory have had a very considerable impact in several countries on good practice concerning how to obtain evidence from (alleged) witnesses/victims, more research and definitely some good practice guidelines need to be developed on interviewer behaviour. This necessary work should focus not only on how interviewer behaviour may affect what the child witnesses say or recall but also on how they say it. A very interesting, but as yet poorly researched, question is whether variations in interviewer behaviour may cause children to demonstrate what O'Barr (1982) described in his seminal book as either a powerful or powerless speech style, the former probably having a more positive impact on juries and relevant professionals (see also Erickson et al., 1978; Ruva & Bryant, in submission).

Another important question is whether a suspicious manner demonstrated by interviewers can affect witness behaviour in a way that is then falsely taken as reducing the witnesses' perceived credibility. Exciting research involving adult suspect interviewees by Winkel and Vrij and by Akehurst and Vrij (cited in Bull, 2002b) suggests that it might.

A further question is whether interviewing a child via a live video link (that is, interviewer and child are not in the same room), as now occurs in criminal trials in some countries (for a review, see Doherty-Sneddon & McAuley, 2000), reduces the likelihood that the interviewer's manner will affect the child.

SUMMARY AND CONCLUSION

This chapter has reviewed key areas concerning the interviewing of vulnerable witnesses, including children, and psychology's contribution to understanding their weaknesses and to building on their strengths. However, much remains to be done.

CHAPTER 6

PSYCHOLOGICAL FACTORS IN EYEWITNESS TESTIMONY

Evidence in criminal trials is often based upon eyewitness testimonies. An example of a recent case in the UK that relied heavily on eyewitness evidence is that of Barry George, convicted in July 2001 of the murder of television presenter Jill Dando. The police held live identity parades after George's arrest in May 2000. A live parade is one in which a witness is asked to look at several people (the suspect and volunteers who resemble the suspect) standing in a row behind a one-way mirror (they cannot see through the mirror). None of the five witnesses picked George. In the summer of 2000, the police presented four other witnesses with a video-identity parade, from which one witness identified George. When questioned in court, this witness stated she had seen George for a total of 5 or 6 seconds from under an umbrella (it was raining at the time). Three witnesses who had also had fleeting glances of the suspect had lingered on George's photograph during the parade but had not picked anyone from the line-up. Despite this, the three non-identifications were presented by the prosecution in court as near-misses. The prosecution claimed that the descriptions given by all four witnesses were consistent. The descriptions were general (for example, "Mediterranean" appearance) and could apply to a large percentage of the general population of men living in the UK. All witnesses were given feedback after the line-up in that they were told that George was the suspect. The witnesses who had not identified George became increasingly confident that George was the one they should have picked from the line-up and one of these witnesses went as far as identifying George as he stood in the dock during the trial (the *Independent*, 11 July 2002). George appealed his conviction in 2002, but the Court of Appeal upheld the conviction and concluded that Barry George, and no other, murdered Jill Dando. George's supporters are now planning an appeal to the House of Lords, Britain's highest court (Reuters, 30/07/02).

It has been estimated that around 77 000 people a year in the USA are charged with crimes solely on the basis of eyewitness evidence (Goldstein, Chance & Schneller, 1989; Wells et al., 1998). Mistaken identifications continue to be a significant source of miscarriages of justice in England and Wales also (Davies, 1996). Eyewitness identification is a potentially powerful form of evidence (Wells et al., 1998). An eyewitness who claims, "That is the person I saw fire the gun," is providing direct evidence of guilt, as it directly links the suspect with the crime. In contrast, physical evidence such as a fingerprint indicates only that the suspect touched something; it does not directly link the suspect to the crime, as the touching could have happened for reasons unrelated to the crime.

Despite its persuasiveness and potential power, eyewitness testimony can be inaccurate. In 1976, the British government's Devlin Report tried to explain why honest eyewitnesses can be mistaken (Clifford & Bull, 1978). More recently, the introduction of DNA testing procedures has shed further light on this issue. DNA forensic analysis has been conducted on people who were convicted prior to its introduction in the 1990s. These tests have resulted in the exoneration of people innocent of the crime for which they were convicted. Wells et al. (1998) described the first 40 cases in the USA in which DNA was found to exonerate a previously convicted person (five of these persons were sentenced to death). Of these 40 cases, 36 (90 per cent) involved eyewitness identification evidence in which one or more witnesses falsely identified a person. One person was identified by five separate witnesses. In a more recent analysis, Scheck, Neufield and Dwyer (2000) described 62 exoneration cases (eight persons were sentenced to death). In 52 of these 62 cases, mistaken identification occurred, involving, in total, 77 mistaken eyewitnesses. These findings led Wells et al. (1998: p. 605) to conclude that "eyewitness identification evidence is amongst the least reliable forms of evidence and yet it is persuasive to juries". While the DNA studies generally support this conclusion, Wells et al. (2000) point out that we do not know how representative these case studies are. DNA exoneration is only possible in a fraction of cases, mostly sexual assault cases. Crimes such as murders, muggings and robberies rarely leave DNA trace evidence, so it is not possible to use this type of evidence in these crimes to question the reliability of witness evidence (Wells et al., 2000). A large part of what we know about eyewitness identification comes from empirical research on the factors influencing eyewitness performance.

ESTIMATOR VARIABLES AND SYSTEM VARIABLES IN EYEWITNESS IDENTIFICATION

There are many reasons why false identifications occur. On the one hand, a long delay between the encounter and the recognition test, or the fact that the witness was intoxicated when he or she witnessed the crime, may impair the witness's memory of the culprit. These and similar factors are called "estimator variables" (Wells, 1978). Estimator variables are factors over which the criminal justice system exerts little or no control. Wells called these factors estimator variables because, although these variables may be manipulable in research, they cannot be controlled in the actual criminal situation and their influence on identification accuracy can at best be estimated only post hoc. On the other hand, the witness may have made a wrong identification because the police conducted a line-up which was biased in some way. This and similar factors are called "system variables" (Wells, 1978). System variables are factors that can, in principle, be directly controlled by the criminal justice system to increase the accuracy of eyewitness evidence (for example, by conducting a fair, unbiased line-up).

The nature of system and estimator variables implies that expert witnesses have different roles with regard to these two types of factor. One task is to inform others (jurors, for example) about the impact of system and estimator variables on eyewitness accuracy (see Chapter 8). This does happen, but only in a small fraction of criminal cases (see Chapter 9). A second task is to inform others (practitioners, for example) how to prevent errors caused by system variables—for example, by telling the police how to conduct proper line-ups or identification parades. Guidelines are now available to law-enforcement personnel in several countries. For the first time, the US Department of Justice has published national guidelines for the preservation and collection of eyewitness evidence (Technical Working Group for Eyewitness Evidence, 1999). Many of these recommendations have been in use in England and Wales since the introduction in 1986 of the Police and Criminal Evidence Act 1984 and associated Codes of Practice (see Home Office, 1995, for the latest version).

Another way of classifying the factors which influence eyewitness identifications is by the stage of memory at which they influence identification accuracy. Memory for persons may be seen as a three-stage process involving encoding, storage and retrieval (Sporer, Köhnken & Malpass, 1996). Stage 1 (encoding) refers to a witness's attention and perception at the time of the event in question. At stage 2 (storage), the witness stores the information in memory. At stage 3 (retrieval), the witness attempts to retrieve information from storage. Errors can occur at each of these three stages. Estimator variables focus primarily on the first two stages, whereas system variables focus primarily on stage 3.

ESTIMATOR VARIABLES

By 1995, there were over 2000 publications in psychology addressing eyewitness reliability. These studies have consistently confirmed that eyewitnesses can be mistaken. In the last 20 years, numerous books, meta-analyses and reviews about the impact of estimator and system variables on eyewitness identification have been published (Kebbell & Wagstaff, 1999; Memon & Wright, 2000; Narby, Cutler & Penrod, 1996; Ross, Read & Toglia, 1994; Sporer, Malpass & Köhnken, 1996; Thompson et al., 1998; Wells et al., 1998; Wells et al., 2000; Westcott & Brace, 2002). See Cutler and Penrod (1995) for a meta-analysis of studies examining identification accuracy in realistic field settings. Estimator variables can be classified into seven categories: stable witness characteristics, malleable witness characteristics, style of presentation, stable target characteristics, malleable target characteristics, environmental conditions and post-event factors.

Stable Witness Factors

Witness characteristics such as intelligence, gender and race are not particularly useful predictors of identification accuracy. They have been found to be weakly, if at all, related to making false or correct identifications. However, the *age* of a witness may be important. Under some conditions, children will remember less and make more errors in recall than older adults (see Chapter 5). In terms of eyewitness identification, a meta-analysis of findings (Pozzulo & Lindsay, 1998) concludes that children (5 years and older) do not differ significantly from adults with respect to correct identification. However, there is a stronger tendency for children to make a choice from line-ups in which the culprit is absent. For example, Beal, Schmitt and Dekle (1995) reported that kindergarten-age children who made a correct identification in a target-present (TP) line-up nevertheless went on to identify an innocent suspect in a subsequent target-absent (TA) line-up. Moreover, they were as likely to choose someone from a TA line-up when they were given an extra opportunity to look at the perpetrator, a finding which suggests that inattention or poor encoding are not responsible for their errors.

Like children, seniors (adults aged 60–80 years) also have a tendency to make more choices from TA line-ups. A series of studies conducted in our laboratory have shown that senior citizens (adults aged 60–80 years) make more false identifications than younger adults in both TP and TA line-ups (Memon & Bartlett, 2002; Memon et al., in press; Searcy, Bartlett & Memon, 1999, 2000; Searcy et al., 2001). Ageing is typically associated with a reduction in cognitive resources (Craik & Byrd, 1982) and an increased reliance on "familiarity" as a basis for making a decision, as opposed to conscious remembering of a prior episode as a basis for making a decision (Jacoby, 1999; Mandler, 1980; Searcy et al., 1999). There is evidence to suggest that older adults rely more on familiarity (Bartlett & Fulton, 1991), and this is not such an effective strategy when the accuracy of an eyewitness identification is critical. For example, a face may appear familiar because it is someone that shops in the same supermarket as we do or looks like someone we know. What is critical in an eyewitness situation is to be able to remember where one has seen the face before. The theoretical significance of this point will be discussed later.

Malleable Witness Factors

One example of a malleable witness factor may be the level of blood alcohol in a witness at the time of the crime. Alcohol intoxication can have a negative effect on encoding and storage (Cutler & Penrod, 1995). Dysart et al. (2002) examined the effects of alcohol consumption on identification accuracy from show-ups. Participants in the high blood-alcohol condition were more likely than those in the low blood-alcohol condition to make a false identification from a TA show-up. They discuss two possible accounts of their findings. One is a tendency for intoxicated persons to focus on salient cues or features (such as hairstyle) in their environment during encoding (alcohol-myopia hypothesis). The innocent people in the TA show-ups were chosen by their similarity to the target (as is usual practice), a fact which may have led intoxicated participants to use salient cues, such as hairstyle, as a basis for their decisions. An alternative hypothesis is that alcohol consumption resulted in what is referred to as a lax criterion. Decisions were being made on the basis of little evidence. This resulted in people making more identifications overall, although this does not explain why there was no elevated choosing rate in the TP condition among the intoxicated group (Dysart et al., 2002). Research on the effects of alcohol is beset with problems. Besides the ethical issues, there are problems of sample selection, random allocation to conditions and individual differences in alcohol tolerance. This may be why the Dysart et al. (2002) findings have not yet been replicated (Dysart, Lindsay & MacDonald, 2002).

Style of Presentation: Consistency and Confidence

Eyewitnesses are usually interviewed more than once. It is possible that these different accounts reveal inconsistencies in recall for certain details. Lawyers can highlight these inconsistencies in order to discredit the eyewitness (Cutler & Penrod, 1995). However, lawyers may be wrong in making this assumption. Research has revealed that inconsistencies in testimony are not always related to accuracy (Fisher & Cutler, 1996).

Witnesses may differ in the level of confidence about the accuracy of their decision; that is, they may be convinced that the suspect they identified was the culprit, or they may be less certain about their own decision. There is a belief among laypersons, as well as public defenders, defence attorneys, prosecutors and other practising lawyers, that there is a strong positive relation between eyewitness identification confidence and eyewitness identification accuracy. Jurors also rely heavily on witnesses' confidence to infer witness accuracy (Cutler, Penrod & Dexter, 1990; R.C.L. Lindsay, 1994b; Luus & Wells, 1994a). In fact, after reviewing the literature, Wells et al. (1998: p. 620) concluded that "the confidence that an eyewitness expresses in his or her identification during testimony is the most powerful single determinant of whether or not observers of that testimony will believe that the eyewitness made an accurate identification." The findings are perhaps not surprising. A witness who says, "I'm sure that's the one who robbed the shop," makes a more convincing impression than a witness who says, "I think he is the one who robbed the shop, but I might be wrong." While the bulk of the eyewitness literature indicates a weak relationship between confidence and accuracy (see Sporer et al., 1995), a more recent trend in the research is that in some situations confidence may to some extent be a good predictor of accuracy (D.S. Lindsay, Read & Sharma, 1998). Let us take the earlier work first. Sporer et al. (1995) have found that the confidence–accuracy relationship is stronger for choosers (witnesses who make an identification in a line-up) than for non-choosers (witnesses who reject line-ups; that is, they say that the culprit is not present in the line-up). This result has recently been replicated by Weber and Brewer (in press). Wells et al. (1998) noted that the distinction between choosers and non-choosers is forensically important. Choosers appear more often in court than non-choosers because non-identifications (the result of not choosing) do not support criminal prosecutions. The trial in the UK of Barry George was an exception in this case. As pointed out in the opening paragraph of this chapter, the prosecution called all witnesses, including three who had not identified the suspect from the identification parade.

D.S. Lindsay et al. (1998) attempted to identify conditions under which a witness's subjective judgement of confidence may be meaningfully related to objective accuracy. According to the optimality hypothesis (Deffenbacher, 1980), the more optimal the encoding and retrieval conditions for person identification, the greater the likelihood of a positive confidence–accuracy relation. An alternative interpretation of the optimality hypothesis suggests that the gains in the confidence–accuracy relationship with increased exposure may be due to an increased opportunity for variability in encoding across participants rather than merely enhanced encoding (Read, D.S. Lindsay & Nichols, 1998). Lindsay et al. (1998) and Read et al. (1998) present convincing evidence that reliance on homogeneous samples (college students) and controlled settings in eyewitness studies actually minimises variability in witnessing conditions, thereby reducing the chances of finding a confidence–accuracy relationship.

It is generally accepted among researchers that confidence ratings are malleable. For example, witnesses who are questioned repeatedly become more confident in the accuracy of their reports (Shaw & McClure, 1996); briefing witnesses about the types of questions they may encounter boosts their confidence (Wells, Ferguson & R. Lindsay, 1981), and information that a co-witness has identified the same person increases confidence (Luus & Wells, 1994b). Interviewer feedback can also influence witness confidence (see section below on Investigator Bias).

Stable Target Characteristics

The gender of the suspect or perpetrator has no effects on face recognition accuracy, but facial distinctiveness does have an effect. Faces that are rated as highly attractive or highly unattractive are better recognised than typical faces (see Chapter 2 for more on the effects of attractiveness). A typical face will result in a high probability of false identification. An example is the FBI search for Andrew Cunanan, who allegedly murdered fashion designer Gianni Versace in

Miami, Florida. There were thousands of falsely reported sightings of Cunanan, who had very typical facial features (Brigham, Wasserman & Meissner, 1999). However, while a distinctive feature may make it easier to recognise a face, it may also make it more difficult to construct a fair line-up, because the police have to find other people with similar distinctive features (Brigham et al., 1999).

Malleable Target Characteristics

Malleable target characteristics are important predictors of identification accuracy. Studies of face recognition have shown that recognition performance is severely affected by disguises (hats, masks, glasses and so on) and changes in facial appearance between the crime and recognition test (see Narby, Cutler & Penrod, 1996; Shapiro & Penrod, 1986, for reviews). When people are asked to describe faces from their memory they refer mostly to hairstyle (in 27 per cent of the cases), followed by eyes (14 per cent), nose (14 per cent) and face shape (13 per cent) (Ellis, 1984; Shepherd & Ellis, 1996). In line with this, face recognition research has shown that people are primarily reliant on external features, such as hair, when they are faced with the task of recognising an unfamiliar face (O'Donnell & Bruce, 2000; Shepherd, Ellis & Davies, 1982); therefore, simple appearance changes such as different hairstyles, or the addition or removal of facial hair, may be especially detrimental to recognition performance.

Environmental Conditions

Most experiments regarding estimator variables have examined the impact of environmental factors on identification accuracy. Three estimator variables will be examined here: exposure duration, presence of a weapon and how serious the event is perceived to be (crime seriousness). A meta-analysis of face recognition studies (Shapiro & Penrod, 1986) identified the expected linear relationship between exposure duration and hit rates (that is, when the amount of time spent viewing a target increases, so, too, does the hit rate). It also uncovered a counterintuitive finding, in relation to false alarm rates (incorrect choices of faces that were not shown earlier), which indicated that as exposure to a face increased so, too, did the false-alarm rate. Therefore, it is surprising that only a handful of studies have manipulated exposure duration in an eyewitness context (see Memon et al., 2002). Moreover, while researchers tend to report the length of the stimulus event, they rarely report actual exposure to the target's face. However, in a live situation, it is difficult to gauge accurately the focus of witnesses' attention and hence the exposure of the target.

Only two studies have systematically manipulated exposure duration, namely, those by Read (1995) and by Memon, Hope and Bull (in press). Read (1995) tested the hypothesis that a longer exposure to a face may lower participants' decision criteria on the basis of their reasoning that they saw the person for longer and so should be able to recognise him or her. Read (1995) found that participants who interacted with salespersons for a longer time (4–15 minutes as compared to 30–60 seconds) made more correct choices from TP line-ups but more false choices from TA line-ups. Memon et al. (2002) compared eyewitness performance where a culprit's face was viewed for either 12 seconds or 45 seconds. They report an increase in hits from 32 per cent with short exposure to 90 per cent with the longer exposure to the face. However, contrary to Read (1995), there was no corresponding increase in choosing rates (false alarms) in the TA group in the long-exposure condition. In fact, there were almost twice as many false alarms in the short-exposure than the long-exposure condition (that is, 85 per cent versus 45.5 per cent).

There has been a great deal of interest in the "weapon-focus" effect (see Pickel, 1999; Steblay, 1992, for reviews). This effect refers to the visual attention that eyewitnesses give to a perpetrator's weapon during the course of a crime. The two most popular explanations are that the presence of a weapon (i) increases level of arousal in witnesses and (ii) focuses their attention on that weapon (see also Christianson, 1992). The effects were compellingly demonstrated by Maass and Köhnken (1989). Participants were approached by an experimenter who was holding at hip level either a syringe or a pen, and who threatened the participant. Later, the participants were asked to identify the experimenter in a TA line-up and to recall details about the experimenter's face and hand. Prior to the experiment, participants had answered some questions about their fear of injections. The results revealed that twice as many participants in the syringe-present condition (64 per cent) than in the pen-present condition (33 per cent) made a false identification in the line-up task. Moreover, the more afraid participants were of injections, the more hand cues and the less facial cues they accurately recalled.

A study conducted by Loftus, Loftus and Messo (1987) supported the focus of attention explanation. Their study showed that even in harmless situations (in situations in which no arousal is involved) witnesses' eyes are automatically (like a magnet) drawn to a weapon. Participants saw slides of a customer who approached a bank teller and pulled out either a handgun or a chequebook. The number and duration of eye fixations on the gun or chequebook were recorded. They found that participants made more and longer eye fixations on the gun than on the chequebook.

More recent research (Pickel, 1999; Reisberg, Heuer & Laney, 2000) has considered an alternative explanation of the weapon-focus effect. Pickel (1999) argues that the "driving force" behind the effect is that weapons take witnesses by surprise. Because the weapon appears out of context, the witnesses' visual attention is drawn to it, leaving fewer attentional resources to process other details. Pickel (1999, Experiment 2) found that witnesses' descriptions were poorer if a target carried an object that was inconsistent with his occupation. She showed the same target dressed as either a police officer or a priest and carrying either a gun or a cellphone. Witnesses remembered less about the priest when he carried a gun rather than a cellphone. The scores for witnesses who saw the police officer were the same whether he had a gun or a cellphone.

The external validity of the laboratory research on weapon focus has recently been questioned. An archival analysis of eyewitness identification in actual criminal cases (Behrman & Davey, 2001) reports no significant difference in the rates with which a suspect was identified in cases in which a weapon was involved and crimes without a weapon (the percentages were 48 and 51, respectively). This finding is inconsistent with the laboratory data and suggests that further work is required to understand when a weapon-focus effect may occur and when it may not.

Crime seriousness (another estimator variable) may also be related to identification accuracy. It is important to know whether or not the results of eyewitness studies can generalise to different cases and to situations where an eyewitness's decision can have serious consequences. One of the first studies to examine this variable was that of Leippe, Wells and Ostrom (1978). Leippe et al. examined the effect of the value of an item stolen in a mock theft on line-up identification. Participants were told either that the object was valuable or that it was relatively worthless. The authors found the only effect of the manipulation was that witnesses who were told in *advance* of seeing the video that the item was valuable were more likely to make a correct identification. Those told the same thing *after* the video were not more likely to identify the target, suggesting that the manipulation did not affect decision processes. Foster et al. (1994) varied the perceived salience of the identification decision itself by telling half their witnesses that the results of the experiment in which they were participating would be used at a real trial as evidence of the likelihood that the target could be identified from a surveillance videotape. Although the witnesses were informed that their decision would have consequences, their line-up performance was not different from that of controls. More recently, Searcy, Bartlett and Siepel (2000) showed young adults (18–30 years) and senior adults (60–80 years) a videotape of a young man apparently breaking into a house, and then told them that he had committed either a minor theft or a murder within the house. In a subsequent line-up task, those who were trying to recognise a murderer were more likely to make an identification attempt than those trying to recognise a petty thief. Accuracy rates were higher in the murder condition than the theft condition, but only for young adults. Seniors made more false identifications than younger adults, particularly in the murder condition. These data suggest that crime seriousness affects participants' propensity to choose, but it is not clear whether this is due to the characteristics of the crime or to the characteristics of the criminal, as the manipulation was confounded. The suspect in the murder story was described as having a criminal history, whereas the suspect in the minor theft story was not.

There is some evidence to suggest an *own-age bias* in face recognition. Wright and Stroud (2002) showed young adults (18–25-year-olds) and older adults (35–55-year-olds) crime videos. The participants then viewed TP and TA line-ups comprising young or older targets. The participants were more accurate at identifying the target when viewing TP line-ups composed of people their own age (own-age bias), but the findings did not extend to TA line-ups. Memon, Bartlett and Rose (2002) found young and older adults were more likely to pick "other-age" faces in line-ups, but did not find any evidence that faces from the witness's own age group were any more accurately identified than faces from the other age group.

In contrast to the small amount of research on gender and age of face, there is an extensive literature on the effects of cross-race bias. Identifications of someone of the same race are more accurate than identifications of someone of another race (see Meissner & Brigham, 2001b, for a recent review). The effect appears to be stronger for white than for black people. For example, Cross, Cross and Daly (1971) found an own-race bias in white participants, who were more accurate at identifying faces of their own race, but not in black participants. Chance and Goldstein (1996) suggested that the effect is caused by differences in frequency and, particularly, quality of contact between members of different groups. For example, Lavrakas, Buri and Mayzner (1976) found that in explaining white participants' other-race recognition performance, *quality* of contact was more important than *frequency*: "Being white and actually having black friends was found to be more positively related to recognition of black faces than merely having grown up in an integrated neighbourhood or having gone to school with blacks" (p. 480). In a meta-analysis of 39 published studies involving around 5000 participants, Meissner and Brigham (2001b) report that people are 1.38 times more likely to recognise correctly someone of their own race and 1.50 times less likely to identify falsely someone of their own race. White participants were more likely to demonstrate an own-race bias, especially with respect to false-alarm responses. McClelland and Chappell (1998) have proposed a model of the processes underlying own-race bias. They argue that individuals store features of a stimulus in memory, and as these features are repeatedly processed, their perceived familiarity increases. This increases the strength of the represented feature but decreases the likelihood of a response to a novel stimulus. McClelland and Chappell (1998) argue that own-race faces are thus stored more accurately and efficiently due to their familiarity. This framework is broadly consistent with work on discrimination training and prior experience as ways of reducing the own-race bias (Chiroro & Valentine, 1995).

One of the limitations of the cross-race identification literature is that it has relied heavily on laboratory studies of face recognition in which participants are shown multiple sets of targets and later shown a larger set of faces and asked to select those faces seen earlier. The participants are usually students (typically Caucasian) and are usually expecting some kind of recognition test. There are few exceptions. Recently, a field study of own-race bias was conducted in South Africa and England (Wright, Boyd & Tredoux, 2001). Adopting a procedure based on Yarmey (1993), Wright et al. asked one of two confederates (black or white males) to walk up to members of the public (a black or a white person) and ask them a series of questions. The second confederate then approached the same persons and asked them about the stranger with whom they had just spoken. They found an own-race bias, with black and white participants for a black and white confederate. The effect was obtained in both England and South Africa, countries with different race profiles and political histories. Wright et al. (2001) suggest that it would be interesting to track the size of the own-race bias in South

Africa, given the increase in interracial contact following the abolition of apartheid. Racial integration may reduce the own-race bias (Meissner & Brigham, 2001b), but, as stated above, the quality of contact may be more important than the quantity of contact.

Post-Event Factors

Common sense suggests that memory declines over time. Research has revealed that this time-delay effect indeed exists. The longer the time between witnessing a crime and making an identification, the more identification errors occur.

Witnesses are sometimes asked by the police to search through mugshots to identify the culprit. However, research has shown that previous exposure to the suspect (in the media, in mugshots or in an earlier line-up) affects identification accuracy in subsequently presented line-ups. Several experiments (Brigham & Cairns, 1988; Gorenstein & Ellsworth, 1980) have shown that when witnesses view a line-up after having looked at mugshots, they are inclined to identify a person whose mugshot they have previously seen (regardless of whether that person is the perpetrator). There are probably two reasons for this "repeated identification" effect (Köhnken, Malpass & Wogalter, 1996). It occurs because the witnesses recognise the photograph but forget the circumstances in which they originally saw it (the "unconscious-transference" effect; Loftus, 1976), or it may occur because, once witnesses come to a decision and express it, they feel committed and may be less willing to change the decision later (the "commitment" effect; Kiesler, 1971). Recent studies, however, question whether "commitment" alone can account for the mugshot-exposure effects. Memon et al. (in press) set out to identify the mechanisms responsible for false choosing in a photograph identification parade after prior exposure to a set of mugshots. They showed participants a crime video and then divided them into two conditions. In one condition, participants were asked to look through a mugshot album, and then asked whether the thief from the crime video was among the photographs. He was not there, but some witnesses nevertheless chose someone. In the other condition, witnesses did not see the mugshot album. Two days later, all witnesses were presented with a six-person photograph line-up. Again, the thief was not among the photographs. However, one of the faces from the mugshot albums (an innocent face) appeared in the photograph line-up. In line with predictions, exposure to this innocent face (referred to as the "critical foil") prior to the line-up increased the rate of false choices of that critical foil. A new finding was that witnesses who made *any* selection from the mugshot album were more likely to make a false choice of the innocent face than those witnesses who made no mugshot choice. Participants' prior commitment to choosing the critical foil was not a necessary prerequisite for the mugshot effect (cf. Dysart et al., 2001). This effect is interesting because it is counter to intuition. One might have predicted that witnesses presented with a line-up in which the face they saw earlier is absent will not pick anyone from the line-up. Yet Memon et al. (2002) found that mugshot choosers are highly likely to make line-up choices whether or not the previously chosen face was present.

Changes in experiential context may make an identification difficult. When someone "knows" a person from one context, say, as an employee in a shop, it is sometimes difficult to recognise the same person in another context, such as away from the shop. Research has shown that context reinstatement (going back to the original context) can, on occasion, improve identification accuracy (see Brown, 2003; Searcy et al., 2001, for alternative findings). Context can be reinstated physically (by returning to the scene of crime when performing the identification task) or, if that is not appropriate, reinstated mentally (imagining the scene of crime when performing the identification task). The cognitive interview technique (described in Chapter 5 of this volume) is a mental reinstatement technique. (See Malpass, 1996, for a review of the effects of reinstatement techniques.)

Additional information about the event (correct or incorrect) given to witnesses in a post-event interview might distort their memory. This is referred to as the post-event information effect. In one of the earliest studies, Loftus and Palmer (1974) showed participants a film of a traffic accident, and they then answered questions about the event, including the question, "About how fast were the cars going when they *contacted* each other?" Other participants received the same information, except the verb "contacted" was replaced by either "hit", "bumped", "collided" or "smashed". Although all participants saw the same film, the wording of the question affected their answers. The speed estimates (in miles per hour) were 31, 34, 38, 39 and 41, respectively. One week later, participants were asked whether they had seen broken glass at the accident site. Although there was no broken glass visible at the accident site (so that the correct answer was "no"), 32 per cent of the participants in the "smashed" condition said they had seen it. Hence, the wording of the question had influenced their "memory" of the incident. This finding is sometimes referred to as the "misinformation effect" because participants will often report the post-event information when they are asked for details of the event (see Ayers & Reder, 1998; Wright & Loftus, 1998, for reviews). Various mechanisms have been proposed. For example, the "trace-alteration account" (Loftus, Miller & Burns, 1978) posits that post-event information alters or updates original event details. More recently, it has been argued that recalling misinformation may *inhibit* memory for the original information (Saunders & MacLeod, 2002). Others have argued that misled witnesses remember the event details just as well as the witnesses who were not misled, but also remember the suggested detail and follow this suggestion, but leaving their original memory intact for retrieval under the right conditions (Bekerian & Bowers, 1983; McCloskey & Zaragoza, 1985). Source-monitoring accounts (Johnson, Hashtroudi & Lindsay, 1993) are consistent with this approach. A source-monitoring error occurs when participants say they *witnessed* something with their own eyes when in fact they *read* or *heard* about it. For example, when they asked about the accident in which Diana, Princess of Wales, was killed, Ost et al. (2002) found that 44 per cent of participants reported that they had seen a non-existent film of the car crash. Source-confusion errors can have serious consequences and on occasion result in false beliefs and memories (see Chapter 7).

There continues to be a debate as to the theoretical mechanisms underlying the misinformation effect and the extent to which misinformation alters the memory trace, exerts a social influence or is a combination of the two (for more details, see Chapter 7). From an applied perspective, the important issue is that eyewitness reports can be biased by post-event information. Suggestive questions asked by the police could interfere with the witness's original memory of the event and should therefore be avoided. Unfortunately, not only the police but also others (friends and acquaintances) will talk with the witness about the event. Their suggestive information may distort the witness's memory as well. A good example is provided by recent research on the memory-conformity effect (Gabbert, Memon & Allan, in press). Gabbert et al. investigated memory-conformity effects between pairs of participants, who were led to believe that they were seeing the same video of a crime scene, but they were actually shown one of two variants. Although the two video clips contained exactly the same sequence of events, they were filmed from different angles to simulate different witness perspectives. Critically, this manipulation allowed different features of the event to be observed for each participant. After viewing the event, participants were asked to recall the event, either alone or in pairs. An individual recall test was then administered to examine the effects of the co-witness discussion on subsequent memory reports. A significant proportion (71 per cent) of witnesses who had discussed the event reported "erroneous" details acquired during the discussion (that is, details that they could not have seen in the video). For example, 60 per cent of witnesses reported that they saw the suspect stealing despite the fact that the version of the video that they were shown did not show the suspect committing any crime. Their co-witness had seen the suspect steal some money.

Another post-event factor that can affect eyewitness identification is the verbal description of a culprit that is typically obtained prior to an identification parade. Police officers rely heavily on verbal descriptions of faces. Occasionally, a very detailed description of a suspect is obtained from a witness to enable the police to create a composite of the suspect, such as an E-fit (electronic facial identification technique) or an identikit. Verbally describing a stimulus can sometimes impair our ability visually to recognise that stimulus. This effect, termed "verbal overshadowing", was first demonstrated by Jonathan Schooler and colleagues with faces and has been extended to memories for colours, music and fine wines (see Meissner & Brigham, 2001a, for a review). In a typical study of the effects of verbalising on recognition, participants view a difficult-to-verbalise stimulus such as a face. Later, some participants are asked to describe the face in as much detail as possible while others engage in an unrelated activity. Finally, all are given a recognition test in which they have to distinguish targets from visually similar distracters. The standard finding across a series of experiments was that those participants who had described a face were less likely to recognise that face among other faces (Schooler & Engstler-Schooler, 1990). According to Schooler and Engstler-Schooler (1990), the verbal task of describing a face somehow *interferes* with the subsequent visual task of trying to distinguish this face from similar faces (see Memon & Bartlett, 2002, for a discussion of the mechanisms).

The verbal-overshadowing hypothesis has captured the attention of numerous researchers over recent years, and attempts to replicate it have met with mixed success. Examples of a failure to replicate the verbal-overshadowing effect include studies of child witnesses (Memon & Rose, 2002) and young and older adults (Memon & Bartlett, 2002). Recent evidence suggests that retrieval instructions may be the key to understanding how the accuracy (or inaccuracy) of verbal descriptions may moderate the verbal-overshadowing effect. Meissner, Brigham and Kelley (2001) investigated whether the accuracy in verbalisation of a previously seen stimulus is related to subsequent identification performance. They found that forced recall (that is, instructions to recall as much as possible without screening for accuracy) increased erroneous information, and this reduces the likelihood of subsequent identification. Thus, variations in actual retrieval instructions may influence the accuracy of target descriptions, and this accuracy, in turn, determines whether or not verbal overshadowing occurs.

SYSTEM VARIABLES

As mentioned earlier, system variables are factors that are under the control of the criminal justice system (Wells, 1978). These factors are often related to the retrieval stage (the third memory stage), and include issues such as how properly to interview witnesses and how to conduct recognition tests (line-up tests). Psychological theory and research about interviewing are discussed elsewhere (see Chapter 5), and we restrict ourselves here to theory and research on conducting line-up tests. In the USA, it is estimated that more than 200 people per day become criminal defendants after being identified from line-ups or photospreads (Goldstein et al., 1989; Wells et al., 2000). According to Cutler and Penrod's (1995) categorisation, five biases may occur in line-up tests: line-up instruction bias, foil bias, clothing bias, presentation bias and investigator bias.

Line-up Instruction Bias

As soon as witnesses are requested to come to the police station for a line-up test, they are likely to think that the police have reason to believe that they have apprehended the perpetrator (Malpass & Devine, 1984). Malpass and Devine (1981) were the first to show that situations in which witnesses believe that the perpetrator is in the line-up reduce accuracy, especially when the perpetrator is not present in the line-up. This research is referred to as the biased information condition, although the police may not have given any such instructions. Memon, Hope and Gabbert (2002) used a post-line-up questionnaire to examine participants' post-identification cognitions regarding the line-up identification task. Participants were asked to provide responses to a series of questions relating to their beliefs about the line-up task. In some studies, the target was present in the line-up; in some studies, absent. Two questions were of particular interest. One question sought to determine whether witnesses expect that the guilty parties will always be present and thereby assume their job is to identify them (rather than first of all discern whether they are in fact present). A further question asked witnesses whether they would have made the same identification decision in real life.

The results across four studies ($n = 636$) indicate that 90 per cent of mock witnesses expected the target to be present in the line-up despite clear instructions that the target might not be present. However, 95 per cent of participants did recall the instruction that the perpetrator might not be present! Only 17 per cent said they felt under pressure to choose from the line-up, and 78 per cent indicated that they would be happy to make the same decision in real life. The overall accuracy rate was only 48 per cent (that is, only 48 per cent of participants made the correct identification decision). Of those who said they would make the same decision in real life, 47 per cent were incorrect in their line-up decision ($n = 220$). However, there was a significant association between accuracy and responses to this question. Participants were more likely to say that they would *not* make the same decision in real life when they were incorrect. Nonetheless, this relatively small number (given the large sample) should not overwhelm the basic finding that a large proportion of witnesses were quite happy to indicate that they would make the same decision in real life even though they were actually inaccurate in their identification decision. Thus, even when safeguards are in place (such as the "may or may not be present" instructions required by the Police and Criminal Evidence Act 1984), witnesses' beliefs and expectations may influence their decision making. Courts, police and lawyers need to be aware of this.

Foil Bias

A suspect in a line-up deserves a fair test, that is, a test in which the suspect does not stand out inappropriately from the other innocent people ("foils") in the line-up. Although this sounds obvious, biased line-ups do occur. One of the most notorious examples was the black suspect in an all-white line-up used by police in Minneapolis (Ellison & Buckhout, 1981). The police justified this line-up by explaining that there were no other blacks in the building when the line-up was constructed and, since there are few blacks in Minneapolis, the line-up was representative of the population! Constructing a fair line-up is not easy. For example, which foils do you need to select? People who look like the suspect or people who fit the description that the witness gave of the perpetrator? Initially, there were disagreements on this issue (see Brigham & Pfeifer, 1994; Lindsay, Martin & Webber, 1994; Wells et al., 1994, for a discussion), but, according to Wells et al. (2000), an answer has emerged. The foils should fit the verbal description of the perpetrator given by the eyewitness before viewing the line-up. Wells et al. (1998) point out that a proper selection of foils who fit a comprehensive description of the suspect could result in the selection of near "clones", a result which might make the recognition of the actual culprit too difficult. Selecting foils on the basis of the verbal description of the witness guarantees more variability among the members of the line-up because there will be some differences between witnesses in their choice of descriptors and in the amount of detail, and a wider range of foil faces can be used to match the description. Clark and Tunnicliff (2001) also recommend that when constructing a TA line-up for the purposes of research, the innocent foils should be selected on the basis of a match to a description of the perpetrator, and not a match to the suspect. They found the false identification rate was lower in the former situation.

There are several problems associated with the match-to-description technique. For example, if the suspect has a distinctive feature that the witness did not describe, the foils may not have that feature. In such a case, the suspect will stand out. Moreover, certain features of the suspect might be in the witness's memory but not reported in a pre-line-up description. Furthermore, the witness might give a very vague description of the culprit—witnesses typically give only five descriptors, such as gender, approximate age, race, information about hair and facial hair, and height or build (Sporer, 1996; Wells et al., 2000). Alternatively, the witness's description of the culprit may sometimes be so specific that finding a reasonable set of distracters is virtually impossible. Finally, in cases where more than one eyewitness was involved, their descriptions of the culprit may well differ from each other.

Given the problems of composing a fair line-up, it is highly desirable to test the validity (fairness) of the line-up prior to the identification procedure. An effective way of doing this is by conducting the line-up with pseudo-witnesses or mock witnesses (people who have not seen any of the line-up members before). In a totally fair line-up, each of the members of the line-up should be chosen as "the culprit" at the level of chance, that is, in a six-people line-up, each of the members should gather one-sixth (16.7 per cent) of the mock witnesses' votes.

Another question is, how many foils are needed? The more people in the line-up, the less likely it is that the suspect will be chosen by chance. That is, when only two people are present (the suspect and one foil), there is a 50 per cent chance of a random identification of the suspect, but this chance is lowered to 20 per cent when five people are in the line-up. Of course, recruiting many foils can be difficult and expensive. A line-up of at least six people (one suspect and five foils) is usually recommended by experts (Wells et al., 1994).

Clothing Bias

An important question is how the members of a line-up should be dressed to ensure a fair identification procedure. It is obvious that suspects should not stand out from the foils by their clothing. It is therefore recommended that all members of the line-up wear similar clothes. But should they all wear clothes similar to those worn by the perpetrator at the scene of crime, or is it better to have clothes which differ from those worn by the perpetrator at the scene of crime? Lindsay, Wallbridge and Drennan (1987) and Yarmey, Yarmey and Yarmey (1996) concluded that it is better if the people in the line-up do not wear clothes similar to those worn by the perpetrator at the scene of crime because witnesses may misidentify someone on the basis of recognising the clothing. In addition, having subjects wear different clothes gives the police the opportunity to conduct a second test (apart from the line-up) in which the witnesses are requested to identify the clothes worn by the perpetrator.

Presentation Bias

It is a common procedure to present suspect and foils simultaneously. In a conventional simultaneous line-up, all members are viewed at the same time. Thus, there may well be a tendency for witnesses to select the member of the line-up who most resembles their memory of the culprit relative to other members of the line-up (Wells & Seelau, 1995). In a sequential line-up, members are presented one at a time followed by a witness decision (yes/no) after each face is viewed. The witness is not told how many faces will be presented. According to Lindsay & Wells (1985), the sequential procedure reduces false identifications in those situations where the police do not have the perpetrator. Participants in the Lindsay and Wells (1985) study witnessed a theft and were asked to identify the culprit afterwards from six photographs (the photograph of the thief was not present). Half of the participants were presented with a simultaneous presentation, and the others with a sequential presentation. Fifty-eight per cent of the participants in the simultaneous condition made a wrong identification, whereas only 17 per cent of the participants in the sequential condition made a wrong identification. The reason seems obvious. In the simultaneous condition, the witness knows from the beginning the size of the set from which the choice may be made and is looking for the person who most resembles the culprit. In a sequential presentation, the size of the set is unknown. It is important that the witness is not informed about the number of alternatives that will be presented in a sequential line-up; otherwise, the pressure would be increased on someone who feels an obligation to choose when the line-up is coming to the end. A recent meta-analysis (Steblay et al., 2001) of 24 studies (15 unpublished) concludes that sequential testing reliably reduces false choices in TA situations but also lowers correct identifications in TP conditions.

Steblay et al. argue that under test situations that simulate real-life situations (use of crime simulation and appropriate cautionary instructions) the difference between sequential and simultaneous line-ups is likely to be minimised or eliminated. However, evidence does not always support this hypothesis. For example, Memon and Gabbert (in press) used a simulated crime event shown on video and found a 30 per cent decrease in correct identifications by younger adults, and a 27 per cent decrease by older adults. A previous study (Memon & Bartlett, 2002) using a realistic crime simulation and cautionary instructions also obtained lower correct identification rates with a sequential line-up. Furthermore, Lindsay et al. (1997; Experiment 2), using a live event, found that the sequential line-up reduced the hit rate by 27 per cent for children and 35 per cent for adults in comparison with a simultaneous line-up. Thus, it is not always the case that the sequential line-up outperforms the simultaneous line-up, even when real-life conditions are approximated.

We have already discussed the single-suspect line-up, that is, a line-up with one suspect and some foils (preferably at least five foils). Other types of line-up are all-suspects line-ups (a line-up in which all members are suspects) and the show-up (in which the witness is shown only one person, namely, the suspect). Although both the all-suspects line-up and the one-suspect line-up are used by the police, they lead, compared to a line-up with one suspect and some foils, to more false identifications of a lookalike innocent suspect (Yarmey et al., 1996) and should therefore be avoided. Both types of line-up are inappropriate because they do not give an opportunity to discriminate between accurate and inaccurate witnesses. A guessing witness who mistakenly identifies a line-up member known to be innocent will usually do no harm to this person. It is a different story, however, if the innocent person who is mistakenly identified by the witness is a suspect, because he or she will then be accused of the crime. In an all-suspects line-up and in a show-up, each incorrect decision will automatically lead to such an accusation, because each member is a suspect. In a one-suspect line-up, it is likely that a guessing witness will identify a foil (for example, the chances are 5 out of 6 that a foil will be identified by a guessing witness in a one suspect plus five foils line-up).

Investigator Bias

If the persons conducting the line-up (such as police officers) know which member of the line-up the suspect is, they may, perhaps unintentionally, pass on this information to an eyewitness through their nonverbal behaviour. For example, when the witness is observing the suspect, the investigator may at that moment become anxious about whether or not the witness will recognise the suspect. This anxiety will change the investigator's behaviour, in turn, leading the witness to believe that this particular person is the suspect (see Harris & Rosenthal, 1985; Rosenthal, 1976). Indeed, a line-up administrator's knowledge of a suspect's identity can increase false identification rates (Phillips et al., 1999). Moreover, line-up administrators' beliefs about a culprit's position within a line-up have been found to affect witnesses' confidence in their line-up choices (Garrioch & Brimacombe, 2001).

The effects of interviewer feedback on eyewitness confidence is particularly interesting. For example, receiving confirming or disconfirming feedback about the identification after the identification task increases and decreases confidence, respectively, in adults (Wells & Bradfield, 1998) and children (Hafstad, Memon & Logie, 2002). The witness in the Barry George trial was told she had picked the suspect immediately after the live parade. This witness appeared highly confident when she presented her testimony in court ("Cutting Edge", Channel Four, 19/08/02). In a laboratory analogue of the pressure that may be experienced in the courtroom, Shaw, Woythaler and Zerr (in press) have shown how testimony may alter eyewitness confidence without changing eyewitness accuracy.

The fact that confidence can be manipulated by those who conduct the line-up means that confidence is, at least partly, controllable by the criminal justice system, a fact which makes it, in part, a system variable. The results of Phillips et al. (1999) suggest that only investigators who are blind to the suspect's identity should be present at identification parades. In England and Wales since PACE, the person conducting the line-up must not be part of the "team" dealing with the investigation (see Davies & Valentine, 1999). In fact, one might say that a well-conducted line-up has much in common with a good psychological experiment (Wells & Luus, 1990). For example, both include a control group (a line-up with mock witnesses in order to test the fairness of the line-up); they have an experimenter who is blind to the hypotheses (an investigator who does not know who the suspect is); and the questions are phrased in such a way that they do not demand a particular answer (the procedure does not imply that the culprit for certain is in the line-up).

SUMMARY AND CONCLUSION

Psychological eyewitness research has now produced a substantial insight into which factors may influence the accuracy of eyewitness accounts. Eyewitness researchers have examined the effects of estimator and system variables on witness performance. While the majority of studies have been laboratory based, there are some data from the field which converge with some of the findings from these experimental studies. For example, the recent archival analysis of over 200 police cases (Behrman & Davey, 2001) supports the existence of the cross-race identification effect, but there is no evidence to support the weapon-focus effect noted in several laboratory studies. Further field data are needed. Research has been directed not only at identifying the sources of errors but also at ways of minimising them. In accordance with this, guidelines have been developed to aid investigators in the collection of eyewitness identification evidence in the UK and the USA (e.g., PACE, 1984; Wells et al., 1998). This has been a significant step forward.

CHAPTER 7

FALSE MEMORIES

The 1990s saw an increasing number of reports of recovered memories from adults of childhood sexual abuse accompanied by a fierce debate as to the authenticity of these memories. It is a debate that has elicited considerable controversy in the courts, in academic circles and in professional practice due to its personal, social and political implications. A criminal case based on the recovered memory of a murder was instrumental in bringing the debate to the attention of the public and courts. In 1990, George Franklin was convicted of the murder of a child, primarily on the evidence of his daughter Eileen, who claimed she had repressed the murder of her friend for 20 years (Maclean, 1993). The conviction was overturned by a successful appeal in 1995, but the case nevertheless remains a poignant example of the impact of a recovered memory in the legal context. In the academic domain, recovered memories have presented memory researchers with some challenging questions. The debate has focused attention on conditions under which memories are recovered and the power of suggestion in the creation of false memories. False memories are typically defined as incorrect beliefs about past events that have been incorporated and experienced as genuine memories (Heaps & Nash, 1999; Lampinen, Neuschatz & Payne, 1998). In other words, what is a false memory may appear to us to be a true or accurate reflection of our past (Payne et al., 1997). That is not to say that all memories that are repressed or recovered after a period of being "unavailable" are false memories. The important issue concerns the manner in which the memory was recovered and what evidence exists to support the veracity of the memory.

Until recently, there was a heated debate about the origin of these so-called recovered memories, and recent research has attempted to address the question of whether memories for traumatic events are any different from memories for non-traumatic events (see Read, 2001, for a special issue of *Applied Cognitive Psychology* on this topic). This chapter will briefly review some of the theories about recovered memories and the methods used to study them. The conditions under which false memories arise will then be discussed. Experts who are invited to give advice to the courts as to the nature of a recovered memory have the job of making clear what they mean by a recovered memory. This may include information about what makes that memory different from any other memory, the process by which the memory was recovered and the reliability of that memory. The final section of this chapter will briefly examine the ways in which expert testimony based on scientific research can inform the courts about the reliability of recovered memories.

REPRESSION, AMNESIA AND MEMORY FOR EARLY CHILDHOOD EXPERIENCES

One of the major problems in working in the area of recovered memories is that of defining terms such as "amnesia", "recovery", "repression" and "forgetting" (Memon & Young, 1997). The term "amnesia" is confusing since it is also used in cases of psychogenic amnesia or functional amnesia, which refers to "a temporary loss of memory precipitated by a psychological trauma" (Schacter, 1996). It is also used to refer to amnesia due to organic causes (for example, the result of brain injury). The term "recovered memories" broadly refers to the reporting of memories of childhood events for the first time by adults who have previously been unable to recall these events or the circumstances surrounding them. The definition of "repression" is crucial in establishing whether or not there is supporting evidence for recovered memories. Freud was inconsistent in his use of this term. In his early writings, he clearly stated that repression involved the intentional rejection of distressing thoughts and memories from conscious awareness (also referred to in the literature as "suppression" or "repression proper"). Gradually, Freud began to use the term "repression" in reference to unconscious defence mechanisms designed to exclude threatening material from protruding into conscious awareness ("primary repression"; Brewin & Andrews, 1998). The assertion that this is involuntary distinguishes repression from suppression (see Erdelyi, 1990, for a full discussion of Freud's writings on the subject). In recent years, the terms "discovered memories" (e.g., Schooler, Ambadar & Bendiksen, 1997) and "non-continuous memories" (Read, 2000) have been used in place of the terms "recovered" and "repressed" memories.

One of the most frequently asked questions in the debate about recovered memories is whether these memories require special mechanisms to explain their existence and quality. This is a central question since it is the assumption that such memories are "special" that makes them stand apart from "normal" everyday memories in the eyes of the courts. Brewin, Dalgleish and Joseph (1996; p. 671) define "trauma" as "any experience that by its occurrence has threatened the health or well-being of the individual". If memories for traumatic experiences are no different from other types of memories, the study of everyday autobiographical memories and eyewitness memory may provide some useful answers (see Chapters 5 and 6).

Another common question is whether or not one has memories for events that happen in the first 2 or 3 years of life or "infantile amnesia" for early childhood events. Until recently, it was thought that infantile amnesia may explain failures of memory in some of the clinical case studies. However, the recent work of Fivush and colleagues would caution us from specifying a childhood amnesia barrier for preschoolers and has drawn our attention to the ways in which young children's memories are shaped by parents' conversations with their child (see Fivush & Reese, in press, for a review). Recent research suggests that 3-year-olds are able to give accurate detailed reports about familiar recurring events as well as single episodes (Fivush, 1998). In one study, Fivush and Schwarzmueller (1998) asked 8-year-olds to recall an event they had been interviewed about when they were 3, 4, 5 or 6 years of age. Children recalled detailed events that had occurred more than 5 years ago. Other research has shown that a mother's reminiscing style predicts a child's later reminiscing. For example, mothers' use of open-ended prompts is associated with children's talking about past memories (Farrant & Reese, 2000). Fivush and Reese (in press) point out there are clearly individual differences, some parents engaging in highly coherent and emotionally laden reminiscing and others in very sparse questions with little emotional information. This may account for individual differences in memories for early childhood traumas (see Howe, Courage & Peterson, 1994).

Repression and Memory Loss

A review of 60 years of experimental tests of "repression proper" led to the conclusion that at this time there is no controlled laboratory evidence supporting repression (Holmes, 1990). This review of research is often cited in the recovered-memory literature as evidence against the Freudian interpretation of repression as an unconscious mechanism but without any clarification of what these null effects mean. Are we to conclude that there is no evidence for repression? Can we generalise from these laboratory studies (which, for example, use threatening words as emotional stimuli) to real trauma? A scientist should answer "no" to both these questions but proceed to see whether evidence can be obtained from other sources of data. Another method used to gather evidence on the role of repression in memory loss has been case studies, but let us look first at the experimental studies.

Inhibitory Processes in Everyday Cognition: Experimental Studies

Brewin et al. (1996) and Brewin and Andrews (1998) have reviewed the cognitive psychology literature which suggests that repression and dissociation imply the presence of cognitive mechanisms that inhibit the activation of representations of traumatic events. They argue that these mechanisms have parallels in everyday cognitive processing, thus providing us with yet another interpretation of repression. Relevant research reviewed by Brewin et al. (1996) includes studies of retrieval-induced forgetting in which participants are typically presented with different categories of words and exemplars of them in the study phase. In the next phase, they have to practise retrieval of some items from the studied categories by completing words that formed part of the category exemplars (for example, Animal-Ho—). In a subsequent memory test, participants' recall of unpractised items is impaired relative to recall of the practised items and items from the control (baseline). It is concluded from this that there are "active inhibitory processes" which serve to reduce the activation level of practised versus unpractised words (Anderson & Spellman, 1995). Brewin et al. (1996) elaborate on inhibitory mechanisms in the discussion of their dual-processing model of post-traumatic stress disorder (PTSD). According to Brewin et al., PTSD is characterised by "an alternation between re-experiencing and avoiding trauma related memories" (p. 4). It is proposed that traumatic memories are represented in two ways: (i) a conscious experience (verbally accessible memories) that can be deliberately retrieved from the memory store and (ii) a non-conscious processing of the situation resulting in automatic activation of memories in specific contexts (referred to as "specific situationally accessible knowledge"). The dual-representation theory predicts that the latter would remain intact even when verbal memories are incomplete. Brewin et al. (1996) argue that "premature inhibition strategies" may be employed to avoid thinking about the trauma. Intrusive memories will be prevented from surfacing, but this does not mean that the memories cannot be reactivated later in life. This is a significant theoretical development in our understanding of memory for traumatic events. This work also informs us about how individual differences in coping strategies (Brewin & Myers, 1996) may contribute to memory deficits and other symptoms in trauma victims.

Case Studies in Clinical Contexts

A completely different approach to the study of inhibitory processes has been to identify cases of adults who are likely to have suffered some trauma and to question them about what may be in their memory "gaps" for this experience. This research provides us with an interesting insight into the nature of (presumed) previously inaccessible memories but does not allow us to determine whether we are dealing with primary repression, repression proper or merely forgetting due to lack of retrieval cues and the passage of time. For example, Briere and Conte (1993) asked 450 adult clinical clients reporting sexual abuse histories whether there were any conditions under which they could not remember the experience. Almost 60 per cent identified some period in their lives before the age of 18 when they had no memory of abuse. However, in addition to the demand characteristics inherent in this situation, asking someone to identify a time when they did not remember is a complex question. Does it mean a time when they did not think about the event, a time when they did not tell anyone or a time when they were unsure? In other words, it is not clear what a "yes" answer to this question means. The memory status of these patients prior to entering therapy is not clear either, and the fact that the patients were undergoing group therapy with others who had "survived" sexual abuse in childhood is problematic. Surveys of qualified therapists (e.g., Poole et al., 1995) indicate that a significant minority of clients in therapy may have undergone some form of memory recovery therapy such as hypnosis, the risks of which are well documented in earlier reviews (e.g., Lindsay & Read, 1994). Moreover, expectations and demand characteristics may have resulted from the therapy received, and these may have influenced the answers to questions about amnesia (Lindsay and Read, 1994). Indeed, the highest estimates of amnesia in the Briere and Conte (1993) study came from adults who had received extended therapy for abuse. Moreover, as pointed out by Read (1997), in none of the surveys have the respondents volunteered gaps in memory as being a source of psychological distress.

Williams (1994) had the opportunity to follow up women with a known history of childhood abuse (recorded as part of a mental health survey). Few of the participants in Williams's study had received extended therapy. Williams asked the women during the course of a single interview whether they had been abused. No specific technique was used to help them remember, and the question did not allude to a specific episode of abuse. Hence, when 38 per cent denied abuse, it is not clear whether they were referring to a particular instance of abuse. Williams assumes that her participants were referring to periods of time during which they avoided thinking about the abuse. Therefore, this study does not constitute evidence for primary repression but is more consistent with a suppression of the memory. There could also be other reasons why the women had not disclosed memories of abuse to Williams, such as embarrassment or threat, or because they had forgotten about the episode. It is interesting to note that in this study the women who always remembered the abuse recalled more supportive interactions surrounding their abuse experience from their mothers than those claiming to have forgotten for a period of time. The recent research of Fivush and colleagues (see above) strongly suggests that the absence of discussion may contribute to the forgetting of traumatic experiences.

In a prospective study, Widom (1997) examined the accuracy of adult recollections of childhood physical and sexual abuse, using officially documented and substantiated cases. Widom's analysis was part of a larger cohort study. In the first phase, court records identified a large group of abused children. Only substantiated cases were included in the sample. In all cases, the children were less than 11 years of age at the time of abuse. The cases included physical abuse, sexual abuse and neglect. In the second phase (20 years on), 2-hour follow-up interviews were conducted during which structured and semi-structured questionnaires were completed. The questions were designed to cue recall. For example, respondents were presented with a list of explicitly sexual behaviours and asked whether they had experienced any of the behaviours listed up to the time they finished primary school. Sixty-three per cent of respondents who were known to have suffered sexual abuse reported at least one sexual experience before the age of 12 as compared to 47 per cent of those who had been known to have been physically abused. To test the validity of the retrospective reports, Widom looked to see whether the three outcomes most frequently associated with child sexual abuse would be prevalent (depression, alcohol problems and suicide attempts). For women, official reports of child sexual abuse predicted alcohol problems and suicide attempts. Men were not at increased risk of any of the three outcomes, although the sample size was smaller here, and the men were less likely to disclose information about sexual abuse. Widom reports that of those respondents with documented histories of physical abuse, 40 per cent did not report the abuse. Again, the reason for failure to report is not clear. It could be due to embarrassment, need to protect a loved one or lack of rapport with the interviewer, or because the respondent forgot the experience.

Another method of investigating the forgetting of traumatic memories is to detail claims of individuals who reportedly forgot their traumas and subsequently recalled them. The forgetting has to be estimated retrospectively in these cases (Schooler & Eich, 2000). Schooler and Eich (2000) suggest that independent corroborative evidence of cases should be sought whenever possible. One case that was corroborated by a taped confession from the perpetrator was that of Ross Cheit, who recovered a memory of being molested by a counsellor (Horn, 1993). The problem here, however, is that individuals may distort the extent of forgetting. In other words, they may exaggerate or underestimate the degree of forgetting. Schooler et al. (1997) sought and found independent corroboration of sexual abuse in several cases by seeking out other individuals who had knowledge of the abuse before the memory was "discovered". In several cases, however, Schooler and colleagues discovered that individuals knew about their traumatic experiences and had discussed them with others, but they had simply forgotten they had done that when questioned later. Schooler hypothesised that this might be a variant of the hindsight bias effect when in hindsight people claim they would have estimated a probability of occurrence of a given behaviour that is higher than would have been estimated in foresight (Fischoff, 1982). In this case, Schooler argues it would be more of a "forgot-it-all-along effect" whereby individuals underestimate their prior knowledge. For example, people find that they become very upset when recalling a past experience and they do not remember reacting this way before. They may deduce from their reaction that this is the first time they have recalled the experience (see Arnold and Lindsay, 2002, for a laboratory analogue of this effect).

ADULTS' MEMORIES FOR TRAUMATIC AND NON-TRAUMATIC EVENTS

One of the problems of the retrospective studies reviewed so far is that few provide base rates of periods of forgetting or amnesia for non-traumatic life events (Read & Lindsay, 2000). There is increasing evidence to suggest that traumatic and non-traumatic events may be equally likely to be accompanied by a period of complete or partial amnesia. Read (1997) surveyed over 400 adults in the community and reports that 60 per cent reported a gap in their memory for at least one major life event. Importantly, 23 per cent of the events were recurring activities (such as music lessons). Participants also described periods of forgetting for emotional events such as parental conflict. Just over a third of respondents said this was simply due to forgetting. Sixty-five per cent said they had simply not thought about the event and would be able to recall were they given a reminder.

Another limitation of the retrospective studies described above is that engaging in efforts to retrieve childhood events is a confounding factor because it may change the way in which people view their inability to remember a prior experience (Read & Lindsay, 2000). Contrary to intuition, some evidence suggests that the *more* events people recall from their childhood, the *less* complete they judge their memories for childhood events to be (see Belli et al., 1998). Read and Lindsay (2000) asked a subset of the same community sample from the Read (1997) study to reminisce and engage in retrieval activities directed towards remembering more. Following a 4-week period of active memory retrieval, reports of prior periods of poor memory for target events increased substantially.

Reverie and Bakeman (2001) interviewed a sample of 110 undergraduates to test the hypothesis that those who had histories of trauma (sexual, physical abuse and parental conflict) would show greater deficits in memory. They found that neither type, severity nor frequency of trauma predicted memory elaboration, although the range of trauma sampled was heavily weighted toward mild trauma. Porter and Birt (2001) directly asked the question, are traumatic memories special? They interviewed 306 undergraduate students about two life experiences: their most traumatic and most positive experience (the order was counterbalanced). Measures of trauma severity were taken. They found traumatic memories were richer, more coherent and detailed than memories for positive events (cf. Bryne et al., 2001). The two types of memories were equally vivid. These results contradict the view held by some trauma theorists that traumatic memories are recalled in an impaired and fragmented fashion.

Finally, a recent study on young children's memories for positive as compared to negative life events supports the results of the adult memory studies. Fivush et al. (in press) report an interview study of 5–12-year-olds growing up in inner-city neighbourhoods with a high incidence of community violence. They found that children can give detailed reports about positive and negative experiences. Positive events were typically excursions (such as a visit to an amusement park) while negative events were more varied, including illness or death of family members, parental separation, loss of a pet, minor accidents and bullying incidents. Children reported different kinds of details for the negative and positive experiences. When narrating positive experiences, the children reported more descriptive information pertaining to objects and people. When narrating negative experiences, the children included more information about their thoughts and emotions. The negative events were recalled more coherently than positive events overall, and older children with better language skills recalled the negative events more coherently. Fivush et al. suggest this is because negative events require more explanation, and people need to make sense of these events and work through them. That the older children's narratives were more coherent suggests they can do this better. Contrary to expectation, few age differences were found, and there were no apparent differences as a function of time since the event occurred or of reported family discussion about the event. The authors point out a few shortcomings of their study. The negative events were quite variable, and it was not possible for the researchers to obtain any objective ratings of stress for the events (they relied on mothers' ratings). Moreover, the children were only asked about emotionally negative events that were acknowledged by their family or community. It may be that more private events such as sexual abuse did not form part of this study. Nevertheless, this study, together with the evidence reviewed earlier, strongly suggests that memories for traumatic experiences do not differ markedly from memories for non-traumatic experiences.

In summary, there is considerable controversy surrounding the validity of retrospective reports and a need for appropriate control conditions to get the base rates of forgetting for non-traumatic events. Without such controls, it is not possible to say that memory for traumatic events involves a special mechanism (Read & Lindsay, 2000). Indeed, studies of adults' memories of traumatic and of more mundane childhood events do not suggest that traumatic experiences yield fundamentally different kinds of memories. However, more research is needed using a broader range of events and more representative samples. Retrospective studies of adults in clinical settings have relied on select samples, and these studies cannot rule out alternative accounts of why there may be gaps in memory for episodes of trauma. Recent studies of adult memories for autobiographical memory suggest that both traumatic and non-traumatic memories can be equally vivid, and gaps in memory can occur for both positive and negative life events. Some alternatives to the repression hypothesis will now be explored.

Normal Mechanisms of Forgetting

It has been well established through decades of careful research that forgetting can occur over short and long delays through deficits in encoding, storage or retrieval processes, or a combination of these (see Brainerd et al., 1990, for a review). A retrieval cue is effective to the extent that there is an overlap between it and the encoded information (Tulving & Thomson's [1973] encoding specificity hypothesis). Thus, mentally reinstating the physical and personal contexts that existed at the time an event was witnessed can aid retrieval, as in the cognitive interview (see Chapter 5). Schacter and colleagues have recently completed research in their laboratory that provides a nice illustration of how properties of retrieval cues can influence what is recalled about the past (see Schacter & Scarry, 2000, for a review). In their experiments, college students looked at photographs of people (in which they were slightly smiling or frowning) and heard them speak in either a pleasant or irritating tone of voice. Later, they saw the same photographs again and tried to recall the tone of voice. Those faces seen with a slight smile tended to be attributed a pleasant voice and vice versa, despite the fact that there was no relationship between facial expression and tone of voice (cited in Schacter, 1996).

While retrieval cues may be effective in bringing back memories, we know that false recollections increase with the passage of time (Barclay, 1986), and retrospective biases at the time of recall can influence our memories for past events (Schacter & Scarry, 2000). For example, recollections of past political views can be distorted by beliefs held currently (Levine, 1997). According to Schacter and Scarry (2000), mere exposure to material about everyday activities such as brushing one's teeth can alter one's recollections of how often one has brushed one's teeth in the past (see Ross, 1989). A third area of research is based on the misinformation paradigm of Loftus and colleagues (e.g., Belli, 1989). Research using various types of procedures where misleading information is presented after an event is experienced shows how easily it is to bias recollection; for example, it may be biased through subtle changes in the wording of questions (see Chapter 6 for a review). As a direct result of concerns about the possibility that false memories can be created, several laboratories have developed paradigms to study systematically whether or not it is possible to implant an entirely false memory in the mind of an adult (see also Chapter 5, for a review of research on child witness suggestibility). It is this research which will be reviewed next.

IMPLANTING FALSE MEMORIES

It is well established that misleading information and the demands of an interview can result in memory distortions (see Chapters 5 and 6). However, how easy or difficult is it to implant an entirely false memory? The typical procedure in the memory-implantation studies is described by Loftus and Pickrell (1995). In the first part of their study, an older relative presents participants with four stories about their childhood. Three stories are "true" and one is a "false" event (for example, getting lost in a shopping centre). All participants are interviewed twice and asked to recall as much as they can. Loftus and Pickrell report that 68 per cent of the true events are remembered, while 25 per cent of false events are fully or partially recalled at the first and second interview. These findings have been replicated. For example, Hyman, Husband and Billings (1995: Experiment 2) implanted memories of an accident at a wedding reception in which a punchbowl was overturned on the parents of the bride. Memory for true events was highly accurate over three separate interviews. For the false "punchbowl" events, no participants provided false recollections during the first interview whereas 25.5 per cent did so by the third interview. (The false recalls varied in clarity, with six of the 23 rated as "very clear".) Interestingly, subjects who incorporated general details that fitted the event script into their first or second interview were more likely to have false recollections by the third interview.

Hyman and Pentland (1996), in an extension of the earlier studies of memory implantation, were interested in whether guided-imagery procedures resembling the ones sometimes used in therapy would increase the recall of true and false memories, and whether "hypermnesia" (or net increases in recall) would occur over repeated interviews (Payne, 1987). The guided-imagery procedure is one where recall is cued by using specific questions designed to evoke images of the experience. Students were interviewed three times about a series of "true" events based upon information supplied by their parents and a false event (the accident with the punchbowl). They were given basic cues (age, nature of event and locations). If participants in the imagery condition failed to recall the event, they were asked for detailed descriptions of it (and were asked questions about what happened). The control group were asked to sit quietly and think about the event for a minute. For true events, there were no significant differences between the imagery and control conditions in the percentage of true events recalled, but there was a tendency for additional information to be reported following the first interview (this is most marked in the imagery condition), suggesting a form of hypermnesia. Not surprisingly, memories provided by participants in the imagery condition were rated as higher in image clarity than memories provided in the control condition. Turning to the false events, these were scored as clear false memory, partial memory, no memory and no memory but trying (a memory recovered from the first to the third interview was referred to as a recovered memory). The number of clear false memories increased across interviews in both conditions (there were no clear differences in partial memories, although some individuals went from partial memories to clear memories). By the third interview, 37.5 per cent in the imagery condition and 12.4 per cent in the control condition had created a false memory. Those who created a false memory tended to rate their image as clearer and were more confident about the memory. The data are compatible with source monitoring theory (see below).

Imagination Inflation

Within the context of a suggestive interview, imagination is a simple and effective procedure that can alter the autobiographical beliefs of a significant minority of individuals. It has been demonstrated that asking people to imagine "critical" events increases their certainty that the imagined event was actually experienced. This effect of pure imagination on confidence has been termed "imagination inflation". In the first study on imagination inflation, Garry et al. (1996) asked participants to imagine certain childhood events. They first gave a number of participants a copy of the Life Events Inventory (LEI) to complete. The LEI is a 40-item self-report questionnaire asking about a variety of events that may have happened to respondents before the age of 10 years (for example, you broke a window with your hand). For each event, they circle one of eight options (1 = definitely did not happen and 8 = definitely did happen) to indicate how certain they are that the event stated had actually happened to them. From this pre-test data, eight target items were chosen; that is, a significant number of individuals responded that these events probably did not occur. In the second session (2 weeks later), the participants were randomly split into two groups, one of which was given four of these target events, and asked to imagine them (the other group acted as a control). Finally, the experimenter told both groups that their original LEI had been misplaced, and asked them to complete another copy. Thirty-four per cent of those in the imagination group increased their confidence that the events had occurred to them personally, as compared to 25 per cent in the control group, who did not imagine the items (a statistically significant difference). In much the same way that imagination can be used to predict possible future events, it also seems to affect an individual's prediction of whether a past event occurred or not. This finding has been replicated in several studies (for a recent review of the results of imagination-inflation studies, see Garry & Polaschek, 2000).

In a more recent study, Porter et al. (1999) attempted to obtain a false recovered memory for a highly stressful, emotional event. The events were a serious medical procedure, getting lost, being seriously harmed by another child, a serious animal attack, a serious indoor accident and a serious outdoor accident. The participants were interviewed and asked about one real and one false event (from the above list). There were also an additional two interviews asking specifically about the false event. The authors state that context reinstatement, guided-imagery techniques and "mild pressure" were used to encourage repeated attempts to recover the memory. During the third session, participants were asked to give a report of the incident, and 26 per cent of them recovered a full memory for the false event, while another 30 per cent recalled various aspects of it. These findings would seem to suggest that caution should be exercised when imagination-based therapies are used in recovered memory situations. However, the results of Porter et al. need to be interpreted with caution because the criteria for a "full memory" were low. In other words, a description could be coded as a memory even when relatively few details were present. This problem may apply to a number of the studies described in this section.

In the studies reviewed so far, imagination was just one of the components of a much more complex procedure aimed at inducing a new autobiographical memory. For example, in Hyman and Pentland's (1996) study, participants were given truthful information (provided by parents) about a number of events that had happened to the participants during their early childhood. However, along with the descriptions of the real events presented to the participants, the experimenters inserted descriptions of false events. Prior to imagining, participants were told that all the events had been provided by their parents, thus indicating that the events had in fact occurred, even if they did not remember them happening. The provision of this information was aimed at changing the belief about the occurrence of the false event, but belief change was not measured in these studies. Instead, after imagining the suggested event, memory reports for the false event were reassessed and were found to be more frequent than those found in a no-imagination control condition. This demonstrates that the combination of imagination and a belief-altering suggestion can result in the creation of memory for events that did not happen. However, it does not demonstrate that imagination per se has an effect on memory. In order to address this question, Mazzoni and Memon (2003) included a control condition aimed at controlling for simple exposure to the event, thus allowing us to establish whether imagination per se was responsible for changes in belief and memory. The study was run in three sessions with a 1-week delay separating each test session, and all participants were tested individually. In week 1, participants completed a pre-test LEI presented along with several other questionnaires and filler tasks, so as to disguise the purpose of the study. In week 2, the participants were allocated to one of two groups. The first group were asked to imagine a relatively frequent event (a tooth extraction) and were merely exposed to information about an event that never occurs (skin extraction). A second group were asked to imagine the skin event and were merely exposed to information about the tooth event. This design enabled us to examine the effects of imagination for both the frequent (tooth) event and the event that we know does not occur (the skin event). Participants in both groups rated the likelihood of occurrence of each of the two critical events and a series of non-critical events before and after the manipulation. In week 3, participants were asked to describe any memories they had for the events, and a further LEI was completed. For both the skin and tooth events, the imagination manipulation increased the number of memories reported, as well as beliefs about the event's occurrence (as measured by changes in LEI ratings before and after the manipulation). Compared to simple exposure, imagination produced a significantly greater shift in autobiographical beliefs and increased the number of false autobiographical memories. Participants were almost twice as likely to report memories after imagination than exposure.

The results reported by Mazzoni and Memon (2003), suggesting that mere familiarity that may arise as a result of exposure, cannot explain the increases in false beliefs and memory. An examination of the content of the memory reports suggests that participants may have been influenced by their prior knowledge and schema for the critical events. Memories for the frequent (tooth) event were relatively detailed. (For example, "I was lying on the dentist's chair and the dentist kept on singing silly songs and at the end I got lots of stickers. I got injections and they were really sore.") Memories about the non-occurring (skin) event also contained a surprising degree of detail and appeared to refer to real events. (For example, "It was taken at school and I was very scared. I remember crying but the nurse gave me a sweet and it helped.") Most of the false memories included elements such as the presence of a nurse, somebody dressed in white, pain and the smell of disinfectant. In other words, there was reference to actions and activities that commonly occur in a medical setting.

One theory about increases in memory errors following exposure to information is an increase in fluency or familiarity (Jacoby, Kelley & Dywan, 1989). The participants in the Mazzoni and Memon study (2003) had certainly experienced other medical procedures; thus, in recalling the skin event, they may have merely made a source-confusion error (Johnson, Hashtroudi & Lindsay, 1993; Mitchell & Johnson, 2000). In other words, they were recalling aspects of genuine personal medical experiences that had taken place in completely different situations.

MECHANISMS RESPONSIBLE FOR THE CREATION OF FALSE MEMORIES AND BELIEFS

Hyman and Kleinknecht (1999) have argued that three processes may be responsible for the creation of a false memory. The first is plausibility—an individual must accept a suggested event as plausible. Second, an image and narrative of the false event must be constructed. Third, a source-confusion error must be made. These processes are interactive. For example, clarity of the image may influence assessment of plausibility (Garry et al., 1996). Mazzoni and Kirsch (2003) have put forward a similar model and also point out that the process by which false beliefs and memories are produced may be no different from the processes by which accurate memories are retrieved.

The role of plausibility in the creation of a false memory is a question that is often raised in the research. One of the first studies to look at event plausibility was a study by Pezdek, Finger & Hodge (1997). They gave Jewish and Catholic high-school students detailed descriptions of some true events from their early childhood and two additional false events. One of the false events was described as a Jewish ritual and the other as a Catholic ritual. Seven Catholic students, but no Jewish students, remembered the Catholic false event, while three Jewish students and one Catholic student remembered the Jewish false event. Only two students recalled both false events. Similarly, when older family members read descriptions of one true event and two false events to a younger family member, it was found that the more plausible event was successfully planted, while individuals were more likely to reject the less plausible event. Pezdek et al. conclude from this study that plausible events are more likely to result in the creation of a false memory. However, research by Mazzoni and colleagues has shown that plausibility judgements are malleable. Mazzoni, Loftus and Kirsch (2001) provided their participants with written information that led them to believe highly implausible events (such as demonic possession) were more common than is generally believed in the population from which the participants were sampled. The authors collected assessments of plausibility over a 3-month interval along with several other assessments in different contexts, so as not to draw attention to the purpose of their study. The written information significantly increased judgements of plausibility. Moreover, Mazzoni and Memon (2003) have shown that imagination can influence adults' memory reports of plausible and frequently occurring childhood events, as well as implausible and non-occurring events.

Social Influences on Memory

The recent research conducted in the laboratories of Beth Loftus in the USA and Maryanne Garry in New Zealand suggest that a minority of people may be vulnerable to memory distortion if they are questioned by "suggestive" techniques. However, the conditions under which these memories develop is not fully clear. In an attempt to understand the social contexts in which false memories may occur, researchers have extended the earlier work by using a variety of other techniques to create false memory reports.

Wade et al. (2002) exposed 20 people to a false childhood event (a ride in a hot-air balloon) by creating a fake photograph. Over three interviews, participants were asked to think about the photographs and to try to recall the event depicted in the photographs (and three true events) using guided imagery. Fifty per cent of the participants created a full or a partial memory report of the fake balloon ride. To be a full memory report, the report had to contain an elaboration of details not in the photograph. Participants who gave such reports would typically begin with a fragmented description of the balloon event, which they embellished during the subsequent interviews. The extent to which the interviewers prompted participants during these interviews is not clear. Wade et al. suggest that seeing the photograph led people to search their memory for the event with a lower criterion for concluding whether or not it was a real memory. One example of the use of a lower or lax criterion is when decisions about the veracity of a memory are made on the basis of familiarity. This, in turn, can lead to source-confusion errors, as discussed earlier.

Assefi and Garry (in press) have shown how mere suggestions about alcohol consumption can affect people's memories for an event. Participants drank a plain-water tonic beverage, but half were told it was alcohol. Participants then took part in an eyewitness experiment. The group that were told they had taken alcohol were significantly more influenced by misleading post-event information and were more confident about their responses overall than those participants told they had drunk water. Assefi and Garry did check to see whether the belief that alcohol was consumed would affect the degree of attention paid to the eyewitness event. However, there was no difference in the performance on control items among the alcohol and tonic instruction groups, ruling out this hypothesis. Again, a lower criterion may be the reason for the susceptibility to misinformation effects here. Another study, recently conducted in the Garry laboratory (Vornick et al., in press) found that when post-event information was introduced aurally, ratings of the speaker influenced susceptibility to this information. Speakers rated high on a scale of power and attractiveness were more likely to mislead participants than those rated low on these dimensions.

Finally, an innovative set of studies was conducted by Braun, Ellis and Loftus (2002). These authors were interested in how advertising can change our memories of the past. Advertisers manipulate our memories and emotions by autobiographical referencing. For example, Disney World (Orlando) used the "Remember the Magic" campaign (1996), showing people having fun in the theme park, meeting Mickey Mouse and so on. Braun et al. reasoned that this may cause people to imagine themselves experiencing these things and alter their own experiences of their visit to Disney World. They conducted two studies. In the first study, participants viewed an advertisement for Disney World, which subsequently led them to believe they shook hands with Mickey Mouse as a child relative to a control group who did not see the advertisement. Of course, it is possible that if they did go to Disney World as a child, they would have come across Mickey Mouse. They would not have come across Bugs Bunny, however, because he is not a Disney character. In Experiment 2, participants were led to believe that they shook hands with Bugs Bunny (impossible). Relative to controls, participants viewing the Bugs Bunny advertisement were significantly more likely to believe they had shaken hands with Bugs Bunny at Disney World.

Therapy in Which Memories are Recovered

Do the same general principles that govern suggestibility for laboratory events also govern suggestibility in clients who may be undergoing various forms of therapy to "recover" memories? There is no reason to believe that people undergoing therapy are any less suggestible than the participants in the memory implantation studies described above. If anything, they may be more vulnerable. Guided imagery or visualisation techniques may be used successfully in therapeutic contexts in the relief of symptoms of PTSD in rape victims (e.g., Foa et al., 1991). However, they are also used by some practitioners as part of repressed-memory therapy, and this use for memory recovery is problematic. The conditions under which false reports are created in the false-memory experiments are not unlike those in which a therapist using "memory-recovery techniques" may elicit memories from adults (see Lindsay & Read, 1994; Poole et al., 1995). The therapist is more likely to have enlisted the trust and confidence of a client than an experimenter (after all, this is an essential part of the client–therapist relationship). This suggests that demand characteristics may have a greater impact in this setting.

Mazzoni et al. (1999) were interested in whether an authority figure (a clinical psychologist) might affect an individual's recall of past events. One group of participants (labelled the "Dream" group) had their dreams interpreted and were given a highly personalised suggestion that a critical childhood event (for example, being bullied before the age of 3 years) had occurred in their life. The participants in the control group did not receive this sort of personalised suggestion. There were two "clinical psychologists" interpreting the dreams. One was Mazzoni, who is a trained clinical psychologist with 16 years of experience. The other was a student trained by the clinical psychologist to use the identical dream-interpretation procedure. Regardless of who their "clinical psychologist" was, the dream group had a higher tendency to believe the critical experience had actually occurred, with approximately 50 per cent of this group producing memory reports of the event.

Finally, there have been concerns about the use of hypnosis to recover memory (see Kebbell & Wagstaff, 1998). There have been many reports of patients recovering memories of bizarre events following hypnosis, including memories of trauma in a past life (Fiore, 1989), alien abduction (Fiore, 1989; Mack, 1994) and ritualistic abuse (Shaffer & Cozolino, 1992). Spanos and colleagues (Spanos, 1996; Spanos et al., 1999) simulated the conditions under which hypnotic suggestion and age regression may be used to retrieve memories. They wanted to generate in participants a belief that they could retrieve memories of an event from the day after their birth. They randomly assigned high, medium and low hypnotisable participants to hypnotic and non-hypnotic induction conditions. Eight-seven per cent of the age-regressed participants generated false memories of infancy, and half reported strong beliefs in the reality of their recovered memories. However, hypnotisability did not affect the number of infancy experiences that could be classified as memories or as fantasies.

Given concerns regarding the use of suggestive practices in therapy, some clinicians (e.g., Courtois, 1997) have provided detailed guidelines for therapists with clients with possible histories of child abuse. In these guidelines, they caution against unduly suggestive approaches to memory work. We will have to wait and see what effects these guidelines have in the long term, especially since some people may be more suggestible than others.

Individual Differences

Research has increasingly considered the specific role that individual differences may play in the creation of false memories and the characteristics that distinguish those who are most susceptible from those who are less susceptible (see Eisen, Winograd & Qin, 2002; Heaps and Nash, 1999, for reviews). One measure that has commonly been used in false-memory implantation studies is the Dissociative Experiences Scale (DES). The DES (Bernstein & Putnam, 1986) measures an individual's tendency to experience dissociation. It is one of the most widely used self-administered scales and has been subjected to the most methodological scrutiny (Ross, 1997). Dissociation has also been implicated as a factor contributing to the gaps in memory noted in studies of recovered memory clients and has been linked to a variety of traumatic experiences (see Eisen et al., 2002, for a recent review). Dissociation can be described as the isolation of experience, memory, or mental content from conscious awareness (Spiegel & Cardena, 1990). Individuals prone to dissociation appear to be unable to distinguish between memories, fantasies, events and thoughts (Whalen & Nash, 1996). Therefore, it could be said that there is a positive correlation between dissociation and imagination inflation (see also Heaps & Nash, 1999). Individuals who are prone to dissociation may be more likely to accept external suggestions as personal memories (Bernstein & Putnam, 1986; Hyman & Pentland, 1996; Kihlstrom, Glisky & Angiulo, 1994).

The DES was devised for, and piloted on, clinical populations (Carlson & Putnam, 1993; Wright & Loftus, 1999). In normal populations, the majority of scores are skewed and clustered at the low end of the scale. Moreover, as the DES is such a widely used test, cultural differences should be taken into account when it is given to a wide range of participants. A version of the DES that is suitable for use with normal populations has now been developed (see Wright & Livingston-Raper, 2001).

Hyman and Billings (1998) found that individuals with higher scores on the DES were more likely to have a false memory. It is theorised that individuals who show high levels of dissociation may find themselves more likely or willing to accept external information as personal memory. However, despite being more susceptible to suggestion, high DES scorers do not show reduced accuracy in everyday memories (Platt et al., 1998).

Porter et al. (2000) were interested in the association between personality and susceptibility to memory distortion. They applied the "five-factor model" of personality. The five factors in this model are neuroticism, extraversion, openness, agreeableness and conscientiousness. Porter et al. used a sub-sample of the participants from the memory-implantation study described above who had created a full or partial memory of an event (such as a serious animal attack). Porter et al. found that participants who experienced a complete false memory had significantly lower extraversion scores than those who had experienced a partial memory. They also looked to see whether the personality characteristics of the nine interviewers were related to participants' susceptibility to false memories. Interviewers who were successful in implanting memories scored higher on extraversion, presumably because these interviewers were more confident, persuasive, friendly and so on. Analysis of the videotapes confirmed this hypothesis. Porter et al.'s work is a nice illustration of the interaction between particular individuals and specific interviewing approaches.

The focus of this section has been on the impact of retrieval conditions on remembering. A number of different paradigms have been used to demonstrate how, through repeated questioning by suggestive techniques, a false memory may occur. While the participants limit to some extent the ecological validity of these studies (the participants are typically younger than clients undergoing therapy, and the events being reported are fairly innocuous, as compared to sexual trauma), the interviews do simulate the social psychological pressures to comply with suggestions. Future studies of this kind may provide some clues as to the cognitive and personality characteristics of individuals that may predict vulnerability to suggestion. Moreover, much can be gained by looking more carefully at the way in which individuals' beliefs and attributions about memory may be shaped by their experiences of remembering and forgetting. As pointed out by Winograd and Killinger (1983), there is an important sense in which no memory is false—if information is part of the cognitive system and is part of an individual's beliefs about what happened, its presence needs to be explained. Therapists need to avoid using any suggestive practices in memory-recovery therapy, so that the truth can be reached without contaminating it. In the forensic context, not only is it important to establish whether or not an event has occurred but also to determine precisely what happened. In the final section of this chapter, we illustrate the significance of accuracy and memory for details with reference to some recent cases of recovered memory that have gone to trial.

VERIFYING THE ACCURACY OF RECOVERED MEMORIES IN THE COURTROOM

The case of George Franklin cited in the opening paragraph of this chapter provides a telling example of conflicting therapeutic and legal agendas.

Franklin was accused of the murder in 1969 of Susan Nason, largely on the basis of memories recovered 20 years after the event by Franklin's daughter, Eileen. Although it is not clear when Eileen's memories began to return, she claims that the initial recollection occurred when she recognised an expression on her own daughter's face as being identical to that of her friend Susan before she was killed. Eileen was seeing a therapist and acknowledged that she had undergone hypnosis. More importantly, her reports of what she remembered clearly changed during the course of the investigation and the trial (Maclean, 1993). This is not surprising given that she was questioned repeatedly by a number of different people with conflicting motives. The prosecution's case that George Franklin murdered Susan Nason tallied with the history of abuse in the Franklin family and the involvement of Franklin in behaviours consistent with paedophilia. Franklin was convicted of first-degree murder in November 1990, but this was overturned in 1995, partly because the defence had not been permitted to introduce newspaper accounts of the crime scene that would have shown that Eileen's memories may have come from this source. The latter contained details similar to those given by Eileen after she recovered the memories.

Eileen's recovered memories may have tallied with other memories in her life as well as many of her emotions and perceptions in adulthood. Pennebaker and Memon (1995) point out that this criterion may be sufficient in the clinical setting where one is attempting to understand the patient's distress and world-view. However, if recovered memories are to be the basis for confronting presumed past abusers and for instituting legal actions, actions which are likely to have a devastating impact on the course of the client's or other people's lives, the therapist has a moral obligation to play detective and seek additional data that could confirm or disconfirm the recovered memories.

The preceding discussion raises the question of how it is possible to tell the difference between a true and false account (see also Chapter 2). Newby and Ross (1996) argue that rememberers and observers will invoke a variety of truth criteria to assess the validity of recollections and will often be wrong. They illustrate this with reference to the memories of alien abductions, in which a rememberer may use criteria such as context, vividness, memorability and originality to assess the validity of these accounts in the absence of external evidence. Of course, the same criteria could be used by observers to discredit the memories. Thus if people truly believe in their memory, what we, as scientists, ought to be able to do is study the conditions under which it was obtained and comment on the accuracy of the report. However, trying to distinguish true and false memories on the basis of truth criteria is not going to tell us much about the accuracy of the memory (see Ross, 1997, for a discussion). Unless external corroboration is available, neither cognitive nor clinical psychologists can distinguish between false memories, on the one hand, and genuine memories, on the other hand. This is the major area where the results of future research are awaited.

SUMMARY AND CONCLUSION

The aim of the research reviewed here has been to review some of the mechanisms that may account for recovered memories and to examine their likely accuracy in relation to the literature on the encoding and retrieval of traumatic events. It was concluded that the evidence for primary repression is sparse and that intentional forgetting or suppression may account for the previous unavailability of childhood memories. Ethical constraints prevent researchers from simulating the threat experienced in real-life situations. However, an increasing number of studies have shown that memory-enhancement techniques, such as imagery, suggestive interviewing and the provision of false information, can result in the creation of illusory memories.

CHAPTER 8

JURY DECISION MAKING

Trial by a jury of one's peers has long been considered in many countries to be the centrepiece of the judicial system (Penrod & Heuer, 1998). Empirical research on juries has focused largely on the variables that may influence the decisions of individual jurors and juries—for example, the characteristics of the participants (actual jurors or a jury-eligible sample, defendants, judges and lawyers), case characteristics, trial procedures, pre-trial information and the deliberation process (Devine et al., 2000). This chapter will describe some of the empirical research on jurors and juries. It will also review the different research methods and theoretical approaches relating to the processes governing jury decision making. We will begin with a brief review of the jury system in different countries (see Vidmar, 2002, for more details).

THE JURY SYSTEM IN DIFFERENT COUNTRIES

Most Western European countries (France, Italy, Germany and Portugal) adhere to what is referred to as the "escabinado system", in which a mixture of laypersons and judges make decisions in criminal cases. Verdicts and sentencing are decided under a non-unanimous rule (Montero-Aroca & Gomez-Colomer, 1999). In Germany, juries are referred to as "judges without robes" (Hertel, Brundt & Kaplan, 2002). Austria, Russia and Spain have recently adopted some elements of the American lay jury system, in which citizens decide a verdict under majority or unanimity rule (Martin, Kaplan & Alamo, 2003; see Thaman, 2000, for a historical review). Spain and Russia do, however, retain parts of the escabinado system. For example, the jury is required to answer a list of questions instead of reaching a single guilty/not guilty verdict (Thaman, 2000). There has been relatively little research to compare the influence and effectiveness of the "trained" and lay jurors within the escabinado system (but see Kaplan & Martin, 1999; Martin et al., 2003). Juries in Spain are made up of nine jurors and two alternates; in Russia juries comprise 12 jurors and two alternates (Thaman, 2000).

In Scotland, potential jurors (persons aged 18–85) are randomly selected from the electoral register. The Scottish criminal jury is made of up 15 persons while the English jury comprises 12. In England and Wales, juries must try for at least 2 hours to reach a unanimous verdict. After 2 hours, a 10–2 majority will be accepted, but nothing less. Otherwise the jury is hung. The Scottish jury may reach a majority verdict on the basis of a bare majority of eight to seven. However, the Scottish system allows the jury in criminal trials a choice of three verdicts: guilty, not proven and not guilty. The Contempt of Court Act prohibits anyone from obtaining, disclosing or soliciting any of the particulars of the deliberations in the jury room. Similar legislation exists in Australia and Canada. In New Zealand, jury secrecy limits but does not preclude empirical research (Young, Cameron & Tinsley, 1999). In contrast, in the USA, the constitutional right to freedom of expression means interviews with jurors are permissible although there may be restrictions imposed by the courts.

Trial by jury is much rarer in the UK than in the USA. In England, juries are used in about 2 per cent of criminal trials where the accused pleads not guilty. In New Zealand, less than 1 per cent of all criminal cases are tried by juries. In contrast, in the USA, criminal defendants have the right to have charges against them judged by a jury of their peers, although they can choose a judge (bench trial) if the prosecutor agrees. The same applies in civil lawsuits. In the USA, the traditional jury is made up of 12 persons with a unanimous verdict, but in some states, juries can be as small as six persons and a majority of only three-quarters is sufficient (Wrightsman, Nietzel & Fortune, 1998).

In the USA, there are two stages in the identification of jurors for a trial. First, a panel of prospective jurors is compiled from a list based on voter registration lists and licensed drivers. A process referred to as "voir dire" is then used to select the jurors. The task is more one of elimination, and jurors who are likely to be biased are excluded.

A lucrative industry has been built up around "scientific" jury selection in the USA. The clients in this industry are lawyers seeking advice on jury selection from psychologists and others with expertise in the characteristics of jurors that might influence trial outcome. Sometimes an attitude survey is conducted in the community to identify relationships between demographic factors and attitudes that may influence decisions in a particular case.

The philosophy governing jury selection in Scotland, England and Wales is quite different from that governing the process in the USA. In Scotland, the view is that the accused and prosecutor must accept jurors that emerge randomly from the selection process (Duff, 2000). In England, the scope for jury challenges during the selection process is restricted to the prosecution, but it is of limited use in practice (Lloyd-Bostock & Thomas, 1999). There is no equivalent to the American jury-selection procedure. In Scotland, it is assumed that the broad background from which jurors are drawn means that any prejudices and biases cancel each other out, and the majority verdict ensures that it is unlikely that one prejudiced juror can influence case outcome (Duff, 2000). Such lack of information about jurors means that no attempt can be made by either side to "stack" the jury in its favour.

In Germany, a list of representative members of various communities (such as age, gender, occupation and status) is compiled and sent to the court. The jurors are assigned to different courts and serve for 4 years (a maximum of 12 days a year). They are sometimes under considerable time pressure and could serve on several cases in one day (Hertel et al., 2002).

EMPIRICAL RESEARCH ON JURIES: METHODOLOGY

Four primary methods have been used by researchers to study jury decision making. The most popular technique is to conduct experimental jury studies with "mock" jurors. These are studies in which a trial or part of a trial is presented to participants in a written form or by videotape. The participants are told to play the role of juror and reach a decision based on the evidence. The major advantage of mock-jury studies is that they allow specific variables to be manipulated with a high level of control over, for example, defendant characteristics, juror characteristics and case characteristics. They also provide an opportunity to systematically test interventions such as the usefulness of allowing jurors to take notes. However, mock-jury studies are limited in a number of ways. Apart from the artificial nature in which evidence is presented (written transcripts/videotaped trials), the jurors know their decisions will have no consequences and hence may not be motivated in the same way as real jurors. The mock studies have largely focused on individual decisions, neglecting the impact of the deliberation process. These shortcomings have raised concerns about the ecological validity of research findings (see below). Furthermore, the reliance on student samples has been criticised, although a review of the literature reveals little research that has obtained differences between studies that use student samples and studies using more representative samples or different trial media

(Bornstein, 1999). This is an important finding because the external validity of research in psychology and law can affect how the judiciary views this research. One example of a judicial perspective on external validity is the US Supreme Court decision in *Lockhart* v. *McCree* (1986), which concerned the selection of jurors in death-penalty cases. The research literature was rejected because it included only student samples and did not present any data on jury deliberations (see Studebaker et al., 2002, for an excellent discussion on the external validity of jury research).

Case studies and archival sources are another way of studying the processes governing jury decisions (see Vidmar, 2002). However, the analysis here is post hoc with no control of variables governing the decision making of jurors or juries. Some examples of these will be provided later in this chapter. A third method is post-deliberation interviews and surveys of ex-jurors. A good example is a survey of 48 jury trials (ranging from attempted burglary to murder) conducted in New Zealand in 1998, during which jurors were provided with pre-trial questionnaires, the opening and closing phases of the trial were recorded, and post-deliberation (post-verdict) interviews were conducted (Young et al., 1999). A wealth of data was gathered, including jurors' comments on how ill-prepared they felt for the trial, the lack of information on how to select a "foreperson", the advantages of note-taking during the trial and the pressure from other jury members to reach a verdict during deliberations.

A fourth method that can be used to study juries is the field experiment involving real juries (for example, the Penrod and Heuer, 1998, study described later in this chapter). Field studies can provide ecologically valid data, but lack of control means that confounding variables cannot be eliminated and may not even be identified. There is also a question about how representative the data gathered from these studies are. Even surveys of ex-jurors may be limited by the biases of the respondents. Moreover, studies of real jurors are possible only in jurisdictions which permit access to jurors and ex-jurors. Ideally, then, for any given topic, various approaches should be used, and it is important to replicate findings, using different participant pools and stimulus material (Robson, 2002).

JUROR CHARACTERISTICS

Gender

The relationship between demographic variables and jurors' verdicts tends to be weak and mediated by other factors such as case type (Horowitz, 1980). One characteristic of jurors that might be important in some types of cases is their gender. Mock juror research suggests female jurors are more likely to find a rape defendant guilty (Ugwuegbu, 1979). This finding is supported by studies of jury panels. Mills and Bohannon (1980) analysed data from questionnaires returned from 117 women and 80 men randomly selected from Baltimore, Maryland, juries. When individual (pre-deliberation) verdicts were collected, women gave more guilty verdicts for rape and murder (78 and 71 per cent, respectively) than men (53 and 50 per cent, respectively). Moreover, a higher proportion of the individual guilty verdicts of the women matched the jury verdict. In a follow-up study conducted in Florida, Moran and Comfort (1982) found no sex differences for verdict or pre-deliberation verdict. Moran and Comfort did, however, find an interaction between sex of juror and other variables, such that male jurors who convicted had more children and a lower income. Female jurors who convicted had a stronger belief in retributive justice. The latter is a system based on establishing guilt and administering punishment, as compared to restorative justice, which seeks to determine harm to the victim and offender, and identify how both can be helped.

One hypothesis that has been tested in research is that women vote for conviction in cases of child sexual abuse more often than men. For instance, Epstein and Bottoms (1996) conducted a study in which mock jurors heard a child sexual abuse case, rendered a pre-deliberation verdict and then deliberated. Pre-deliberation of male and female jurors differed significantly, with women more likely to convict the defendant (71 per cent) than men (51 per cent). A further analysis was conducted after the deliberation, looking at those jurors predisposed to convict as a function of their own gender and whether they deliberated with jurors who were of the same or opposite gender as themselves. There were no significant effects. Epstein and Bottoms (1996) also noted a tendency for all jurors' judgements to become more lenient following deliberation (leniency bias) and found no evidence of men influencing the responses of women.

Age

Research conducted in the UK by Sealy and Cornish (1973) indicated a significant relationship between age and verdict, the most consistent finding being a higher portion of not-guilty verdicts among the youngest groups. The nature of the crime may be important, however. In the USA, Mills and Bohannon (1980) found that jurors' guilty verdicts increased with age, especially with rape cases. However, Moran and Comfort (1982) did not find a correlation between age and verdict in the state courts of Miami, Florida. Similarly, in England, Baldwin and McConville (1979) found that the age of jurors had no effect on verdict. Age of juror may, however, be related to other relevant factors, such as how much people recall of the case facts (see Darbyshire et al., 2000).

Race

There is some evidence from laboratory studies that racial bias affects determination of guilt. One of the problems of an experimental study on the effects of race is that social desirability may lead people to conceal bias. Daudistel et al. (1999) examined real-life felony cases adjudicated in Texas to examine possible relationships among juror and defendant ethnicity, conviction rates and sentences. The cases included crimes against property and persons, and drug-related and sex offences. In Texas, jurors not only render decisions on guilt but also decide on sentence length for offenders who are convicted. Both juror and defendant ethnicity contributed to trial outcomes. The latter affected length of sentences, Hispanic (of Latin American origin) jurors recommending twice as long sentences for Anglo (white, non-Hispanic) defendants as Hispanic defendants. As the number of Hispanics on the jury increased, so, too, did the length of sentences for Anglo defendants.

HOW THE SOCIAL PERCEPTIONS OF JURORS MAY INFLUENCE DECISIONS

Research in the area of social cognition concerned with the impact of attitudes and stereotypes on person perception, impression formation and categorisation (Fazio, 2001; Wilson et al., 2000; Ybarra, 2002) provides the necessary theoretical tools to understand how jurors might be influenced by a variety of extralegal or nonevidentiary factors. Research in social cognition has amply demonstrated that social perceivers are often unaware of biases in their social perceptions, and that incidental exposure to stereotyped knowledge can unconsciously and selectively influence judgement (Banaji, Hardin & Rothman, 1993). For example, the awareness of stereotypes about particular groups can influence judgements even when the stereotype is not endorsed by the social perceiver (Devine, 1989). Research on attribution theory, or people's naive theories about the causes of behaviour, has demonstrated that there is a tendency for people to draw inferences about character from behaviour while neglecting to take into account situational factors that could have influenced the behaviour (Fein, McCloskey & Tomlinson, 1997; Gilbert & Malone, 1995; see Ybarra, 2002, for a review). Moreover, attempting to suppress unwanted knowledge can have a counter-intuitive outcome (see below). Hence, the courtroom setting is a highly appropriate context in which to consider how the attitudes and information brought to the trial by the jury interact with their processing of evidence both relevant and irrelevant to the matter in hand. Some specific examples of social biases that may distort juror perceptions and decisions follow.

SOCIAL IDENTITY AND JUROR DECISIONS

According to social identity theory (SIT), people's sense of who they are comes from their group memberships (Tajfel & Turner, 1986). We maintain a positive self-image or identity by viewing our own groups (in-groups) more favourably than out-groups. SIT has also been used to explain the tendency for people to discriminate between their in-group and out-groups. If we apply this theory to the jury context, it could be argued that jurors behave more leniently towards defendants with whom they can identify (that is, their in-group). This is what Kerr et al. (1975) refer to as the "similarity-leniency hypothesis", and it may account for the effect of juror and defendant ethnicity reported by Daudistel et al. (1999). A counter hypothesis is the black-sheep effect (Marques, 1990), which occurs when an in-group member is perceived by other members of the group as a threat to their positive self-image and therefore is viewed even more negatively than a defendant who comes from an out-group.

Kerr et al. (1995) report that strength of evidence may be important in the black-sheep effect. In a mock-jury study, they found that black jurors and white jurors were comparatively harsher towards same-race defendants when the evidence was strong. When the evidence was weak, there was evidence of in-group bias.

Taylor and Hosch (2002) tested the similarity-leniency and black-sheep hypotheses by using archival data from the files of 448 closed non-capital felony cases adjudicated in Texas. Defendants were classified as being Hispanic or Anglo on the basis of the files. Evidence strength was calculated by summing across six variables. The strength of prosecutorial evidence, defendants' ethnicity and the ethnic composition of the jury were examined. Strength of evidence was the only significant predictor of guilty decisions. No evidence was found regarding guilt in support of the similarity-leniency hypothesis or the black-sheep effect. Defendant ethnicity did, however, influence recommended sentence length, Anglo defendants receiving an average of 10 years more than Hispanics regardless of juror ethnicity. This study suggests that variables that have been found to influence individual juror decisions may not be useful in examining the collective decisions of jurors. The fact that the Taylor and Hosch (2002) study was based on actual cases further questions the ecological validity of simulation research. However, there are also some limitations of the Taylor and Hosch study. First, because they relied on archival data, the number of cases within each cell of the experimental design was limited. Second, juror group membership was decided by surname. However, not all people who are culturally Hispanic have Hispanic surnames, and the opposite may also be true. Finally, the study relied only on jury decisions; individual juror data were not available. Nevertheless, this study does set the agenda for future research in this area.

PRIOR CHARACTER EVIDENCE

In England and Wales, as part of the government's anti-crime drive, the White Paper on Criminal Justice (July 2002) proposes changes in the law to allow the previous convictions of defendants to be revealed to jurors in some cases. This is surprising, given that the potential for this kind of evidence to bias jurors is well documented in the research literature. The most comprehensive investigation using the mock-jury paradigm in the UK was commissioned by the Home Office in 1996 and published by Lloyd-Bostock (2000). A series of mock-jury studies investigated the effect of hearing previous conviction evidence on jury verdict outcomes. The research also examined the impact on the credibility of the defendant as well as the propensity to commit the crime charged. The studies found that jurors who were told that the defendant had a recent similar conviction were more likely to believe that the defendant was guilty. The effect was most pronounced if the prior conviction was a sexual offence against a child. However, if the previous conviction was for a dissimilar crime, jurors rated the defendant as less likely to be guilty. Participants were also asked to estimate the likelihood that the defendant would commit different kinds of offences in the future. When defendants had a previous conviction, they were perceived to be significantly more likely to commit similar offences in the future and less likely to commit dissimilar offences. Furthermore, a defendant with a previous conviction of sexual assault against a child was viewed as less trustworthy, less truthful and more deserving of punishment. Lloyd-Bostock (2000) concludes that information about a prior conviction may evoke criminal stereotypes, and she cautions against revealing a defendant's criminal record. Further research is warranted on this topic.

One of the major limitations of the Lloyd-Bostock study was that the defendant's prior record consisted of only one conviction and the information about the conviction was limited to the time of the offence and its nature. It is important to examine how a record of multiple convictions for different offences might influence decisions. Another limitation of the research is that it did not examine how previous conviction evidence might influence the weighting given to other forms of evidence. However, the findings are consistent with earlier research. Studies conducted in North America have similarly found that jurors informed of a defendant's previous conviction are more likely to find the defendant guilty of subsequent charges—particularly where the charge was for a similar offence (e.g., Borgida & Park, 1988; Greene & Dodge, 1995). Research has also demonstrated that even the judge's warning the jury about the potential bias arising from the previous conviction does not reduce prejudicial bias introduced by prior conviction evidence (Hans & Doob, 1976).

In the USA, recent changes to the Federal Rules of Evidence 413–415 mean that conviction evidence can now be admitted in sexual assault and child abuse cases and is deemed evidence of "propensity" to reoffend. However, a recent review of these rules and their application observes that the absence of guidelines regarding the admission of prior conviction details may only serve to jeopardise the fairness of the current trial (Eads, Shuman & DeLipsey, 2000). Quite rightly, the authors point out that "propensity is not established merely because in the past an individual committed an act or is alleged to have committed an act of sexual impropriety" (Eads et al., 2000: p. 215), and they cite the low recidivism rates for rape found in other studies as confirming this conclusion. Prior conviction evidence may also influence sentencing decisions. For example, drawing on a large sample of capital penalty trials from Georgia, Barnett (1985) noted an association between prior felony convictions and probability of receiving the death sentence. The only field study which did not find an association between prior conviction and verdicts was one in which the prior conviction was unrelated to the case at hand (see Devine et al., 2000, for a review).

PUBLICITY BEFORE AND DURING THE TRIAL

The protected freedom of the press in the USA means that a high degree of publicity may enter the courts. Examples of recent US trials in which media publicity conveyed specific prejudicial facts include the Oklahoma bombing trial and the O.J. Simpson trial. It is interesting to note that for criminal cases, research looking at the content of the news media stories generally indicates a slant favouring prosecution (Imrich, Mullin & Linz, 1995).

The English and Scottish judiciary treats very seriously any potentially prejudicial publicity before or during a trial. The position is governed primarily by legislation (the Contempt of Court Act 1981) which makes it an offence to publish anything that creates a "substantial risk" that the course of justice in any active proceedings will be "seriously impeded" or prejudiced. In practice, even if there is a minimal risk, proceedings can be brought forth under the act (Duff, 2000). Despite this, in Scotland, there has never been a successful application to prevent a trial proceeding because of prejudicial pre-trial publicity. In one case (*Stuurman* v. *H.M. Advocate* [1980]), the court imposed large fines on the news media for causing the greatest risk of prejudice, and only a few weeks later decided that the accused could receive a fair trial. An example of a trial that received a great deal of media publicity in England is *R*. v. *Maxwell* (1990), a civil case in which fraud charges were brought against the sons of a business tycoon for embezzlement of large sums of pension funds. Adverse coverage of the defendants was seen in television and newspaper reports throughout England and Wales. In England, courts have increasingly recognised that publicity may cause substantial prejudice and have demonstrated a willingness to intervene. For example, in *R*. v. *McCann*, the Court of Appeal overturned the conviction of alleged Irish terrorists because the trial judge did not discharge the jury following a sudden wave of publicity in the closing stages of the case.

Empirical Research on Pre-Trial Publicity (PTP)

The increasing number of empirical studies on the effects of pre-trial publicity (PTP) led Steblay et al. (1999) to conduct a meta-analysis to determine whether PTP influences juror verdicts. A total of 44 studies with data from 5755 participants was included in the meta-analysis. Participants exposed to negative PTP were significantly more likely to judge the defendant guilty than participants exposed to less or no negative PTP.

The bulk of research on PTP has focused on criminal cases. There has been some recent work on PTP in civil cases in the USA. Media attention to cases involving civil litigation (class action suits concerning tobacco companies, manufacturers of silicon breast implants, etc.) have received extensive publicity. Bornstein et al. (2002) conducted a jury simulation study, using undergraduates as jurors presented with a lawsuit against a chemical company for causing ovarian cancer. Participants were assigned to one of three conditions in which they read an article containing basic information about the case (control), an article containing negative information about the plaintiff or an article containing negative information about the defendant. Pilot studies were conducted to ensure that the defendant and plaintiff PTP articles produced significant bias compared to the control article. As predicted, participants who read the plaintiff PTP were less likely to find the plaintiff liable (25 per cent) than participants who read the control (46 per cent). Participants who read the defendant PTP were most likely to find the plaintiff liable (75 per cent). Furthermore, PTP significantly influenced ratings of the plaintiff and defendant. PTP that contained more negative information about the defendant produced a more negative impression overall of the defendant and a more positive impression of the plaintiff. Instructions to disregard the PTP did not reduce bias, but they did reduce the overall number of verdicts against the defendant when they were presented before and after the trial evidence. In addressing some of the shortcomings of their study, the researchers suggest that perhaps their study actually underestimated the dangers of PTP in a real civil trial. Longer, more realistic trials are likely to have greater amounts of both PTP and trial evidence, as well as a longer passage of time between exposure to PTP and trial. These conditions are associated with larger PTP effects (see Steblay et al., 1999).

How do beliefs or impressions generated during the course of a trial come to influence juror verdicts following PTP? This question was addressed in a recent study conducted in Aberdeen, Scotland. Using the mock-jury paradigm, Hope, Memon and McGeorge (submitted, a) exposed some jurors to a prejudicial newspaper article about a defendant before they served in a murder trial. Jurors in the control condition read a neutral article of equal length unrelated to the defendant or trial. The pre-trial information was presented along with several "filler" tasks, and participants were told the study was focusing on individual differences in comprehension. Approximately half an hour later, jurors were presented with a modified version of an actual murder trial transcript (*New Jersey v. Bias* [1992]). The trial presented evidence from six witnesses and the defendant. A procedure developed by Carlson and Russo (2001) was used to track juror assessments of the evidence presented during the course of the trial and verdicts. After each witness's evidence, jurors were asked to determine whether that evidence had favoured the prosecution or the defence. They were asked to consider all of the evidence they had received up to that point and identify who they felt was the "leader" (prosecution or defence).

Finally, they were asked how confident they were that the party they thought was currently the leader would win the case. Analysis of post-trial responses indicated that jurors exposed to negative pre-trial information returned significantly more guilty verdicts. However, consistent with earlier research, participants reported that they had not been aware of being unduly influenced by the pre-trial information. In addition, pre-decisional distortion (as calculated from the in-trial evaluations of evidence) appeared to be exacerbated by negative pre-trial publicity for testimony favouring the case of the prosecution. An examination of juror evaluations of the evidence revealed that the testimony from two prosecution witnesses was "over-evaluated" in terms of its perceived favourability to the prosecution by jurors exposed to negative pre-trial information.

Most of the research on the effects of PTP has focused on case-specific publicity. There is comparatively little work on the cumulative effects of news broadcasts and media attention. An exception is Kovera's (2002) research on general publicity related to a rape trial. In the first of two studies, she found that mock jurors (undergraduates) who watched a pro-defence rape trial reported they would need more evidence to convict a defendant of rape than participants who watched a pro-prosecution rape trial. In a second study, Kovera showed how important a juror's attitudes about the social issue in question are. Participants were exposed to a series of news stories about a variety of social issues. One of the stories was varied to study the effects of exposure to media information about rape. Some participants were shown a pro-prosecution rape story and some a pro-defence rape story. Participants were asked to judge the importance of all the social issues while a computer recorded their reaction times. Participants were also asked to complete a questionnaire which measured their attitudes towards rape. In the next part of the study, they were exposed to a videotaped simulation of a rape trial and were asked about their beliefs, and a verdict was obtained. The judgements made by participants with polarized attitudes towards rape (that is, pro-defendant and pro-victim) were unaffected by exposure to the rape media. Only participants with neutral attitudes towards rape were influenced by rape media exposure. Those with neutral attitudes who watched a rape news story judged rape to be a more important social issue than participants who held pro-victim or pro-defendant attitudes. Moreover, there was no effect of media publicity on jurors' response latencies or the length of time it took them to respond to the rape judgement, as compared to other judgements. This suggests that the accessibility of an attitude or how quickly information concerning one's beliefs about a case come to mind is not solely responsible for media effects on juror decisions.

The Kovera (2002) study also provided some data on the processes underlying media influence on jury decision making. One factor that is almost always predictive of jurors' verdicts is complainants' credibility. However, the defendant's credibility was only predictive of jurors' verdicts when jurors had been exposed to rape news. Kovera concludes that media exposure of rape altered the standards participants used to make their evaluations of a defendant's guilt. The practical conclusion from this is that any publicity about rape prior to a trial, regardless of its slant, can influence individual witnesses' appraisals and decision making (see also Hope, Memon & McGeorge, submitted, b). The usual limitations of simulation research can be applied to this study. For example, Kovera did not look at jury deliberation processes, and there is evidence to suggest that the decisions of individual jurors may change following deliberation (e.g., London & Nunez, 2000). One study has found that deliberations may attenuate the biasing effects of case-specific PTP (Kramer, Kerr & Carroll, 1990). Moreover, Kovera obtained the effects of publicity with a 2-minute news story. In the real world, jurors would be exposed to multiple news stories about sexual offences repeatedly from a variety of sources and over a period of many years. A further interesting question in the real world is what happens when the stories take opposing perspectives. To our knowledge, there is little (if any) research on this question.

The external validity of mock-jury studies on the effects of PTP has been questioned (Studebaker et al., 2002). Studebaker et al. (2002) point to four shortcomings of simulation research on the effects of PTP: (i) student participants are over-represented; (ii) group deliberations are under-represented; (iii) the delays between presentation of PTP and trial are too short, and (iv) PTP presented via audio or video media is under-represented. To address these shortcomings would require considerably more time to conduct the study and resources (for example, to recruit community participants). In the meantime, a fruitful approach would be to do what Vidmar (2002) has done and examine the effects of PTP in a wider context, looking for examples in real trials.

Evidence from Real Trials

The advantage of simulated jury research is that researchers can in a more controlled way study the effects of different variables (for example, age, race, gender and other characteristics of the victim and defendant). However, one of the limitations of mock-jury research is that there are no consequences associated with the decisions jurors make. Thus, Vidmar (2002) has examined data from real trials. He reviews a number of civil and criminal cases to examine the effect of prejudice arising from PTP and mid-trial publicity. These cases reveal deficiencies in the manner in which prejudicial publicity has been studied in many jury-simulation studies. Vidmar's analysis shows that potential juror prejudices involve more than just the effects of publicity in the mass media. He provides a useful framework with which to construe the effects of prejudice on juror decisions. Vidmar argues that it is important to consider four categories of prejudice. The first is "interest prejudice", which arises from the juror's having a direct or indirect interest in the outcome of the trial. The juror's being a relative or victim of the accused in a criminal case is an example. A second type of prejudice is specific prejudice. This exists when jurors hold attitudes about specific issues in the case that prevent them from being impartial. Information about a defendant's prior criminal record is one example (see above). The evidence need not necessarily be factual; it could also be based on rumour or a juror's own life experiences. For example, Culhane and Hosch (2002a) conducted a jury-simulation study to assess whether victims of similar crimes (property crimes) or victims of some other type of crime are as impartial as jurors who have not been victimised. They found that jurors who had been victims of theft or who reported knowing a friend or relative who had been a victim of theft were more likely to convict than those who had never been a victim of theft or did not know a victim. Note, however, that only 9 per cent of the sample of jurors in this study had been, or knew, victims, so the frequency of the effect is likely to be low.

A third type of prejudice is "generic prejudice", which involves the transferring of pre-existing attitudes, beliefs and stereotypes about the person to the trial setting. Racial prejudice is one example of generic prejudice, and, again, this can arise without any negative publicity, as indicated earlier. Generic prejudice can also be directed against people accused of certain crimes, such as child sexual abuse. Vidmar (2002) describes a Canadian case involving a physician charged with homosexual offences who denied being a homosexual. The judge subsequently allowed a question about attitudes towards homosexuality to be put to the jurors, several of whom stated that they could not be impartial. Jurors may also hold generic prejudices that are more specific. One example is prejudice against the insanity defence (Gertner & Mizner, 1997). In *U.S. v. Allsup* (1997), an appeal court reversed a conviction on the grounds that the judge refused to question jurors about their attitudes towards the insanity defence. Studies of attitudes towards the insanity defence in the USA reveal a high level of rejection of it (e.g., Hans & Slater, 1984).

The fourth type of prejudice discussed by Vidmar (2002) is "conformity prejudice". This exists when potential jurors perceive a strong community reaction in favour of a particular outcome of a trial and feel pressure to reach a verdict consistent with the community feelings. A good example is the trial of Timothy McVeigh for the bombing of a public building in Oklahoma, an act which caused the death of many people. The judge in this trial concluded that the entire state of Oklahoma was united as a family in the face of the disaster, and that the strong emotional responses generated by the trial were consistent with normative values. The judge stated that, regardless of the trial outcome, identification with the community can result in jurors feeling a sense of obligation to achieve an acceptable result (*U.S. v. McVeigh* [1996]). Vidmar (2002) acknowledges that more than one form of prejudice may be present in a particular trial, and that the combined effect of two or more types of prejudice could be greater than any one form.

THE STORY MODEL

The most pragmatic theoretical explanation currently available of the process by which pre-trial publicity comes to influence the decision-making process is Pennington and Hastie's (1986) story model. Briefly, this model describes how individual jurors attempt to generate a plausible event sequence or scenario of the crime in question. A three-staged model of decision making is proposed. In the first stage, jurors collect information at the trial and combine this information with their general knowledge to construct a "story" of the case (Smith, 1991). In the second phase, jurors form theories of the law based on the judge's instructions and their own lay theories of moral and legal justice. Their theories may include accurate knowledge as well as misconceptions and distortions (Smith & Studebaker, 1996). Finally, the stories are used to reach a verdict. Pennington and Hastie (1986) asked jurors to participate in a study while they were waiting to serve in a trial in the Massachusetts Superior Court. They were shown a video of a homicide trial and asked to reach individual verdicts. Analysis identified four story structures mapping onto four final verdicts: first-degree murder, second-degree murder, manslaughter and not guilty. The verdicts were strongly related to individual stories and shared story structures associated with those verdicts.

Wiener et al. (2002) have recently tested the Pennington and Hastie (1986) model by collecting qualitative data. They interviewed jury-eligible citizens in the St Louis, Missouri, area who were willing to invoke the death penalty. Participants were asked to imagine a scenario in which a jury justly convicted a perpetrator of committing first-degree murder. They were asked to think about a crime story involving someone they knew or one they had read about or watched on television. They were then asked to describe the events leading up to the killing. A codebook comprising of 13 variables was developed, including the theme, type of weapon, location, manner in which deaths occurred, number dead, relationship of defendant to victim(s) and so on. Although a skeletal theme was apparent, no single notion emerged as the shared prototype for first-degree murder. The modal responses comprised a spousal killing with the defendant acting out of a "hot" emotional state. The authors noted that in 10 or more stories the storytellers mentioned several aggravating circumstances (for example, the murder was committed while the defendant was engaged in committing another felony). Yet only one mitigating circumstance (for example, the defendant acted under duress) emerged in 10 or more stories. Wiener et al. (2002) point out the practical relevance of these research findings. In most US states that have capital punishment, there is a second (penalty) phase if a defendant has been found guilty. Jurors are asked to determine whether the state has proved "beyond a reasonable doubt" the existence of specific aggravating circumstances. If there are, these should be weighed against any mitigating circumstances to determine sentence (Wiener et al., 1998). The research of Wiener et al. (2002) suggests that jurors may find it more difficult to understand mitigating circumstances because they do not store this information in their stories. The authors argue that jury instructions would be more effective if information about mitigating as well as aggravating factors was presented to jurors in a story format (see also Hope et al., submitted, a).

While the story model has largely been supported by juror research, more recent work on the process by which juries transform information to find verdicts has found limited evidence that stories are central to juries' verdict resolution (Macoubrie, 2002).

EVIDENCE

Strength of Evidence

So far this review has focused on how characteristics of jurors or beliefs about defendants' character can influence juror decision making. The next session looks at the role played by the quality of the evidence in jury decision making. Not surprisingly, strength of evidence is positively correlated with jury verdicts. The interesting question for psychologists has been how important strength of evidence is in relation to the many factors that may bias juror verdicts.

Different studies have manipulated strength of evidence in a variety of ways. Simulation studies have manipulated strength of evidence by varying the eyewitness identification evidence, corroborating witnesses, specific aspects of defendant behaviour, additional evidence such as a confession or polygraph, and the presence of expert testimony, as well as the number of incriminating and exonerating facts present in the trial stimulus materials (see Devine et al., 2000, for a review). The research has led to the general conclusion that the impact of many forms of bias would be attenuated when strength of evidence is high and accentuated when evidence is moderately strong (Devine et al., 2000). There is a large literature looking at how content of witness testimony influences juror decisions. One factor that has been researched is the effect of conflicting testimony. Leippe (1985) compared four conditions in which witnesses testified. In the first, the victim was the only witness. In the second, a victim and bystander testified against the defendant. In the third, the victim testified but was contradicted by a bystander. In the fourth, the victim and bystander testified against the defendant, but a second witness contradicted them. Contradictory testimony reduced conviction rates from 50 per cent to 10.3 per cent where there was one contradictory witness testimony.

Jurors can be swayed by the testimony of a confident eyewitness (Cutler, Penrod & Dexter, 1990). They may also assume that a consistent witness is a reliable one, even though consistency is not always a powerful predictor of eyewitness accuracy (Fisher & Cutler, 1996). So what effect do inconsistencies in eyewitness testimony have on juror decision making? Berman and Cutler (1996) conducted a mock-jury study to address this question. Participants viewed from one to four versions of a videotaped trial in which the primary evidence against the defendant was the testimony of an eyewitness. One group heard consistent testimony from the eyewitness (the control condition). A second group of participants heard eyewitness statements that were given from the witness box but not previously mentioned by the witness during the investigation (the novel condition). A third group heard statements given in the witness box that contradicted the witnesses' own statements during the investigation. The fourth group heard eyewitnesses contradict themselves in the box. Berman and Cutler found that participants exposed to any form of inconsistent testimony were less likely to convict. Participants exposed to inconsistent testimony found the defendant less culpable and the eyewitness less convincing. These findings complement the results of Leippe (1995). The strongest effects occurred for contradictions, whether between statements in the box or between statements made in the box and before the trial. Berman and Cutler draw on attribution theory in an attempt to provide a theoretical explanation of their findings. According to the discounting hypothesis (Kelley, 1972), the presence of other potential causes of behaviour (discounting cues) leads observers to attach less importance to any given cause. For example, if jurors are presented with statements in the witness box that did not appear in earlier reports given by the witness, they may reason that a good explanation exists for this, such as that the previous investigator may not have asked about the novel information earlier. This kind of explanation may serve as a discounting cue; hence, jurors may thus be more willing to excuse inconsistencies of the novel information kind than contradictions in the witness box.

More recent research on the effects of testimonial inconsistencies on juror decision examines possible interactions between testimonial consistency and other variables that may influence juror judgements. Brewer & Hupfeld (in press) examined the relationship between testimonial consistency (an evidential factor) and an extra-evidential factor, namely, social identity. They drew upon the heuristic–systematic processing model of Chaiken, Liberman and Eagley (1989) to determine when people might rely on extra-evidential factors. Systematic processing involves careful, detailed and analytic scrutiny of information, while heuristic processing is guided by simple, intuitive decision rules. The latter does not involve the cognitive effort associated with systematic processing. According to Chaiken et al. (1989), both processing modes can be activated, but heuristic processing can bias systematic processing under some circumstances. In the courtroom context, Brewer and Hupfeld (in press) argue that, while jurors are motivated to process information systematically under some conditions (such as complexity of information or time restrictions), they may rely on heuristic processing. In their study, mock jurors took part in a trial which focused exclusively on eyewitness evidence (which was consistent or inconsistent) for the prosecution. They also manipulated jurors' identification with the witness by providing a witness who was seen to be from the same group as the jurors (a postgraduate student), from an out-group (a right-wing political secretary) or neutral. Jurors in the inconsistent testimony condition heard contradictory statements or previously unreported facts. The consistent testimony condition did not contain any inconsistencies, but neither was there any corroborative evidence. Both consistency and group identity influenced juror decisions. Regardless of group identity, inconsistent prosecution witnesses were judged low in effectiveness, and guilty verdicts were rare in this condition. Consistent testimony was associated with higher rating of witness effectiveness and more guilty verdicts, particularly when the testimony was delivered by in-group and neutral witnesses. The authors conclude that these findings are broadly consistent with the heuristic–systematic processing model. Jurors are motivated to process evidence systematically, and when they detect inconsistencies, they do not engage in any heuristic processing. When they analyse the evidence and it is consistent but complex or unambiguous, they cannot achieve sufficient "judgemental complex" (Chen & Chaiken, 1999) or confidence to make a decision, so other information may be relied upon (in this case, information about the witness's group affiliation).

Inadmissible Evidence and Instructions to Disregard

We have shown that juror perceptions and decisions can be influenced by a variety of non-evidentiary factors presented in the courtroom (such as prior conviction evidence) and outside (such as PTP). Rules of evidence state that information is admissible if it is relevant and has probative value (Kassin & Studebaker, 1998). This situation obviously places jurors in a morally (and psychologically) difficult situation. The inadmissible evidence may provide them with sufficient information to convince them to return a verdict of guilty. One way that judges can manage the problem of inadmissible evidence is with specific instructions to jurors to ignore this evidence. In a review of the literature on the effectiveness of such instructions, Kassin and Studebaker (1998) draw our attention to relevant research from the social cognition literature. For example, there is research on the paradoxical effects of suppression of information from our thoughts. Not only do we find it difficult to ignore or suppress information, but also the very attempt to keep unwanted thoughts out of our minds makes the thoughts all the more persistent (Wegner & Erber, 1992; Wegner et al., 1987). Emotionally laden material may be particularly difficult to ignore (Edwards & Bryan, 1997). Most relevant to the current chapter is research showing that people are unable to suppress group stereotypes that are activated when making social judgements (see Macrae et al., 2001, for a review of this literature).

Empirical studies of jurors' ability to ignore inadmissible evidence have reported mixed results, however. In their review of this research, London and Nunez (2000) suggest that this may be due to differences in methodologies. Some researchers have focused on mock jurors prior to deliberation, whereas others have examined the impact of bias on jurors after deliberation. Studies of individual juror decisions suggest that pre-deliberation verdicts are largely unaffected by evidence that is deemed inadmissible (e.g., Edwards and Bryan, 1997). Other studies have shown that after deliberation jurors may disregard inadmissible evidence (e.g., Carretta & Moreland, 1983; Kerwin & Shaffer, 1994). London and Nunez (2000) also report that jury deliberation lessens the biasing impact of inadmissible evidence, and that jurors may change their pre-deliberation verdicts towards disregarding the inadmissible evidence.

There may, however, be individual differences in how jurors respond to instructions to disregard. Sommers and Kassin (2001) conducted a mock-juror study to see whether jurors comply selectively with instructions to disregard inadmissible testimony. In this case, mock jurors were asked to disregard evidence from a wire-tap. The authors found that only jurors with a "high need for cognition" (a tendency to seek, think about and reflect on information) disregarded the inadmissible wire-tap. The group with a high need for cognition also *overcorrected* for the bias. In other words, they gave a lower estimate of the likelihood of guilt in the inadmissible condition than a no-wire-tap control condition.

Do jurors obey judges' instructions not to read newspaper reports or watch television news about a case when a trial is in progress? In a New Zealand survey, some jurors said they went out of their way to ignore media publicity during a trial, while others avidly followed media coverage (Young et al., 1999). Vidmar (2002) describes the case of an air crash involving an American Eagles flight in North Carolina in 1994. American Airlines was contesting liability, arguing that American Eagles is an independent company. The jury had been dismissed for the weekend with instructions not to read or listen to media reports. That weekend, there was a front-page story in the press stating that the judge in the case had stated that the American Airlines advertisements were misleading. The articles quoted statements made in the courtroom by the judge. Vidmar was called by the plaintiffs to submit an opinion about the potential impact of this publicity. The judge dismissed the opinion, stating that he had instructed jurors not to look at any publicity. The jurors were not individually questioned about the publicity, but eventually several jurors admitted they had come across the publicity, either directly or through conversation with family members and friends wishing to solicit their opinions. Jurors will disregard PTP or incriminating information if they are given a reason to be suspicious about the motives underlying its introduction in the media or into the trial itself (Fein, McCloskey & Tomlinson, 1997). Suspicion may be a way of tackling the "dirty tricks" that are used by some attorneys and others to influence jurors, although it is by no means a full remedy. Fein et al. (1997) refer to the O.J. Simpson trial as a case in point. In that trial, the defence team raised suspicions about the motives of the Los Angeles police investigation, and this may have raised doubt in the minds of jurors about the validity of the incriminating evidence.

Alibi Evidence

Recent research has looked at what effect an alibi witness who may or may not have a relationship with the defendant might have on decision making. Culhane and Hosch (2002b) were particularly interested in the instances when a poor or non-existent alibi might support a defence eyewitness's identification. They manipulated several variables in a mock-jury study. The first was type of alibi testimony: identification (defence witnesses who said the defendant was with them), non-identification (witnesses who said the defendant was not with them) and uncertain (witnesses unsure whether the defendant was with them). The second variable manipulated was witness confidence (100 per cent confident versus 100 per cent not confident). The third variable was the relationship of the alibi witness to the defendant (girlfriend compared with neighbour). The strength of evidence was held constant. Participants read a scenario about an armed robbery of a shop. Type of alibi and confidence influenced conviction rates. A witness who gave an alibi (yes, he was with me) resulted in significantly fewer guilty verdicts. The alibi testimony from the neighbour yielded significantly fewer guilty verdicts than when there were no alibi witnesses or when the suspect's girlfriend provided his alibi. Contrary to Culhane and Hosch's predictions, but perhaps not surprisingly, the girlfriend's testimony did not reduce convictions beyond no alibi at all. Culhane and Hosch (2002b) suggest that this implies that in the real world it is unlikely that jurors would believe a defendant's alibi if it was proffered by a relative or a person who has a relationship with the defendant. This study also supports earlier research showing that jurors tend to believe confident witnesses (see Chapter 9).

AIDING JURIES

Evidence suggests that jurors understand less than half of judges' instructions (Reifman, Gusick & Ellsworth, 1992). In particular, jurors struggle with legal jargon, and attempts to simplify the language (for example, rewriting instructions) have been only moderately successful (Charrow & Charrow, 1979). There has been concern about jurors understanding evidence in complex cases, although field research suggests that the length of the trial may be important. In the USA, Cecil, Lind and Bermant (1987) interviewed 180 of 400 jurors who had served in civil trials lasting more than 20 days and compared their responses with a matched sample who had served in shorter trials. Almost half (46 per cent) of the jurors in the long trials rated the evidence as very difficult or difficult, as compared to 29 per cent in the shorter trials.

Jurors' competence to try complex cases, especially complex fraud prosecutions, has been repeatedly questioned. Research conducted by the Roskill Committee (Cambridge University) showed that juror comprehension of complex information could be significantly improved by providing aids such as glossaries and written summaries, and by using visual aids to present information (Lloyd-Bostock & Thomas, 1999).

Penrod and Heuer (1998) reviewed two field studies that were conducted with actual juries. The first study, conducted in Wisconsin, involved a national sample. Jurors were surveyed about how helpful it was to be able to ask questions during a trial. Overall, the jurors were positive about asking questions reporting that they felt better informed and more satisfied that they had sufficient evidence to reach a verdict. However, judges and lawyers did not think juror questions helped get to the truth, and the lawyers in Wisconsin expressed a fear that juror questions would play havoc with their trial strategies, although those lawyers who took part in trials where juror questions were permitted did not see a problem.

Penrod and Heuer (1998) report that juror note-taking was permitted in 135 trials that they reviewed. Most jurors given the opportunity to take notes did so (66 per cent in the Wisconsin and 87 per cent in the national study), and the notes were a fair and accurate recall of the trial proceedings. Note-taking did not improve memory, however, but Penrod and Heuer point out that they took only general measures of recall. Surprisingly, note-taking did not increase juror satisfaction with the trial verdict. Penrod and Heuer (1998) suggest this may be because jurors were already quite satisfied with the procedures and verdicts in the trials they sampled. Note-taking did not have any effect on jury deliberation time either. With respect to the most important outcome measure of juror note-taking, there was no evidence that juror verdicts were influenced by note-taking. Nevertheless, the jurors in the New Zealand survey (Young et al., 1999) reported that they found notes helpful as aids during the deliberation phase.

JUDGE/LAWYER CHARACTERISTICS

As compared to the literatures on juror, victim and defendant characteristics, there has been little research on how judge or lawyer behaviour may influence trial outcomes. In one field study, observers rated various aspects of judges' verbal and nonverbal behaviour from videotaped segments of their jury instructions. Guilty verdicts were associated with judges who were rated by the observers as less professional, less dominant, less competent, less wise and less dogmatic (Blanck, 1985). A small number of studies have looked at lawyers. One study reported an effect of lawyer gender, with higher acquittal rates with male defence counsel (McGuire & Bermant, 1977). Another study looked at the impact of annoying or offensive behaviour of lawyers or judges. Any biases for or against the annoying party, however, dissipated after jury deliberation (Kaplan & Miller, 1978). There is some research looking at the content or style of lawyers' opening statements, although, again, the literature is not consistent. Hans and Sweigart (1993) analysed transcripts of interviews of 99 jurors in 14 civil cases. Jurors reported that opening statements provided them with a framework for understanding and interpreting the evidence, providing support for the story model.

JURY DELIBERATION

Devine et al. (2000) provide a comprehensive review of the jury literature from 1955 to 1999, including studies that have examined the context of jury deliberations. They conclude that juries spend a large part of the deliberation time talking about the facts of the case, the judges' instruction and their verdict preferences. It has also been noted that once jurors enter the deliberation room they quickly assign a foreperson and begin discussion of the facts. Forepersons may be more influential than other jurors (Boster, Hunter & Hale, 1991). Men and persons of higher social status participate more (Hastie, Penrod & Pennington, 1983). The amount of time spent deliberating is influenced by numerous factors, including the composition of the jury, the nature of the crime and the trial's complexity (Ellsworth, 1989; Hastie et al., 1983). The construction and identification of a reliable story accounting for defendant actions and motives is a key focus of the jury discussion (Hastie et al., 1983), although, if a unanimous verdict is needed, deliberations tend to be more evidence driven and follow the three-stage story model (see above). However, a recent study of jury deliberation questions whether jurors apply story elements to resolve verdicts. Macoubrie (2002) undertook an in-depth qualitative analysis of the deliberation of four real juries. The juries had been videotaped by a television company with the permission of the Arizona Supreme Court and the participants. The trials all concerned criminal cases, with three of the juries reaching verdicts and one hung jury. The study found that 3–10 per cent of the juries' deliberation time contained speaker-connected narrative elements. Only one of the four juries' story fragments could be connected to show a large story; the other three juries' dialogues could not be defined as part of a larger story. Macoubrie concludes that stories do not play a critical role in jury decision making. However, she does point out that it may be significant that the juries that did not construct stories were verdict-driven juries (that is, juries that began deliberation with a discussion of the legal charges). Verdict-driven juries may not need to construct stories because they can rely on event facts (Macoubrie, 2002). To date, there has been little research of the kind Macoubrie has conducted. Clearly, further research on jury interaction is warranted.

One function of the jury deliberation process may be to refresh jurors' memories. However, the psychological literature on the effects of group discussion on memory reports mixed results. For example, Stephenson, Clark and Wade (1986) report improvement in free and cued recall after group discussion. Other studies (e.g., Findlay, Hitch & Meudell, 2000) find no differences in the recall performance of individuals and dyads. The validity of the assumption that deliberation may aid memory was recently tested in a jury simulation study (Pritchard & Keenan, 2002). The researchers did this by tracking the fate of individual memories for specific items before and after deliberation, as a function of whether they were discussed. They also examined the effect of jury deliberation on verdicts. Jurors (college students) were shown a 30-minute, edited videotape of an actual murder retrial from "Court TV" (USA). The time of memory test (pre-deliberation versus post-deliberation) and item centrality (central or peripheral) were manipulated within subjects. Pre- and post-deliberation verdicts were obtained. Jurors remembered only 60 per cent of the trial information. There was a slight (3.4 per cent) but statistically significant improvement in memory accuracy after deliberation for central and peripheral information (memory for the two types was equivalent). There were individual differences, however, some jurors showing improvement only on central items after deliberation and some peripheral or both. Jurors made significantly fewer omissions after deliberation, and there was no change in the number of distortions. However, the null effect on distortions could be due to the fact that while some items were being distorted during deliberation, others were being corrected. Indeed, a more detailed analysis showed that items on which jurors made pre-deliberation errors were significantly more likely to be corrected if they were discussed during deliberation. This suggests a positive effect of deliberation on jurors' memories. Juror verdicts became more lenient after deliberation, and jurors with low pre-deliberation confidence were more likely to change their verdicts than jurors with high pre-deliberation confidence. However, there was no correlation between confidence and accuracy; therefore, jurors who have accurate memories of the trial evidence may be changing their verdict due to a lack of confidence in their memories. Pritchard and Keenan (2002) suggest that the courts should be concerned about factors influencing juror confidence when rendering instructions to the jury prior to deliberation, and that jurors ought also to be told not to trust their fellow jurors' confidence as a sign of their memory accuracy.

SUMMARY AND CONCLUSION

Empirical research on the behaviour of jurors and juries suggests that numerous variables may influence juror perceptions and trial verdicts. However, a large body of research has relied upon the use of college samples as jurors and the mock-jury paradigm, raising concerns about the ecological validity. In a recent review of the literature, Bornstein (1999) noted that of the several hundred studies in the literature, only 26 studies actually compared different samples and 11 different trial media (for example, written transcripts and videotaped trials). Diamond (1997) suggests that researchers who are interested in applying their research findings are well advised to conduct their research in two stages. In the first stage, research should be conducted by relatively easy methods (student samples and written transcripts). In stage two, an attempt should be made to replicate the findings with more representative samples and methods (such as videotaped trials). In addition, case studies and surveys of real jurors may provide a richer source of data to enable predictions to be made about the effect of biases and influences on jurors, as well as a more effective way of studying the effectiveness of various judicial remedies and interventions. Furthermore, there is some evidence to suggest that jurors may change their pre-deliberation verdicts after discussion with other jury members. More research is needed on the effects of jury deliberation on verdicts. In the UK, there have been increasing calls for the relaxation of the Contempt of Court Act to enable academic research on the jury deliberation process (e.g., Auld, 2001). Together with the extensive literature on the factors influencing the decision of individual jurors, analysis of the jury deliberation process should provide us with a better understanding of how juries arrive at verdicts.

CHAPTER 9

THE ROLE OF EXPERT WITNESSES

Nijboer (1995) defines expertise as the possession of special qualities—quantity and reliability—acquired through special education and training. Mental health expertise informs a range of topics, such as the connections between mental health and criminal responsibility, children's mental health treatment and placement issues, predictions of future dangerousness, defendant and witness competencies to participate in legal proceedings and the reliability of eyewitness testimony (see O'Connor, Sales & Shuman, 1996, for more examples). This chapter will examine some of the effects of expert witnessing with a focus on expert testimony on the reliability of eyewitness memory. Leippe (1995) defines expert testimony about eyewitness behaviour as follows:

> Expert testimony about eyewitness behaviour occurs when a psychologist admitted by the judge as an expert authority on "eyewitness testimony" takes the stand in a jury trial and presents information about research and theory concerning memory and the variables known to influence memory and memory reports. (p. 910)

As indicated in a review by Penrod and colleagues (1995), the courts in some countries have become more responsive to expert testimony on witness issues over the last 20 years. This chapter is divided into two parts. In the first part, the inquisitorial and adversarial modes of presenting expert evidence are described. The criteria that may be used to determine expertise and to assess the scientific validity of evidence are presented next. The important issues with respect to the admissibility of expert evidence are the qualifications of the expert and the relevance and scientific status of the expert's testimony. In the second part of the chapter, some examples of areas where expert testimony can be helpful will be presented together with ethical concerns about impartial testimony from experts.

ADMISSIBILITY OF EXPERT TESTIMONY

The standards for determining the admissibility of testimony have always been an issue for the courts. Until the middle of the last century, it was rare for the courts to hear testimony on mental issues from experts who were not medical doctors (O'Connor et al., 1996). The qualifications an expert is expected to have vary from one legal system to another. In the UK, the 1993 Royal Commission on Criminal Justice recommended that professional bodies assist the court by maintaining a register of members qualified to act as expert witnesses in particular fields. A psychologist practising in the UK is expected to be chartered by the British Psychological Society on the basis of relevant qualifications and experience in the field in which the psychologist claims expertise. In England and Wales, it is good practice for expert witnesses to give an overview of their qualifications once they are sworn in. In the USA, there are no uniformly adopted standards by which courts operate, but there are requirements that have to be met in order for expert testimony to be admissible. Federal courts follow the *Daubert* ruling. A Supreme Court decision taken in 1993 in *Daubert* v. *Merrell Dow Pharmaceuticals* addressed the standards that federal courts use for the admission of scientific evidence. The *Daubert* case debated the testimony of experts on whether or not the anti-nausea drug Bendectin was responsible for birth defects. *Daubert* gave trial judges the task of making a preliminary assessment of the scientific validity of expert evidence (but see Faigman, 1995). *Daubert* listed four factors which are deemed necessary in testing the validity of expert evidence: falsifiability, error rate, peer review and general acceptance. The first is based on Popper's criterion for distinguishing scientific from non-scientific evidence, the principle of refutability or testability. The second factor is the known or potential error rate of the expert's opinion or the accuracy of the diagnoses given by the expert (Faigman, 1995). A third factor is checking the credibility of an expert's knowledge by looking for evidence of peer review/publication in scholarly journals. The fourth criteria is general acceptance of the data within the scientific community. In its 1999 *Kumho Tire Co., Ltd* v. *Carmichael et al.* opinion, the Supreme Court extended *Daubert's* general holding to include engineers and other non-scientific experts with technical or other specialised knowledge.

Adversarial Versus Inquisitorial Systems

According to Damaska (1973), it was a deep-rooted distrust of judges in the UK and the USA that led to the adversarial system. The latter minimised the role of judges and placed the case in the hands of interested parties. In Continental Europe (all European countries except Britain), judges have a much greater role to play. They are the major channel for information and play an active part in the preparation and evaluation of evidence and in the questioning of witnesses. For instance, in Germany and France, the courts routinely appoint experts. The defendant in the trial is questioned largely by the judge, while the advocate's role is to object to questions and seek supplementary information (see McEwan, 1998, for a discussion of the merits of the adversarial/inquisitorial systems). In the inquisitorial system, the expert psychologist would usually be appointed by the court as an *amicus curiae*, or friend of the court, to appear in an educational role (taking no sides). Experts have more freedom in the inquisitorial system in how they present their evidence, and they are encouraged to re-enact scenarios where possible in order to resolve conflict. Evidence may be presented in person and in the form of a brief which provides a summary of relevant literature and conclusions.

In the USA, court-appointed experts are infrequently employed. This seems to be because of the perceived difficulty in accommodating experts in a system that is used to adversarial presentations of evidence (Cecil & Willging, 1993). A survey conducted by the Federal Judicial Center in 1993 found that the appointment of an expert is often seen as a last resort by judges despite the fact that this may have a strong influence on the outcome of a case (Cecil & Willging, 1993). The survey indicated that court-appointed experts were most often used to get information on technical issues. For example, in personal injury cases, medical experts could be called to assess the nature of the injury and offer a prognosis. This may enable jurors to reach a decision from a more informed perspective.

In Britain, it is rare for psychologists to provide expert testimony on eyewitness issues. The few psychologists who have been involved in eyewitness testimony cases have played an advisory role only, with their activities being limited to consultation with a lawyer (usually the defence counsel) and report writing (but see Bull, 2003). Clinical psychologists in Britain usually work across a wide variety of areas of mental health and also work with individual clients in clinical settings, drawing on their clinical expertise as well as scientific knowledge (Gudjonsson, 1996), and serving as expert witnesses primarily in civil cases (for example, in connection with the mental state/capabilities of the client or in child custody disputes). In criminal cases, clinical psychologists may be asked questions concerning the sanity, competency and dangerousness of the accused.

In the Netherlands, the opinions of expert witnesses are taken at face value by the courts. Experts are court appointed and are the court's own witnesses. As such, they are expected to be neutral. Moreover, most expert witnesses are drawn from a relatively small pool (Crombag, 1993). In France, the system is again different. The judge controls the expert's investigations and monitors the whole process. As soon as the judge considers it appropriate, he or she orders an investigation by an expert, and the judge monitors the expert's work.

EXPERT TESTIMONY: ITS IMPACT ON JURY DECISION MAKING

A large proportion of the debate surrounding expert testimony centres on the empirical question of what, if any, effects expert testimony has on jurors' (in the adversarial system) and judges' (in the inquisitorial system) decision making. One of the central questions is whether scientific research goes beyond common sense and helps them reach a decision. We will illustrate some of the issues by looking at the effects of expert testimony about eyewitness testimony. The variables that can influence the quality of an eyewitness's statement were discussed in Chapter 6. In this chapter, we examine the impact of eyewitness testimony on jurors, judges and lawyers. We also examine the extent to which there is general agreement among experts as to the reliability of research on the impact of various factors on eyewitness performance.

What do jurors and lawyers know about variables influencing the accuracy of eyewitness testimony? Research has indicated that factors which influence memory and identification decisions are not common sense (Devenport, Penrod & Cutler, 1997). For example, Cutler and colleagues (Cutler, Penrod & Stuve, 1988; Cutler et al., 1990) and R.C.L. Lindsay (1994) found that mock jurors were not sensitive to the effects of disguise, weapon-focus, retention interval, instruction bias, foil bias and other factors that influence identification accuracy. (See Chapter 6 for a discussion of how these variables may affect accuracy.) Moreover, these jurors were particularly influenced by how confident the witness was. Witness confidence was the only one of 10 variables that jurors relied upon in Cutler et al.'s (1990) study. However, as noted in Chapter 6, confidence does not predict accuracy. A study by Rahaim and Brodsky (1982) with regard to the knowledge of lawyers revealed similar results. Brigham and Wolfskeil (1983) investigated the beliefs of prosecutors, defence lawyers and law-enforcement personnel about the accuracy of eyewitness identifications. When asked to estimate the percentage of eyewitness identifications they had observed which were probably correct, they found that the vast majority of the prosecutors (84 per cent) felt that "90 per cent or more" of the identifications are probably correct, while 63 per cent of the law officers and only 36 per cent of the defence lawyers endorsed this view. Stinson et al. (1996) presented American judges and lawyers with hypothetical cases. They did not realise that witnesses are more likely to pick someone, guilty or innocent, from photographs when they are shown simultaneously than when they are shown sequentially (see Memon & Gabbert, in press, for a discussion of why this may be the case).

What Do Expert Witnesses Say in Court?

Given that jurors and lawyers are generally not aware of the impact of several factors on eyewitness accuracy (see Chapter 6), it is one of the tasks of the expert to inform them about these issues. To find out what experts tell jurors in court, Kassin et al. (2001) conducted a survey of 64 experts on eyewitness testimony.

Table 9.1. What expert witnesses say in court: statements that expert psychologists reported were reliable enough for them to present in courtroom testimony

Rank	Factor	Statement
1 (98%)	Wording of questions	An eyewitness's testimony about an event can be affected by how the questions put to that witness are worded
2 (98%)	Line-up instructions	Police instructions can affect an eyewitness's willingness to make an identification
3 (98%)	Mugshot-induced bias	Exposure to mugshots of a suspect increases the likelihood that the witness will later choose the suspect in a line-up
4 (94%)	Post-event information	Eyewitness testimony about an event often reflects not only what they actually saw but information they obtained later
5 (90%)	Alcohol	Alcoholic intoxication impairs an eyewitness's later ability to recall persons and events
6 (90%)	Cross-race bias	Eyewitnesses are more accurate when identifying members of their own race than members of other races
7 (87%)	Confidence malleability	An eyewitness's confidence can be influenced by factors that are unrelated to identification accuracy
8 (87%)	Weapon	The presence of a weapon impairs an eyewitness's ability to accurately identify the perpetrator's face
9 (87%)	Accuracy-confidence	An eyewitness's confidence is not a good predictor of his or her identification accuracy
10 (70%)	Child suggestibility	Young children are more vulnerable than adults to interviewer suggestion, peer pressures, and other social influences

Source: adapted from Kassin et al., 2001.

The experts were from the UK, Canada, Israel, Denmark, Germany, Spain, New Zealand, the Netherlands and the USA. Sixty-two of the 64 had a Ph.D. in psychology, and self-reports indicated the experts were leading researchers in their area.

Kassin et al. (2001) asked the experts for their opinions about 30 statements concerning the accuracy of eyewitness testimony. The 10 statements listed in Table 9.1 were seen by the vast majority as highly reliable. Experts expressed a willingness to present these 10 principles as evidence in courtroom testimony.

One should bear in mind that the statements presented in Table 9.1 are based upon findings of research on eyewitness testimony that has almost exclusively been conducted in university laboratories and is therefore artificial in nature. Apparently, many experts felt confident enough to present these findings in court and apply them to real-world cases. However, some experts have suggested a more cautious approach (see Egeth, 1993; Kassin, Ellsworth and Smith, 1994; and Wells, 1993, for a discussion about this issue). For example, there are concerns (Egeth, 1993) about generalising from laboratory findings to the real world, especially with respect to estimator variables (see Chapter 6), which typically occur when the witness actually witnesses the event. These variables can often not be replicated in the laboratory setting (for example, the amount of stress that the witness experiences during a real-life incident). The impact of system variables (factors that can be controlled by the criminal justice system) are easier to examine. More importantly, system variable research can be used to inform law-enforcement personnel how to prevent making mistakes during eyewitness identification parades, as shown in Chapter 6. The next section discusses the expert's role in informing courts about eyewitness issues.

Can Experts Educate Jurors and Law-Enforcement Personnel?

Psychologists disagree over whether receiving information from experts helps the jury. McCloskey and Egeth (1983) and, more recently, R.C.L. Lindsay (1994) and Ebbesen and Konecni (1997) claim that the jury is no better off with help from experts, whereas Cutler and Penrod (1995) and Penrod, Fulero and Cutler (1995) express a more positive view. However, expert testimony probably has a beneficial impact in at least two ways. It can make jurors scrutinise the evidence more carefully, an effect which is beneficial since people tend to place too much faith in eyewitness testimony (Brehm, Kassin & Fein, 2002). Second, it may make people in the criminal justice system realise that applying better methods in their system could improve the accuracy of eyewitness identification evidence. For example, the US Department of Justice published a national guide for collecting and preserving eyewitness evidence in October 1999. The booklet was published by the Technical Working Group for Eyewitness Evidence, a team of over 30 people including researchers, prosecutors, defence lawyers, district attorneys and law-enforcement officers. It includes guidelines on a variety of issues such as how to establish rapport with witnesses, how to interview witnesses, how to prepare mugshot albums (collections of photographs of previously arrested persons), how to instruct witnesses prior to the line-up, how to compose line-ups, how to conduct the identification procedure and so on.

Members of the Technical Working Group for Eyewitness Evidence (Wells et al., 2000) described the resistance they met from others in the working group in preparing the guide. Unfortunately, it is not standard practice for applied researchers to report the opposition they have faced from practitioners they are working with, although such information could be of high value to other researchers. Wells et al.'s (2000) comments are a welcome exception. For example, while they expected resistance from the police, they were surprised to find that the police were quite cooperative, perhaps because they had frequently observed confident eyewitnesses who make mistakes. Prosecutors, in contrast, were among the most reluctant members in the working group, possibly because they were least aware of the problem of mistaken eyewitness identifications.

EXAMPLES OF RESEARCH ON THE IMPACT OF EXPERT TESTIMONY

Child Witnesses

One of the fastest growing areas of research in the eyewitness field has been the study of children as witnesses (see Chapter 5), and as a result of this work, the courts have shown greater sensitivity to the needs of children. Concern about the uncorroborated testimony of child witnesses has led to both prosecution and defence calling physicians, other mental health professionals and social scientists to serve as expert witnesses, either to support or discredit a child's testimony (Ceci & Bruck, 1995). Expert witnesses in child abuse cases, for instance, may be called to educate fact finders on the relevant scientific literature about child-witness testimony and the interviewing of them (see Ceci & Hembrooke, 1998, for recommendations for the proper role of an expert witness in child abuse cases).

Children who have been prepared for courtroom testimony are more comfortable, and appear to be more confident, composed and credible. Courtroom preparation may also facilitate the competency with which a child can communicate in the courtroom (Saywitz, Snyder & Nathanson, 1999). Saywitz and Snyder (1993) describe three approaches to preparation designed to improve accuracy. The first is to give children practice in organising elements of an event into forensically relevant information and reporting as much detail as possible. The second is to facilitate children's communication with videotaped vignettes which illustrate the negative consequences of trying to ask questions not fully understood by the children. The third intervention was to warn children about misleading questions by presenting them with a story about a child who went along with the suggestions of an adult, and highlighting the negative consequences. Saywitz and Snyder also examined more traditional approaches to preparation such as using role-play to teach children about the pre-trial investigative process, the roles and functions of legal professionals and trial procedures. Another technique encouraged children to talk about their fears about going to court and showed them methods to reduce anxiety (such as deep breathing). These techniques improved children's knowledge of the legal system without compromising accuracy, but the traditional approaches did not reduce self-reports of anxiety (Saywitz & Snyder, 1993).

Kovera, Borgida and Gresham (1996) hypothesised that if expert testimony sensitises jurors to an abuse victim's typical response, a prepared child may be judged to be less credible than an unprepared child. Expert testimony and child witness preparation were manipulated in a trial-simulation study. Information about the behaviours that distinguish a prepared from an unprepared witness was obtained by questioning court counsel and child witness advocates. Child witness preparation was manipulated by videotaping the same child twice. On one occasion, the child was asked to appear nervous, hesitant and fidgety during testimony (unprepared version) and later the child was instructed to appear calm, confident and less upset (prepared version). The format of testimony was also manipulated to see whether expert testimony has a greater impact when the expert explicitly links the research findings to the case at hand (concrete testimony). Previous research has suggested that this "concrete" form of testimony would produce a more informed jury (Schuller, 1992). Kovera et al. (1996) exposed mock jurors to a videotaped trial simulation based on a case in Minnesota in which the defendant faced charges of criminal sexual conduct. Among the witnesses was the 8-year-old female alleged victim and the expert. Three versions of expert testimony were created: (i) the standard testimony, in which the expert detailed several common fears of child abuse victims; (ii) the concrete testimony, which applied the information covered in the standard testimony to the case at hand; (iii) the repetitive testimony, in which, after the standard testimony, the expert summarised research findings without explicitly linking the research to the case at hand. Mock jurors who saw the standard or repetitive testimony in conjunction with a prepared witness were more likely to convict the defendant than those who saw the standard or repetitive testimony in conjunction with an unprepared child. Concrete testimony appeared to "sensitise" jurors in that it led to more convictions than standard testimony in the condition where the jurors saw the unprepared child in the witness box. This is an important practical finding, as it suggests that a credibility-enhancing and stress-reduction procedure, such as witness preparation, may produce a witness who does not fit the stereotype of a victim of sexual abuse. This study illustrates the complex way in which the nature of expert testimony may interact with witness variables.

Expert Testimony in Rape Trials

In rape cases (as in cases of child sexual abuse), prosecutors have difficulty in obtaining convictions based solely on a victim's testimony. Moreover, the public hold myths and stereotypes about this type of crime that may influence the victim's credibility (Brekke & Borgida, 1988). Expert testimony may counteract these stereotypes and misconceptions. Adopting a socio-cognitive perspective, Brekke and Borgida (1988) were interested in whether mock jurors would use group probability data (the small number of women who falsely accuse men of rape, the proportion of rapes that involve casual acquaintances, the idea that rape is a crime of violence rather than a crime of passion and so on) in making a decision. Cognitive psychologists have noted that biases in judgements typically occur as a result of the vast amount of information that has to be processed in reaching decisions. One type of bias is known as the base-rate fallacy, which is a tendency to neglect or ignore information that describes most people (base rates) and instead rely on distinctive features of the case being judged (Myers, 1993). Brekke and Borgida were interested in how the base-rate fallacy would operate in a jury context. It was hypothesised that jurors would make the most use of base-rate information in the form of expert testimony when it was presented early in trial proceedings and linked to the case at hand. Participants (jurors) were 208 undergraduates. The type of testimony (standard or "hypothetical") and its timing were manipulated. (The duration of the trial varied according to the type of expert.) All versions of the trial included an opening statement from the judge; opening arguments from prosecution and defence, the defendant's testimony, cross-examination and closing arguments and the judge's final charge to the jury. In the standard form, the expert dispensed testimony in a lecture format. In the hypothetical form, jurors listened to standard expert testimony followed by an explicit attempt to point out the connection between expert testimony and the case under consideration. Mock jurors exposed to the specific hypothetical expert testimony were significantly more likely to vote for conviction and to recommend harsher sentences than were jurors who heard standard expert testimony.

Brekke and Borgida (1988) concluded that expert testimony on behalf of the prosecution may counteract the pervasive effect of rape myths and misconceptions on juror judgements in a simulated trial. This finding was obtained despite the fact that jurors did not rate expert testimony as being useful in reaching their verdicts. Timing was also found to be important, in that the most use was made of it when the testimony appeared early in the trial. This suggests that, rather than store case facts one by one, jurors may try to organise information into a consistent meaningful whole early in the trial (cf. story model, Chapter 8). Expert testimony presented early may serve as a powerful organising theme for jurors' first impression of a case.

ETHICAL ISSUES

According to Loftus (1986), the most important ethical issue surrounding the role of psychologists as experts is whether or not the psychologist should assume the role of advocate or impartial educator. Loftus points out that it is very hard to avoid becoming identified with one of the sides, since the essence of working in an adversarial system is that one side of the case is presented and challenged by the other. Geiselman (1994) has pointed out that it is difficult for an expert to play the role of consultant without straying into the advocate role. Ethical dilemmas are most likely to arise in cases where a defendant stands accused of a serious crime. Geiselman (1994) points out that in such cases an expert's personal opinions and feelings may bias judgements. For example, Geiselman (1994) was asked to testify in the trial of a gang member accused of holding a knife to the throat of a 3-month-old baby while he robbed its mother. The only evidence was her husband's identification. Geiselman refused to take on the case because he could identify strongly with the parents in the case, as he had a baby at home also.

Experts are sometimes selected by lawyers in the adversarial system because of their compatibility with a given view, but this may undermine the authority with which they can speak and leave them open to harassment from lawyers. The most common complaint of experienced forensic scientists and psychiatrists who act as expert witnesses is the way that lawyers use their ability to control what the experts say in court (McEwan, 1998). For example, counsel may insist on yes/no answers and prevent experts from qualifying their answers. They may also mock and humiliate the expert (McEwan, 1998).

THE HIRED GUN EFFECT

One of the roles of an expert is to persuade a jury of the quality of their expertise. The social psychology of persuasion tells us that jurors may well rely more on peripheral cues to process information (Petty & Cacioppo, 2000). In other words, they will use simple guides to help them make decisions, such as the qualifications and appearance of the person who is trying to persuade them. This is most likely when the message they are presented with is difficult for them to comprehend. Consistent with this, Ratneshwar and Chaiken (1991) found that the verdicts and beliefs of mock jurors exposed to complex scientific testimony in a civil case were related to the qualifications of the experts. A scientist with a degree from a prestigious university was more persuasive than an expert who gave the same testimony but whose qualifications were from a less prestigious university.

Cooper and Neuhuas (2000) were interested in the extent to which jurors rely on experts' qualifications and the amount they are being paid, when processing evidence provided by these experts. Experts who frequently testify and are highly paid for their services are sometimes called "hired guns", and Cooper and Neuhaus were interested in the hired-gun effect. Participants were jury-eligible residents of New Jersey. They were presented with a simulated jury case based on a series of public liability cases in New Jersey. The mock jurors were told that both sides had agreed to the facts of the case with the exception of one critical detail. The case revolved around this one issue of whether exposure to a particular chemical was the immediate cause of cancer. They were presented with a 30-minute audiotape of expert testimony. There was one version from the expert taking the plaintiff's side and one version from the defendant's side. The amount that the plaintiff's expert was earning was manipulated. In the low-pay condition, the expert said he was receiving $75 for his time and in the high-pay condition he said he was getting $4800. The testimony began with the experts being questioned about their qualifications and background. The defence expert witness always said he was earning $600. The credentials of the experts were manipulated by varying how well known or prestigious the institution was that conferred their degrees. Cooper and Neuhuas (2000) found that experts who were highly paid for their testimony were viewed by jurors as "hired guns" and were neither liked nor believed. Moreover, witnesses who received high pay as well as having impressive credentials were not believed or liked and were less effective. During debriefing, the mock jurors said this was because they assumed that the highly paid expert from the prestigious institution frequently testified as a paid witness (a hired gun). However, the moderately paid person from the less well-known institution was seen as someone who was testifying simply because of his expertise in a particular area.

OBJECTIVITY IN CHILD ABUSE TRIALS

One potential problem with the adversarial procedure is that experts may form an allegiance with a client and lose their objectivity. There are special concerns in cases where the welfare of children is at stake. For example, it has been alleged that child-centred advocates may express more opinions in favour of the child (Levy, 1989). Kovera et al. (1993) undertook an empirical study to examine to what extent experts' pro-child beliefs would lead them to evaluate a child's evidence favourably. They sampled members of the International Society for Traumatic Stress, many of whom were familiar with post-traumatic stress disorder and other responses to child abuse. They sent a questionnaire to members asking for their opinions about various aspects of child sexual abuse, children's capabilities as witnesses, and the prosecution of child sexual abuse. The major finding of the survey was that while the respondents expressed generally favourable beliefs about child witnesses, the background of the experts predicted their beliefs (although the extent to which these beliefs translate to the courtroom situation is unknown). Respondents who specialised in working with child victims of sexual assault expressed more positive beliefs about children's capabilities, presumably because they are likely to be more knowledgeable about their capabilities and limitations. The Kovera study provides us with some information on experts' beliefs; however, we cannot tell from this study the extent to which beliefs are based on their knowledge of the research, their experiences and so on. Moreover, further research is needed to determine how these beliefs influence decision making in the courts.

SUMMARY AND CONCLUSION

Expert evidence provides a means whereby scientific knowledge can be disseminated and can inform the court's decisions. In an attempt to make their research more applicable, psychologists have relied primarily on the results of laboratory studies, although other methodological approaches have provided useful information. A good example is the work on suggestibility of witness memory (see Chapters 6 and 7). This has gone from traditional laboratory studies, in which participants are presented with slides of an event, to real-life interviews, in which memories are implanted over a period of time (Chapter 7). Similarly, research on techniques for enhancing eyewitness memory have progressed from laboratory studies of factors that influence encoding and retrieval to studies of techniques used by police officers in the field (Chapter 5). Moreover, research on the factors influencing juror verdicts and jury deliberations has advanced our knowledge significantly (Chapter 8). While much of the latter research relies on data collection in simulated settings, there has been a greater effort to use data from real trials to add to our knowledge (see Chapter 8). This chapter illustrated how the many areas of psychological research reviewed in this text can be applied in legal contexts. Continued efforts to communicate the research findings in applied contexts will encourage further collaboration between psychologists and legal professionals, and enhance the use and quality of expert testimony.

REFERENCES

Abwender, D. & Hough, K. (2001). Interactive effects of characteristics of defendant and mock juror on U.S. participants' judgment and sentencing recommendations. *Journal of Social Psychology, 141*, 603–615.

Ackil, J.F. and Zaragoza, M.S. (1995). Developmental differences in eyewitness suggestibility and memory for source. *Journal of Experimental Child Psychology, 60*, 57–83.

Agnew, R. (1984). Appearance and delinquency. *Criminology: An Interdisciplinary Journal, 22*, 421–440.

Ajzen, I. & Madden, T.J. (1986). Prediction of goal-directed behavior: Attitudes, intentions, and perceived behavioral control. *Journal of Experimental Social Psychology, 22*, 453–474.

Akehurst, L. & Vrij, A. (1999). Creating suspects in police interviews. *Journal of Applied Psychology, 29*, 192–210.

Akehurst, L., Köhnken, G., Vrij, A. & Bull, R. (1996). Laypersons' and police officers' beliefs regarding deceptive behaviour. *Applied Cognitive Psychology, 10*, 461–471.

Allen, V.L. & Levine, J.M. (1971). Social support and conformity: The role of independent assessment of reality. *Journal of Experimental Social Psychology, 22*, 453–474.

Anderson, D.E., Ansfield, M.E. & DePaulo, B.M. (1999). Love's best habit: Deception in the context of relationships. In P. Philippot, R.S. Feldman & E.J. Coats (eds), *The social context of nonverbal behavior* (pp. 372–409). Cambridge: Cambridge University Press.

Anderson, M.C. & Spellman, B.A. (1995). On the status of inhibitory mechanisms in cognition: Memory retrieval as a model case. *Psychological Review, 102*, 68–100.

Anne, R., Levine, T., Ching, P. & Yoshimoto, J. (1993). The influence of perceived source reward value on attributions of deception. *Communication Research Reports, 10*, 15–27.

Anson, D.A., Golding, S.L. & Gully, K.J. (1993). Child sexual abuse allegations: Reliability of criteria-based content analysis. *Law and Human Behavior, 17*, 331–341.

Arnold, M. & Lindsay, D.S. (2002). Remembering remembering. *Journal of Experimental Psychology: Learning, Memory, and Cognition, 28*, 521–529.

Asch, S.E. (1956). Studies of independence and conformity: A minority of one against a unanimous majority. *Psychological Monographs, 70*, 416.

Assefi, S. & Garry, M. (in press). Absolute memory distortions: Alcohol suggestions influence the misinformation effect. *Psychological Science*.

Auld (2001). *Review of the Criminal Courts of England and Wales. Report by the Right Honourable Lord Justice Auld*. London: HMSO.

Ayers, M.S. & Reder, L.M. (1998). A theoretical review of the misinformation effect: Predictions from an activation-based model. *Psychonomic Bulletin and Review, 5*, 1–21.

Backbier, E. & Sieswerda, S. (1997). Wanneer en waarom liegen we eigenlijk? *Nederlands Tijdschrift voor de Psychologie, 52*, 255–264.

Baldwin, J. (1992). *Videotaping of police interviews with suspects: An evaluation*. Police Research Series, Paper No. 1. London: Home Office.

Baldwin, J. (1993). Police interview techniques. *British Journal of Criminology, 33*, 325–352.

Baldwin, J. (1994). Police interrogation: What are the rules of the game? In D. Morgan & G.M. Stephenson (eds), *Suspicion and silence: The right to silence in criminal investigations* (pp. 66–76). London: Blackstone.

Baldwin, J. & McConville, M. (1979). *Jury trials*. Oxford: Oxford University Press.

Baldwin, J. & McConville, M. (1980). *Confessions in Crown Court trials*. Royal Commission on Criminal Procedure. Research Study No. 5. London: HMSO.

Banaji, M.R., Hardin, C. & Rothman, A.J. (1993). Implicit stereotyping in person judgment. *Journal of Personality and Social Psychology, 65*, 272–281.

Barclay, C.R. (1986). Schematization of autobiographical memory. In D.C. Rubin (ed.), *Autobiographical memory*. Cambridge: Cambridge University Press.

Barland, G.H. (1988). The polygraph test in the USA and elsewhere. In A. Gale (ed.), *The polygraph test: Lies, truth and science* (pp. 73–96). London: Sage.

Barnett, A. (1985). Some distribution patterns for the Georgia death sentence. *University of California Davis Law Review, 18*, 1327–1374.

Bartlett, F.C. (1932). *Remembering: A study in experimental and social psychology*. Cambridge: Cambridge University Press.

Bartlett, J.C. & Fulton, A. (1991). Familiarity and recognition of faces: The factor of age. *Memory and Cognition, 19*, 229–238.

Bashore, T.R. & Rapp, P.E. (1993). Are there alternatives to traditional polygraph procedures? *Psychological Bulletin, 113*, 3–22.

Beal, C., Schmitt, K. & Dekle, D.J. (1995). Eyewitness identification of children: Effects of absolute judgements, nonverbal response options and event encoding. *Law and Human Behavior, 19*, 197–216.

Behrman, B. & Davey, S. (2001). Eyewitness identification in actual criminal cases: An archival analysis. *Law and Human Behavior, 25*, 433–458.

Bekerian, D.A. & Bowers, J.M. (1983). Eyewitness testimony: Were we misled? *Journal of Experimental Psychology: Learning, Memory, and Cognition, 9*, 139–145.

Bell, K.L. & DePaulo, B.M. (1996). Liking and lying. *Basic and Applied Social Psychology, 18*, 243–266.

Belli, R.F. (1989). Influences of misleading postevent information: Misinformation interference and acceptance. *Journal of Experimental Psychology: General, 118*, 72–85.

Belli, R.F., Winkielman, P., Read, J.D., Schwartz, N. & Lynn, S. (1998). Recalling more childhood events leads to judgements of poorer memory: Implications for the recovered/false memory debate. *Psychonomic Bulletin and Review, 5*, 318–323.

Ben-Shakhar, G. & Furedy, J.J. (1990). *Theories and applications in the detection of deception*. New York: Springer-Verlag.

Berman, G.L. & Cutler, B.L. (1996). Effects of inconsistencies in eyewitness testimony on mock-juror decision making. *Journal of Applied Psychology, 81*, 170–177.

Bernstein, E.M. & Putnam, F.W. (1986). Development, reliability, and validity of a dissociation scale. *Journal of Nervous and Mental Disease, 174*, 727–735.

Blaauw, J.A. (1971). 99 tips voor het verhoor. *Algemeen Politie Blad, 129*, 287–296.

Blanck, P.D. (1985). The appearance of justice: Judges' verbal and nonverbal behavior in criminal jury trials. *Stanford Law Review, 38*, 89–164.

Bond, C.F. & Fahey, W.E. (1987). False suspicion and the misperception of deceit. *British Journal of Social Psychology, 26*, 41–46.

Bordens, K.S. & Bassett, J. (1985). The plea bargaining process from the defendant's perspective: A field investigation. *Basic and Applied Social Psychology, 6*, 93–110.

Borgida, E. & Park, R. (1988). The entrapment defense: Juror comprehension and decision making. *Law and Human Behavior, 12*, 19–31.

Bornstein, B. (1999). The ecological validity of jury simulations: Is the jury still out? *Law and Human Behavior, 23*, 75–91.

Bornstein, B., Whisenhunt, B., Nemeth, R. & Dunaway, D. (2002). Pre-trial publicity and civil cases: A two way street? *Law and Human Behavior, 26,* 3–18.

Boster, F.J., Hunter, J.E. & Hale, J.L. (1991). An information processing model of jury decision making. *Small Group Research, 18,* 524–547.

Brainerd, C.J. & Reyna, V.F. (1998). Fuzzy-trace theory and children's false memories. *Journal of Experimental Child Psychology, 71,* 81–129.

Brainerd, C.J., Reyna, V.F., Howe, M.L. & Kingma, J. (1990). The development of forgetting and reminiscence. *Monographs of the Society for Research in Child Development, 55* (3–4 Serial No. 222).

Braun, K., Ellis, R. & Loftus, E.F. (2002). Make my memory: How advertising can change our memories of the past. *Psychology and Marketing, 19,* 1–23.

Bray, R. & Noble, A. (1978). Authoritarianism and decisions of mock juries: Evidence of jury bias and group polarization. *Journal of Personality and Social Psychology, 36,* 1424–1430.

Brehm, S.S., Kassin, S.M. & Fein, S. (2002). *Social psychology* (5th edn). Boston, MA: Houghton Mifflin.

Brekke, N. & Borgida, E. (1988). Expert psychological testimony in rape trial: A social-cognitive analysis. *Journal of Personality and Social Psychology, 55,* 372–386.

Brewer, N. & Hupfeld, R. (in press). Effects of testimonial inconsistencies and witness group identity on mock-juror judgments. *Journal of Applied Social Psychology.*

Brewin, C.R. & Andrews, B. (1998). Recovered memories of trauma: Phenomenology and cognitive mechanisms. *Clinical Psychology Review, 18,* 949–970.

Brewin, C.R. & Myers, L.B. (1996). Repressive coping and impaired recall of autobiographical and experimental memory. Paper presented at the International Conference on Memory, Padova, 14–19 July.

Brewin, C.R., Dalgleish, T. & Joseph, S. (1996). A dual representation theory of post-traumatic stress disorder. *Psychological Review, 103,* 670–686.

Briere, J. & Conte, J. (1993). Self-reported amnesia for abuse in adults molested as children. *Journal of Traumatic Stress, 6,* 21–31.

Brigham, J.C. & Cairns, D.L. (1988). The effect of mugshot inspections on eyewitness identification accuracy. *Journal of Applied Social Psychology, 18,* 1394–1410.

Brigham, J.C. & Pfeifer, J.E. (1994). Evaluating the fairness of lineups. In D.F. Ross, J.D. Read & M.P. Toglia (eds), *Adult eyewitness testimony: Current trends and developments* (pp. 201–222). New York: Cambridge University Press.

Brigham, J.C. & Wolfskeil, M.P. (1983). Opinions of attorneys and law enforcement personnel on the accuracy of eyewitness identifications. *Law and Human Behavior, 7,* 337–349.

Brigham, J.C., Wasserman, A. & Meissner, C.A. (1999). Disputed eyewitness identification evidence: Important legal and scientific issues. *Court Review, 36,* 12–27.

Brinded, P.M.J. (1998). A case of acquittal following confession in a police videotaped interview. *Psychiatry, Psychology, and Law, 5,* 133–138.

British Medical Journal (1965). Physical disability and crime, *1,* 1448–1449.

Brown, H., Stein, J. & Turk, V. (1995). The sexual abuse of adults with learning disabilities. *Mental Handicap Research, 3,* 179–187.

Brown, J.M. (2003). Eyewitness memory for arousing events: Putting things into context. *Applied Cognitive Psychology, 17,* 93–106.

Bruck, M. & Ceci, S.J. (1999). The suggestibility of children's memory. *Annual Review of Psychology, 50,* 419–439.

Bruck, M., Ceci, S. & Hembrooke, H. (1998). Reliability and credibility of young children's report: From policy to practice. *American Psychologist, 53,* 136–151.

Bruck, M., Ceci, S.J. & Hembrooke, H. (2002). The nature of children's true and false narratives. *Developmental Review, 22,* 520–554.

Bruck, M., Ceci, S. & Melnyk, L. (1997). External and internal sources of variation in the creation of false reports in children. *Learning and Individual Differences, 9,* 289–316.

Bruck, M., Ceci, S., Francoeur, E. & Barr, R. (1995). "I hardly cried when I got my shot!": Influencing children's reports about a visit to their pediatrician. *Child Development, 66,* 193–208.

Bruner, J. S. & Potter, M.C. (1964). Interference in visual recognition. *Science, 144,* 424–425.

Bryne, C.A., Hyman, I. & Scott, K. (2001). Comparisons of memories of traumatic events and other experiences. *Applied Cognitive Psychology, 15,* 119–134.

Buck, J.A., Warren, A.R., Betman, S. & Brigham, J.C. (2002). Age differences in criteria-based content analysis scores in typical child sexual abuse interviews. *Journal of Applied Developmental Psychology, 23,* 267–283.

Buckwalter, A. (1980). *Interviews and interrogations.* London: Butterworth.

Bull, R. (1988). What is the lie-detection test? In A. Gale (ed.), *The polygraph test: Lies, truth and science* (pp. 10–19). London: Sage.

Bull, R. (1992). Obtaining evidence expertly. The reliability of interviews with child witnesses. *Expert Evidence, 1,* 5–12.

Bull, R. (1995). Interviewing people with communication difficulties. In R. Bull & D. Carson (eds), *Handbook of psychology in legal contexts.* Chichester: Wiley.

Bull, R. (1996). Good practice for video-recorded interviews with child witnesses for use in criminal proceedings. In G. Davies, S. Lloyd-Bostock, M. McMurran & C. Wilson (eds), *Psychology, law and criminal justice* (pp. 101–117). Berlin: de Gruyter.

Bull, R. (1999). Police investigative interviewing. In A. Memon & R. Bull (eds), *Handbook of the psychology of interviewing* (pp. 279–292). Chichester: Wiley.

Bull, R. (2001). *Children and the law: The essential readings.* Oxford: Blackwell.

Bull, R. (2002a). Attempts to improve children's facial identification. Presidential Address to the Psychology-Law Division of the International Association of Applied Psychology at the 25th International Congress of Applied Psychology, Singapore.

Bull, R. (2002b). Applying psychology to crime investigation: The case of police interviewing. In I. Mckenzie & R. Bull (eds), *Criminal justice research: Inspiration, influence and ideation* (pp. 221–243). Aldershot: Ashgate.

Bull, R. (2003). Experiences of giving expert testimony in court in criminal trials involving eyewitness and earwitness testimony. Paper presented at the Annual Conference of the European Association of Psychology and Law, Edinburgh.

Bull, R. & Barnes, P. (1995). Children as witnesses. In D. Bancroft & R. Carr (eds), *Influencing children's development.* Oxford: Blackwell.

Bull, R. & Cherryman, J. (1995). *Helping to identify skill gaps in specialist investigative interviewing: Literature review.* London: Home Office.

Bull, R. & Cherryman, J. (1996). *Helping to identify skill gaps in specialist investigative interviewing: Enhancement of professional skills.* London: Home Office Police Department.

Bull, R. & Corran, E. (2002). Interviewing child witnesses: Past and future. *International Journal of Police Science and Management, 4,* 315–322.

Bull, R. & Green, J. (1980). The relationship between physical appearance and criminality. *Medicine, Science, and the Law, 20,* 79–83.

Bull, R. & Horncastle, P. (1989). An evaluation of human awareness training. In R. Morgan & D. Smith (eds), *Coming to terms with policing.* London: Tavistock.

Bull, R. & Rumsey, N. (1988). *The social psychology of facial appearance.* New York: Springer-Verlag.

Bull, R., George, P., Paterson, B. & Knight, S. (2001). *Trying to improve children's facial identifications.* Final report to the Home Office Innovative Challenge Research Fund.

Burke, D., Ames, M., Etherington, R. & Pietsch, J. (1990). Effects of victim's and defendant's physical attractiveness on the perception of responsibility in an ambiguous domestic violence case. *Journal of Family Violence, 5,* 199–207.

Camparo, L., Wagner, J. & Saywitz, K. (2001). Interviewing children about real and fictitious events: Revisiting the narrative elaboration procedure. *Law and Human Behavior, 25,* 63–80.

Cardone, D. & Dent, H. (1996). Memory and interrogative suggestibility: The effects of modality of information presentation and retrieval conditions upon the suggestibility scores of people with learning disabilities. *Legal and Criminological Psychology, 1,* 165–177.

Carlson, E.B. & Putnam, F.W. (1993). An update on the Dissociative Experiences Scale. *Dissociation, 6,* 16–27.

Carlson, K.A. & Russo, J.E. (2001). Biased interpretation of evidence by mock jurors. *Journal of Experimental Psychology: Applied, 7,* 91–103.

Carretta, T.R. & Moreland, R.L. (1983). The direct and indirect effects of inadmissible evidence. *Journal of Applied Social Psychology, 13,* 291–309.

Carroll, D. (1991). Lie detection: Lies and truths. In R. Cochrane & D. Carroll (eds), *Psychology and social issues: A tutorial test* (pp. 160–170). London: Falmer Press.

Carter, C., Bottoms, B. & Levine, M. (1996). Linguistic and socioemotional influences on the accuracy of children's reports. *Law and Human Behavior, 20,* 335–358.

Cavior, H., Hayes, S. & Cavior, N. (1974). Physical attractiveness of female offenders. *Criminal Justice and Behavior, 1,* 321–331.

Cavior, N. & Howard, L. (1973). Facial attractiveness and juvenile delinquency. *Journal of Abnormal Child Psychology, 1,* 202–213.

Ceci, S. & Bruck, M. (1993). Suggestibility of the child witness: A historical review and synthesis. *Psychological Bulletin, 113,* 403–439.

Ceci, S. & Bruck, M. (1995). *Jeopardy in the courtroom: A scientific analysis of children's testimony.* Washington, DC: American Psychological Association.

Ceci, S.J. & Hembrooke, H. (eds) (1998). *Expert witnesses in child abuse cases: What can and should be said in court.* Washington, DC: American Psychological Association.

Ceci, S., Huffman, M., Smith, E. & Loftus, E. (1994). Repeatedly thinking about a non-event: Source misattributions among preschoolers. *Consciousness and Cognition, 3,* 388–407.

Ceci, S., Ross, D. & Toglia, M. (1987). Age differences in suggestibility: Psychological implications. *Journal of Experimental Psychology: General, 117,* 38–49.

Cecil, J.S. & Willging, T.E. (1993). *Court appointed experts: Defining the role of court appointed experts under Federal Rules of Evidence 706.* Federal Judicial Center.

Cecil, J.S., Lind, E.A. & Bermant, G. (1987). *Jury service in lengthy civil trials.* Federal Judicial Center.

Chaiken, S., Liberman, A. & Eagly, A. (1989). Heuristic and systematic information processing within and beyond the persuasion context. In J. Uleman & J. Bargh (eds), *Unintended thought* (pp. 212–252). New York: Guilford.

Chance, J.E. & Goldstein, A.G. (1996). The other-race effect and eyewitness identification. In S.L. Sporer, R.S. Malpass & G. Köhnken (eds), *Psychological issues in eyewitness identification* (pp. 153–176). Mahwah, NJ: Erlbaum.

Charrow, R.P. & Charrow, V.R. (1979). Making legal language understandable: A psycholinguistic study of jury instructions. *Columbia Law Review, 79,* 1306–1374.

Chen, S. & Chaiken, S. (1999). The heuristic–systematic model in its broader context. In S. Chaiken & Y. Trope (eds), *Dual process theories in social psychology* (pp. 73–96). New York: Guilford.

Cherryman, J. (2000). Police investigative interviewing: Skill analysis and concordance of evaluations. Unpublished Ph.D. thesis, University of Portsmouth.

Cherryman, J. & Bull, R. (1996). Investigative interviewing. In F. Leishman, B. Loveday & S.P. Savage (eds), *Core issues in policing* (pp. 147–159). London: Longman.

Cherryman, J. & Bull, R. (2001). Police officers' perceptions of specialist investigative interviewing skills. *International Journal of Police Science and Management, 3*, 199–212.

Chiroro, P. & Valentine, T. (1995). An investigation of the contact hypothesis of the own-race bias in face recognition. *Quarterly Journal of Experimental Psychology, 48A*, 879–894.

Christianson, S. (1992). Emotional stress and eyewitness memory: A critical review. *Psychological Bulletin, 112*, 284–309.

Cialdini, R. (1995). Principles and techniques of social influence. In A. Tessler (ed.), *Advanced social psychology*. New York: McGraw-Hill.

Cialdini, R. (2001). *Influence: Science and practice* (4th edn). New York: Allyn and Bacon.

Clare, I.C.H. & Gudjonsson, G.H. (1992). *Devising and piloting an experimental version of the "Notice to detained persons"*. Royal Commission on Criminal Justice, Research Study No. 7. London: HMSO.

Clark, S. & Tunnicliff, J. (2001). Selecting foils in eyewitness identification experiments: Experimental control and real world simulation. *Law and Human Behavior, 25*, 199–216.

Clifford, B. & Bull, R. (1978). *The psychology of person identifications*. London: Routledge.

Clyde, J. (1992). *The report of the enquiry into the removal of children from Orkney, February 1991*. London: HMSO.

Cooke, P. & Davies, G. (2001). Achieving best evidence from witnesses with learning disabilities: New guidance. *British Journal of Learning Disabilities, 29*, 84–87.

Cooper, J. & Neuhaus, I. (2000). The "hired gun" effect: Assessing the effect of pay, frequency of testifying and credentials for the perception of expert testimony. *Law and Human Behavior, 24*, 149–171.

Courtois, C.A. (1997). Informed clinical practice and standard of care: Proposed guidelines for the treatment of adults who report delayed memories of childhood trauma. In J.D. Read & D.S. Lindsay (eds), *Recollections of trauma: Scientific evidence and clinical practice* (pp. 49–78). New York: Plenum.

Craig, R.A., Scheibe, R., Raskin, D.C., Kircher, J.C. & Dodd, D.H. (1999). Interviewer questions and content analysis of children's statements of sexual abuse. *Applied Developmental Science, 3*, 77–85.

Craik, F.I.M. & Byrd, M. (1982). Aging and cognitive deficits: The role of attentional resources. In F.I.M. Craik & S. Trehub (eds), *Aging and cognitive processes* (pp. 191–211). New York: Plenum.

Crombag, H.F.M. (1993). Expert witnesses as vicarious anchors. *Expert Evidence, 5*, 127–131.

Cross, J.F., Cross, J. & Daly, J. (1971). Sex, race, age, and beauty as factors in recognition of faces. *Perception and Psychophysics, 10*, 393–396.

Culhane, S. & Hosch, H. (2002a). *An alibi witness's influence on juror verdicts*. Submitted.

Culhane, S. & Hosch, H. (2002b). *Crime victims serving as jurors: Is there a bias present?* Submitted.

Cutler, B.L. & Penrod, S.D. (1995). *Mistaken identification: The eyewitness, psychology, and the law*. New York: Cambridge University Press.

Cutler, B.L., Penrod, S.D. & Dexter, H.R. (1990). Juror sensitivity to eyewitness identification evidence. *Law and Human Behavior, 14*, 185–191.

Cutler, B.L., Penrod, S.D. & Stuve, T.E. (1988). Juror decision making in eyewitness identification cases. *Law and Human Behavior, 12*, 41–55.

Damaska, M. (1973). Evidentiary barriers to conviction and two models of criminal procedure: A comparative study. *University of Pennsylvania Law Review, 506*, 506–589.

Darby, B. & Jeffers, D. (1988). The effects of defendant and juror attractiveness on simulated courtroom trial decisions. *Social Behaviour and Personality, 16*, 39–50.

Darbyshire, P., Maughan, A. & Stewart, A. (2000). *What can the English legal system learn from jury research published up to 2001?* www.criminal-courts-review.org.uk.

Daubert v. *Merrell Dow Pharmaceuticals, Inc.* (1993). 113 S CT. 2786.

Daudistel, H., Hosch, H., Holmes, M. & Graves, J.B. (1999). Effect of defendant ethnicity on juries' dispositions of felony cases. *Journal of Applied Social Psychology, 29,* 317–336.

Davies, G. (1991). Research on children's testimony: Implications for interviewing practice. In C.R. Hollin & K. Howells (eds), *Clinical approaches to sex offenders and their victims.* New York: Wiley.

Davies, G.M. (1996). Mistaken identification: When law meets psychology head on. *Howard Journal of Criminal Justice, 35,* 230–241.

Davies, G.M. & Valentine, T. (1999). Codes of practice for identification. *Expert Evidence, 7,* 59–65.

Davies, G.M., Westcott, H.L. & Horan, N. (2000). The impact of questioning style on the content of investigative interviews with suspected child sexual abuse victims. *Psychology, Crime, and Law, 6,* 81–97.

Davis, J., Spitzer, C., Natao, D. & Stasser, G. (1978). Bias in social decisions by individuals and groups: An example from mock juries. In H. Brandstatter, J. Davis & H. Schuler (eds), *Dynamics of group decisions.* Beverly Hills, CA: Sage.

Davis, M. & Hadiks, D. (1995). Demeanor and credibility. *Semiotica, 106,* 5–54.

Davis, S. & Bottoms, B. (2002). Effects of social support on children's eyewitness reports: A test of the underlying mechanism. *Law and Human Behavior, 26,* 185–215.

Deffenbacher, K.A. (1980). Eyewitness accuracy and confidence: Can we infer anything about their relationship? *Law and Human Behavior, 4,* 243–260.

DePaulo, B.M. & Bell, K.L. (1996). Truth and investment: Lies are told to those who care. *Journal of Personality and Social Psychology, 70,* 703–716.

DePaulo, B.M. & Kashy, D.A. (1998). Everyday lies in close and casual relationships. *Journal of Personality and Social Psychology, 74,* 63–79.

DePaulo, B.M. & Kirkendol, S.E. (1989). The motivational impairment effect in the communication of deception. In J.C. Yuille (ed.), *Credibility assessment* (pp. 51–70). Dordrecht, The Netherlands: Kluwer.

DePaulo, B.M. & Pfeifer, R.L. (1986). On-the-job experience and skill at detecting deception. *Journal of Applied Social Psychology, 16,* 249–267.

DePaulo, B.M., Epstein, J.A. & Wyer, M.M. (1993). Sex differences in lying: How women and men deal with the dilemma of deceit. In M. Lewis & C. Saarni (eds), *Lying and deception in everyday life* (pp. 126–147). New York: Guilford.

DePaulo, B.M., Kashy, D.A., Kirkendol, S.E., Wyer, M.M. & Epstein, J.A. (1996). Lying in everyday life. *Journal of Personality and Social Psychology, 70,* 979–995.

DePaulo, B.M., Kirkendol, S.E., Tang, J. & O'Brien, T.P. (1988). The motivational impairment effect in the communication of deception: Replications and extensions. *Journal of Nonverbal Behavior, 12,* 177–201.

DePaulo, B.M., Lanier, K. & Davis, T. (1983). Detecting the deceit of the motivated liar. *Journal of Personality and Social Psychology, 45,* 1096–1103.

DePaulo, B.M., LeMay, C.S. & Epstein, J.A. (1991). Effects of importance of success and expectations for success on effectiveness at deceiving. *Personality and Social Psychology Bulletin, 17,* 14–24.

DePaulo, B.M., Lindsay, J.L., Malone, B.E., Muhlenbruck, L., Charlton, K. & Cooper, H. (2003). Cues to deception. *Psychological Bulletin, 129,* 74–118.

DePaulo, B. M., Stone, J. L., & Lassiter, G. D. (1985a). Deceiving and detecting deceit. In B. R. Schenkler (ed.), *The self and social life* (pp. 323–370). New York: McGraw-Hill.

DePaulo, B.M., Stone, J.I. & Lassiter, G.D. (1985b). Telling ingratiating lies: Effects of target sex and target attractiveness on verbal and nonverbal deceptive success. *Journal of Personality and Social Psychology, 48,* 1191–1203.

Devenport, J.L., Penrod, S.D. & Cutler, B.L. (1997). Eyewitness identification evidence: Evaluating common-sense evaluations. *Psychology, Public Policy, and Law, 3,* 338–361.

Devine, D., Clayton, L., Dunford, B., Seying, R. & Pryce, J. (2000). Jury decision making: 45 years of empirical research on deliberating groups. *Psychology, Public Policy and Law, 7,* 622–727.

Devine, P.G. (1989). Stereotypes and prejudice: Their automatic and controlled components. *Journal of Personality and Social Psychology, 56,* 5–18.

Diamond, S.S. (1997). Illuminations and shadows from jury simulations. *Law and Human Behavior, 21,* 561–571.

Dijker, A., Tacken, M. & van den Borne, B. (2000). Context effects of facial appearance on attitudes towards mentally handicapped persons. *British Journal of Social Psychology, 39,* 413–427.

Doherty-Sneddon, G. & McAuley, S. (2000). Influence of video-mediation on adult–child interviews. *Applied Cognitive Psychology, 14,* 372–379.

Downs, A.C. & Lyons, P. (1991). Natural observations of the links between attractiveness and initial legal judgments. *Personality and Social Psychology Bulletin, 17,* 541–547.

Duff, P. (2000). The defendant's right to trial by jury: A neighbour's view. *Criminal Law Review,* 85–94.

Dysart, J. & Lindsay, R. (2001). A pre-identification questioning effect: Serendipitously increasing correct rejections. *Law and Human Behavior, 25,* 155–165.

Dysart, J.E., Lindsay, R.C.L. & MacDonald, T.K. (2002, March). The effects of alcohol intoxication on identification accuracy from show-ups: A field study. Paper presented at the biennial meeting of the American Psychology-Law Society, Austin, TX.

Dysart, J.E., Lindsay, R.C.L., MacDonald, T.K. & Wicke, C. (2002). The intoxicated witness: Effects of alcohol on identification accuracy. *Journal of Applied Psychology, 87,* 170–175.

Dysart, J., Lindsay, R.C.L., Hammond, R. & Dupuis, P. (2001). Mugshot exposure prior to lineup identification: Interference, transference and commitment effects. *Journal of Applied Psychology, 86,* 1280–1284.

Eads, L.S., Shuman, D.W. & DeLipsey, J.M. (2000). Getting it right: The trial of sexual assault and child molestation cases under Federal Rules of Evidence 413–415. *Behavioral Sciences and the Law, 18,* 169–216.

Eagly, A., Ashmore, R., Makhijani, M. & Longo, L. (1991). What is beautiful is good, but...: A meta-analytic review of research on the physical attractiveness stereotype. *Psychological Bulletin, 110,* 109–128.

Ebbesen, E.B. & Konecni, V.J. (1997). Eyewitness memory research: Probative v. prejudicial value. *Expert Evidence, 5,* 2–42.

Edwards, K. & Bryan, T.S. (1997). Judgmental biases produced by instructions to disregard: The (paradoxical) case of emotional information. *Personality and Social Psychology Bulletin, 23,* 849–864.

Efran, M. (1974). The effect of physical appearance on the judgement of guilt, interpersonal attraction, and severity of recommended punishment in a simulated jury task. *Journal of Research in Personality, 8,* 45–54.

Egeth, H.E. (1993). What do we not know about eyewitness identification? *American Psychologist, 48,* 577–580.

Eisen, M., Goodman, G., Qin, J. & Davis, S. (1998). Memory and suggestibility in maltreated children. In S. Lynn & K. McConkey (eds), *Truth in memory* (163–189). New York: Guilford.

Eisen, M., Winograd, E. & Qin, J. (2002). Individual differences in adults' suggestibility and memory performance. In M. Eisen, J. Quas & G. Goodman (eds), *Memory and suggestibility in the forensic interview* (pp. 205–234). Mahwah, NJ: Erlbaum.

Ekman, P. (1992). *Telling lies: Clues to deceit in the marketplace, politics and marriage.* New York: W.W. Norton.

Ekman, P. & Frank, M.G. (1993). Lies that fail. In M. Lewis & C. Saarni (eds), *Lying and deception in everyday life* (pp. 184–201). New York: Guilford.

Ekman, P. & Friesen, W.V. (1972). Hand movements. *Journal of Communication, 22,* 353–374.

Ekman, P. & O'Sullivan, M. (1991). Who can catch a liar? *American Psychologist, 46,* 913–920.

Ekman, P., Friesen, W.V. & Scherer, K.R. (1976). Body movement and voice pitch in deceptive interaction. *Semiotica, 16,* 23–27.

Ekman, P., O'Sullivan, M. & Frank, M.G. (1999). A few can catch a liar. *Psychological Science, 10,* 263–266.

Elaad, E. (1990). Detection of guilty knowledge in real-life criminal investigations. *Journal of Applied Psychology, 75,* 521–529.

Elaad, E., Ginton, A. & Jungman, N. (1992). Detection measures in real-life criminal guilty knowledge tests. *Journal of Applied Psychology, 77,* 757–767.

Ellis, H.D. (1984). Practical aspects of face memory. In G.L. Wells & E.F. Loftus (eds). *Eyewitness testimony: Psychological perspectives* (pp. 12–37). Cambridge: Cambridge University Press.

Ellison, K.W. & Buckhout, R. (1981). *Psychology and criminal justice.* New York: Harper & Row.

Ellsworth, P.C. (1989). Are twelve heads better than one? *Law and Contemporary Problems, 52,* 207–224.

Endres, J., Poggenpohl, C. & Erben, C. (1999). Repetitions, warning and video: Cognitive and motivational components in preschool children's suggestibility. *Legal and Criminological Psychology, 4,* 120–146.

Epstein, M.A. & Bottoms, B.L. (1996). Gender differences in child sexual abuse judgments: What happens after deliberation and why. Paper presented at the March 1996 meeting of the American Psychology-Law Society, Hilton Head, South Carolina.

Erdelyi, M.H. (1990). Repression, reconstruction and defence: History and integration of the psychoanalytic and experimental frameworks. In J.L. Singer (ed.), *Repression and dissociation: Implications for personality theory, psychopathology and health* (pp. 1–31). Chicago: University of Chicago Press.

Erickson, B., Lind, E.A., Johnson, B. & O'Barr, W. (1978). Speech style and impression formation in a court setting. *Journal of Experimental Social Psychology, 14,* 266–279.

Ericson, K., Perlman, N. & Isaacs, B. (1994). Witness competency, communication issues and people with developmental disabilities. *Developmental Disabilities Bulletin, 22,* 101–109.

Evans, R. (1993). *The conduct of police interviews with juveniles* (Royal Commission on Criminal Justice report). London: HMSO.

Evans, R. (1994). Police interviews with juveniles. In D. Morgan & G.M. Stephenson (eds), *Suspicion and silence: The right to silence in criminal investigations* (pp. 77–90). London: Blackstone.

Eyre, S.L., Read, N.W. & Millstein, S.G. (1997). Adolescent sexual strategies. *Journal of Adolescent Health, 20,* 286–293.

Faigman, D.L. (1995). The evidentiary status of social science under Daubert: Is it scientific, technical or other knowledge? *Psychology, Public Policy and Law, 1,* 960–979.

Faigman, D.L., Kaye, D., Saks, M.J. & Sanders, J. (1997). *Modern scientific evidence: The law and science of expert testimony.* St. Paul, MN: West.

Faller, K., Birdsall, W., Henry, J., Vandervort, F. & Silverschanz, P. (2001). What makes sex offenders confess? An exploratory study. *Journal of Child Sexual Abuse, 10,* 31–49.

Farrant, L. & Reese, E. (2000). Maternal style and children's participation in reminiscing: Stepping stones in children's autobiographical memory development. *Journal of Cognition and Development, 1,* 193–225.

Fazio, R.H. (2001). On the automatic activation of associated evaluations: An overview. *Cognition and Emotion, 15,* 115–141.

Feeley, T.H. & deTurck, M. (1995). Global cue usage in behavioral lie detection. *Communication Quarterly, 43,* 420–430.

Fein, S., McCloskey, A. & Tomlinson, T.M. (1997). Can the jury disregard that information? The use of suspicion to reduce the prejudicial effects of pretrial publicity and inadmissible testimony. *Personality and Social Psychology Bulletin, 23,* 1215–1226.

Feingold, A. (1992). Good-looking people are not what we think. *Psychological Bulletin, 111,* 304–341.

Ferguson, P., Duthie, D. & Graf, R. (1987). Attribution of responsibility to rapist and victim: The influence of victim's attractiveness and rape-related information. *Journal of Interpersonal Violence, 2,* 243–250.

Findlay, F., Hitch, G. & Meudell, P. (2000). Mutual inhibition in collaborative recall: Evidence for a retrieval based account. *Journal of Experimental Psychology: Learning, Memory, and Cognition, 26,* 1556–1567.

Fiore, E. (1989). *Encounters: A psychologist reveals case studies of abductions by extraterrestrials.* New York: Doubleday.

Fischoff, B. (1982). For those condemned to study the past: Heuristics and biases in hindsight. In D. Kahneman, P. Slovic & A. Tversky (eds), *Judgement under uncertainty: Heuristics and biases* (pp. 335–351). New York: Cambridge University Press.

Fisher, R.P. & Cutler, B.L. (1996). The relation between consistency and accuracy of eyewitness testimony. In G. Davies, S. Lloyd-Bostock, M. McMurran & C. Wilson (eds), *Psychology, law, and criminal justice* (pp. 21–28). Berlin: Walter de Gruyter.

Fisher, R.P. & Geiselman, R.E. (1992). *Memory-enhancing techniques for investigative interviewing.* Springfield, IL: Charles C. Thomas.

Fivush, R. (1998). Gendered narratives: Elaboration, structure and emotion in parent–child reminiscing across the preschool years. In C.P. Thompson, D.J. Hermann, D. Bruce, J.D. Read, D.G. Payne & M. Toglia (eds), *Autobiographical memory: Theoretical and applied perspectives* (pp. 70–104). Hillsdale, NJ: Erlbaum.

Fivush, R. & Reese, E. (in press). Reminiscing and relating: The development of parent–child talk about the past. In J. Webster & B. Haight (eds), *Critical advances in reminiscence work.* New York: Springer.

Fivush, R. & Schwarzmueller, A. (1998). Children remember childhood: Implications for childhood amnesia. *Applied Cognitive Psychology, 12,* 455–473.

Fivush, R., Hazzard, A., Sales, J., Sarfati, D. & Brown, T. (in press). Creating coherence out of chaos? Children's narratives of emotionally positive and negative events. *Applied Cognitive Psychology.*

Flin, R., Boon, J., Knox, A. & Bull, R. (1992). The effect of a five-month delay on children's and adults' eyewitness memory. *British Journal of Psychology, 83,* 323–336.

Foa, E.B., Rothbaum, B.O., Riggs, D. & Murdock, T. (1991). Treatment of post-traumatic stress disorder in rape victims: A comparison between cognitive behavioural procedures and counselling. *Journal of Consulting and Clinical Psychology, 59,* 715–723.

Foster, R.A., Libkuman, T.M., Schooler, J.W. & Loftus, E.F. (1994). Consequentiality and eyewitness person identification. *Applied Cognitive Psychology, 8,* 107–121.

Frank, M.G. & Ekman, P. (1997). The ability to detect deceit generalizes across different types of high-stake lies. *Journal of Personality and Social Psychology, 72,* 1429–1439.

Freud, S. (1959). *Collected papers.* New York: Basic Books.

Furedy, J.J. (1993). The "control" question "test" (CQT) polygrapher's dilemma: Logico-ethical considerations for psychophysiological practitioners and researchers. *International Journal of Psychophysiology, 15*, 263–267.

Furedy, J.J. (1996a). Some elementary distinctions among, and comments concerning the "control" question "test" (CQT) polygrapher's many problems: A reply to Honts, Kircher and Raskin. *International Journal of Psychophysiology, 22*, 53–59.

Furedy, J.J. (1996b). The North American polygraph and psychophysiology: Disinterested, uninterested, and interested perspectives. *International Journal of Psychophysiology, 21*, 97–105.

Gabbert, F., Memon, A. & Allan, K. (in press). Memory conformity: Can eyewitnesses influence each other's memories for an event? *Applied Cognitive Psychology.*

Gale, A. (1988). The polygraph test, more than scientific investigation. In A. Gale (ed.), *The polygraph test: Lies, truth and science* (pp. 1–9). London: Sage.

Garrioch, L. & Brimacombe, E. (2001). Lineup administrators' expectations: Their impact on eyewitness confidence. *Law and Human Behavior, 25*, 299–315.

Garry, M. & Polaschek, D.L.L. (2000). Imagination and memory. *Current Directions in Psychological Science, 9*, 6–10.

Garry, M., Manning, C.G., Loftus, E.F. & Sherman, S.J. (1996). Imagination inflation: Imagining a childhood event inflates confidence that it occurred. *Psychonomic Bulletin and Review, 3*, 208–214.

Garven, S., Wood, J., Malpass, R.S. & Shaw, J. (1998). More than just suggestion: The effect of interviewing techniques from the McMartin Preschool case. *Journal of Applied Psychology, 83*, 347–359.

Geiselman, R.E. (1994). Providing eyewitness expert testimony in Los Angeles. *Expert Evidence, 3*, 9–15.

Gerdes, E., Danmann, E. & Heilig, K. (1988). Perceptions of rape victims and assailants: Effects of physical attractiveness, acquaintance, and subject gender. *Sex Roles, 19*, 141–153.

Gertner, N. & Mizner, J. (1997). *The law of juries.* Little Falls, NJ: Glaser Legal Works.

Gilbert, D.T. & Malone, P.S. (1995). The correspondence bias. *Psychological Bulletin, 117*, 21–38.

Goffman, E. (1959). *The presentation of self in everyday life.* New York: Doubleday.

Goldman-Eisler, F. (1968). *Psycholinguistics: Experiments in spontaneous speech.* New York: Doubleday.

Goldstein, A.G. & Chance, J.E. (1971). Visual recognition memory for complex configurations. *Perception and Psychophysics, 9*, 237–241.

Goldstein, A., Chance, J. & Gilbert, B. (1984). Facial stereotypes of good guys and bad guys: A replication and extension. *Bulletin of the Psychonomic Society, 22*, 549–552.

Goldstein, A.G., Chance, J.E. & Schneller, G.R. (1989). Frequency of eyewitness identification in criminal cases. *Bulletin of the Psychonomic Society, 27*, 71–74.

Goodman, G., Batterman-Faunce, J.M., Schaaf, J. & Kenney, R. (2002). Nearly four years after an event: Children's eyewitness memory and adults' perceptions of children's accuracy. *Child Abuse and Neglect, 26*, 849–884.

Goodman, G., Bottoms, B., Schwartz-Kenney, B. & Rudy, L. (1991). Children's testimony for a stressful event: Improving children's reports. *Journal of Narrative and Life History, 1*, 69–99.

Goodman, G., Hirschman, J., Hepps, D. & Rudy, L. (1991). Children's memory for stressful events. *Merrill-Palmer Quarterly, 37*, 109–158.

Goodman, G.S., Rudy, L., Bottoms, B. & Aman, C. (1990). Children's concerns and memory: Issues of ecological validity in the study of children's eyewitness testimony. In R. Fivush & J. Hudson (eds), *Knowing and remembering in young children* (pp. 249–284). New York: Cambridge University Press.

Gordon, N.J., Fleisher, W.L. & Weinberg, C.D. (2002). *Effective interviewing and interrogation techniques*. San Diego, CA: Academic Press.

Gorenstein, G.W. & Ellsworth, P. (1980). Effect of choosing an incorrect photograph on a later identification by an eyewitness. *Journal of Applied Psychology, 65*, 616–622.

Granhag, P.A. & Strömwall, L.A. (1999). Repeated interrogations: Stretching the deception detection paradigm. *Expert Evidence: The International Journal of Behavioural Sciences in Legal Contexts, 7*, 163–174.

Granhag, P.A. & Strömwall, L.A. (2001a). Deception detection: Examining the consistency heuristic. In C.M. Breur, M.M. Kommer, J.F. Nijboer & J.M. Reijntjes (eds), *New trends in criminal investigation and evidence*, vol. 2 (pp. 309–321). Antwerp: Intresentia.

Granhag, P.A. & Strömwall, L.A. (2001b). Deception detection: Interrogators' and observers' decoding of consecutive statements. *Journal of Psychology, 135*, 603–620.

Granhag, P.A. & Strömwall, L.A. (2002). Repeated interrogations: Verbal and non-verbal cues to deception. *Applied Cognitive Psychology, 16*, 243–257.

Greene, E. & Dodge, M. (1995). The influence of prior record evidence on juror decision making. *Law and Human Behavior, 19*, 67–78.

Greenhoot, A.F. (2000). Remembering and understanding: The effects of changes in underlying knowledge on children's recollections. *Child Development, 71*, 1309–1320.

Greenhoot, F., Ornstein, P., Gordon, B. & Baker-Ward, C. (1999). Acting out the details of a pediatric check-up: The impact of interview condition and behavioural style on children's memory reports. *Child Development, 70*, 363–380.

Groth, A. (1981). Rape: The sexual expression of aggression. In P. Brain & D. Benton (eds), *Multidisciplinary approaches to aggression research*. Elsevier: North Holland Biomedical Press.

Gudjonsson, G.H. (1984). A new scale of interrogative suggestibility. *Personality and Individual Differences, 5*, 303–314.

Gudjonsson, G.H. (1987). A parallel form of the Gudjonsson Suggestibility Scale. *British Journal of Clinical Psychology, 26*, 215–221.

Gudjonsson, G.H. (1988). Compliance in an interrogative setting: A new scale. *Personality and Individual Differences, 10*, 535–540.

Gudjonsson, G.H. (1990). One hundred alleged false confession cases: Some normative data. *British Journal of Clinical Psychology, 29*, 249–250.

Gudjonsson, G.H. (1992). *The psychology of interrogations, confessions and testimony*. Chichester: Wiley.

Gudjonsson, G.H. (1993). Confession evidence, psychological vulnerability and expert testimony. *Journal of Community and Applied Social Psychology, 3*, 117–129.

Gudjonsson, G.H. (1994a). Investigative interviewing: Recent developments and some fundamental issues. *International Review of Psychiatry, 6*, 237–245.

Gudjonsson, G.H. (1994b). Psychological vulnerability: Suspects at risk. In D. Morgan & G. Stephenson (eds), *Suspicions of silence* (pp. 91–106). London: Blackstone.

Gudjonsson, G.H. (1995). The effects of interrogative pressure on strategic coping. *Psychology, Crime, and Law, 1*, 309–318.

Gudjonsson, G.H. (1996). Psychological evidence in court. *The Psychologist, 9*, 213–219.

Gudjonsson, G.H. (1997). *The Gudjonsson Suggestibility Scales Manual*. Hove: Psychology Press.

Gudjonsson, G.H. (1999a). Police interviewing and disputed confessions. In A. Memon & R.H. Bull (eds), *Handbook of the psychology of interviewing* (pp. 327–341). Chichester: Wiley.

Gudjonsson, G.H. (1999b). The IRA funeral murders: The confession of PK and the expert psychological testimony. *Legal and Criminological Psychology, 4*, 45–50.

Gudjonsson, G.H. (1999c). The making of a serial false confessor: The confessions of Henry Lee Lucas. *Journal of Forensic Psychology, 10*, 416–426.

Gudjonsson, G.H. (2001). False confessions. *The Psychologist, 14*, 588–591.

Gudjonsson, G.H. (2002). *A psychology of interrogations and confessions.* Chichester: Wiley.

Gudjonsson, G.H. & Lister, S. (1984). Interrogative suggestibility and its relationships with perceptions of self-concept and control. *Journal of the Forensic Science Society, 24*, 99–110.

Gudjonsson, G.H. & MacKeith, J.A.C. (1990). A proven case of false confession: Psychological aspects of the coerced-compliant type. *Medicine, Science, and the Law, 30*, 329–335.

Gudjonsson, G.H. & MacKeith, J.A.C. (1994). Learning disability and the Police and Criminal Evidence Act 1984. Protection during investigative interviewing: A video-recorded false confession to double murder. *Journal of Forensic Psychiatry, 5*, 35–49.

Gudjonsson, G.H. & Petursson, H. (1991). Custodial interrogation: Why do suspects confess and how does it relate to their crime, attitude and personality? *Personality and Individual Differences, 12*, 295–306.

Gudjonsson, G.H. & Sigurdsson, J.F. (1999). The Gudjonsson Questionnaire Revised (GCQ–R): Factor structure and its relationship with personality. *Personality and Individual Differences, 27*, 953–968.

Gudjonsson, G.H., Clare, I., Rutter, S. & Pearse, J. (1993). *Persons at risk during interviews in police custody: The identification of vulnerabilities.* London: HMSO.

Gudjonsson, G.H., Kopelman, M.D. & MacKeith, J.A.C. (1999). Unreliable admissions to homicide: A case of misdiagnosis of amnesia and misuse of abreaction technique. *British Journal of Psychiatry, 174*, 455–459.

Gula, C. & Yarmey, A.D. (1998). Physical appearance and judgment of status as a battered woman. *Perceptual and Motor Skills, 87*, 459–465.

Gumpert, C.H. & Lindblad, F. (1999). Expert testimony on child sexual abuse: A qualitative study of the Swedish approach to statement analysis. *Expert Evidence, 7*, 279–314.

Hafstad, G., Memon, A. & Logie, R. (2002). The effects of post-identification feedback on children's memory. Paper presented at the European Conference on Psychology and Law, Leuven, September.

Hans, V.P. & Doob, A.N. (1976). Section 12 of the Canada Evidence Act and the deliberation of simulated juries. *Criminal Law Quarterly, 18*, 235–253.

Hans, V.P. & Slater, D. (1984). "Plain crazy": Lay definitions of legal insanity. *International Journal of Law and Psychiatry, 7*, 105–114.

Hans, V.P. & Swiegart, K. (1993). Jurors' views of civil lawyers: Implications for courtroom communication. *Indiana Law Journal, 68*, 1297–1332.

Hargie, O. & Tourish, D. (1999). The psychology of interpersonal skill. In A. Memon & R. Bull (eds), *Handbook of the psychology of interviewing* (pp. 71–87). Chichester: Wiley.

Harrigan, J.A. & O'Connell, D.M. (1996). Facial movements during anxiety states. *Personality and Individual Differences, 21*, 205–212.

Harris, M.J. & Rosenthal, R. (1985). Mediation of interpersonal expectancy effects: 31 meta-analyses. *Psychological Bulletin, 97*, 363–386.

Hastie, R., Penrod S. & Pennington, N. (1983). *Inside the jury.* Cambridge, MA: Harvard University Press.

Heal, L. & Sigelman, C. (1995). Response biases in interviews of individuals with limited mental ability. *Journal of Intellectual Disability Research, 39*, 331–340.

Heaps, C. & Nash, M. (1999). Individual differences in imagination inflation. *Psychonomic Bulletin and Review, 6*, 313–318.

Heinemann, W. (1990). Meeting the handicapped: A case study of affective–cognitive inconsistency. In W. Stroebe & M. Hewstone (eds), *European Review of Social Psychology*, Vol. 1. Chichester: Wiley.

Henry, L. & Gudjonsson, G. (1999). Eyewitness memory and suggestibility in children with mental retardation. *American Journal on Mental Retardation, 104,* 491–508.

Herkannen, S.T. & McEvoy, C. (2002). False memories and source-monitoring problems: Criterion differences. *Applied Cognitive Psychology, 16,* 73–85.

Hershkowitz, I., Lamb, M.E., Sternberg, K.J. & Esplin, P.W. (1997). The relationships among interviewer utterance type, CBCA scores and the richness of children's responses. *Legal and Criminological Psychology, 2,* 169–176.

Hertel, J., Brandt, K. & Kaplan, M. (2002). Juries in Germany. Paper presented at the meeting of the European Association of Experimental Social Psychology, 26–29 June, 2002, San Sebastian.

Hess, J.E. (1997). *Interviewing and interrogation for law enforcement.* Cincinnati, OH: Anderson.

Hirsch, A.R. & Wolf, C.J. (2001). Practical methods for detecting mendacity: A case study. *Journal of American Academy of Psychiatry and Law, 29,* 438–444.

Hocking, J.E. & Leathers, D.G. (1980). Nonverbal indicators of deception: A new theoretical perspective. *Communication Monographs, 47,* 119–131.

Holliday, R.E. & Hayes, B.K. (2002). Automatic and intentional processes in children's recognition memory: The reversed misinformation effect. *Applied Cognitive Psychology, 16,* 1–16.

Holliday, R.E., Douglas, K. & Hayes, B.K. (1999). Children's eyewitness suggestibility: Memory trace strength revisited. *Cognitive Development, 14,* 443–462.

Holliday, R.E., Reyna, V.F. & Hayes, B.K. (2002). Memory processes underlying misinformation effects in child witnesses. *Developmental Review, 22,* 37–77.

Holmberg, U. & Christianson, S.A. (in press). Murderers' and sexual offenders' experiences of police interview and their inclination to admit or deny crimes. *Behavioral Sciences and the Law.*

Holmes, D.S. (1990). The evidence for repression: An examination of sixty years of research. In J.L. Singer (ed.), *Repression and dissociation: Implications for personality theory, psychopathology and health* (pp. 85–102). Chicago: University of Chicago Press.

Home Office (2002). *Achieving best evidence in criminal proceedings: Guidance for vulnerable or intimidated witnesses, including children.* London: Home Office.

Home Office and Department of Health (1992). *Memorandum of good practice on video-recorded interviews with child witnesses for criminal proceedings.* London: HMSO.

Honts, C.R. (1994). Assessing children's credibility: Scientific and legal issues in 1994. *North Dakota Law Review, 70,* 879–903.

Honts, C.R., Kircher, J.C. & Raskin, D.C. (1996). Polygrapher's dilemma or psychologist's: A reply to Furedy's logico-ethical considerations for psychophysiological practitioners and researchers. *International Journal of Psychophysiology, 20,* 199–207.

Honts, C.R. & Perry, M.V. (1992). Polygraph admissibility: Changes and challenges. *Law and Human Behavior, 16,* 357–379.

Honts, C.R., Raskin, D.C. & Kircher, J.C. (1994). Mental and physical countermeasures reduce the accuracy of polygraph tests. *Journal of Applied Psychology, 79,* 252–259.

Hope, L., Memon, A. & McGeorge, P. (submitted, a). *Understanding pre-trial publicity: Predecisional distortion of evidence by mock jurors.*

Hope, L., Memon, A. & McGeorge, P. (submitted, b). *In the aftermath of pre-trial publicity: Examining the unexpected manifestations of positive and negative pre-trial information on mock juror decision making.*

Horn, M. (1993). Memories lost and found. *US News and World Report, 29 November,* 52–63.

Horowitz, I.A. (1980). Juror selection: A comparison of two methods in several criminal cases. *Journal of Applied Social Psychology, 10,* 86–99.

Horowitz, S.W., Lamb, M.E., Esplin, P.W., Boychuk, T.D., Krispin, O. & Reiter-Lavery, L. (1997). Reliability of criteria-based content analysis of child witness statements. *Legal and Criminological Psychology*, 2, 11–21.

Howe, M.L., Courage, M.L. & Peterson, C. (1994). How can I remember when "I" wasn't there: Long-term retention of traumatic experiences and emergence of the cognitive self. *Consciousness and Cognition: An International Journal*, 3, 327–355.

Huff, C.R., Rattner, A. & Sagarin, E. (1986). Guilty until proven innocent: Wrongful conviction and public policy. *Crime and Delinquency*, 32, 518–544.

Hyman, I.E. & Billings, F.J. (1998). Individual differences and the creation of false childhood memories. *Memory*, 6, 1–20.

Hyman, I.E. Jr. & Kleinknecht, E.E. (1999). False childhood memories: Research, theory, and applications. In L.M. Williams & V.L. Banyard (eds), *Trauma and memory* (pp. 175–188). Thousand Oaks, CA: Sage.

Hyman, I.E. & Pentland, J. (1996). The role of mental imagery in the creation of false childhood memories. *Journal of Memory and Language*, 35, 101–117.

Hyman, I.E., Husband, T.H. & Billings, F.J. (1995). False memories of childhood experiences. *Applied Cognitive Psychology*, 9, 181–197.

Iacono, W.G. & Lykken, D.T. (1997). The validity of the lie detector: Two surveys of scientific opinion. *Journal of Applied Psychology*, 82, 426–433.

Iacono, W.G. & Patrick, C.J. (1997). Polygraphy and integrity testing. In R. Rogers (ed.), *Clinical assessment of malingering and deception* (pp. 252–281). New York: Guilford.

Imhoff, M. & Baker-Ward, L. (1999). Preschoolers' suggestibility: Effects of developmentally appropriate language and supportiveness. *Journal of Applied Developmental Psychology*, 20, 407–429.

Imrich, D.J., Mullin, C. & Linz, D. (1995). Measuring the extent of prejudicial pretrial publicity in major American newspapers: A content analysis. *Journal of Communications*, 45, 91–117.

Inbau, F.E., Reid, J.E. & Buckley, J.P. (1986). *Criminal interrogation and confessions*, 3rd edn. Baltimore, MD: Williams & Wilkins.

Inbau, F.E., Reid, J.E., Buckley, J.P. & Jayne, B.C. (2001). *Criminal interrogation and confessions*, 4th edn. Gaithersburg, MD: Aspen Publishers.

Irving, B. & McKenzie, I.K. (1989). *Police interrogation: The effects of the Police and Criminal Evidence Act 1984*. London: Police Foundation.

Isaacs, B., Schuller, R. & Turtle, J. (1998). Witnesses with developmental disabilities: The cognitive interview, time delay and suspect identification. Paper presented at the Biennial Conference of the American Psychology-Law Society, Los Angeles.

Jacobson, M. & Popovich, P. (1983). Victim attractiveness and perceptions of responsibility in an ambiguous rape case. *Psychology of Women Quarterly*, 8, 134–139.

Jacoby, L.L. (1999). Ironic effects of repetition: Measuring age-related differences in memory. *Journal of Experimental Psychology: Learning, Memory, and Cognition*, 25, 3–22.

Jacoby, L.L., Kelley, C.M. & Dywan, J. (1989). Memory attributions. In H.L. Roediger & F.I.M. Craik (eds), *Varieties of memory and consciousness: Essays in honor of Endel Tulving* (pp. 391–422). Hillsdale, NJ: Erlbaum.

Joffe, R. & Yuille, J.C. (1992, May). Criteria-Based Content Analysis: An experimental investigation. Paper presented at the NATO Advanced Study Institute on the child witness in context: Cognitive, social and legal perspectives, Lucca, Italy.

Johnson, M.K. & Raye, C.L. (1981). Reality monitoring. *Psychological Review*, 88, 67–85.

Johnson, M.K. & Raye, C.L. (1998). False memories and confabulation. *Trends in Cognitive Sciences*, 2, 137–145.

Johnson, M.K., Hashtroudi, S. & Lindsay, D.S. (1993). Source monitoring. *Psychological Bulletin, 114*, 3–28.

Johnson, M.K., Raye, C.L., Foley, H.J. & Foley, M.A. (1981). Cognitive operations and decision bias in reality monitoring. *American Journal of Psychology, 94*, 37–64.

Jones, E.E. (1990). *Interpersonal perception*. New York: Freeman.

Kalbfleisch, P.J. (1994). The language of detecting deceit. *Journal of Language and Social Psychology, 13*, 469–496.

Kanekar, S. & Nazareth, A. (1988). Attributed rape victim's fault as a function of her attractiveness, physical hurt, and emotional disturbance. *Social Behaviour, 3*, 37–40.

Kaplan, M. & Miller, L. (1978a). Reducing the effects of juror bias. *Journal of Personality and Social Psychology, 36*, 1443–1455.

Kaplan, M.F. & Miller, C.E. (1978b). Judgements and group discussion: effects of presentation and memory factors on polarization. *Sociometry, 40*, 337–342.

Kaplan, M.F. & Martin, A. (1999). Effects of differential status of group members on the process and outcome of deliberation. *Group Processes and Intergroup Relations, 2*, 347–364.

Kashy, D.A. & DePaulo, B.M. (1996). Who lies? *Journal of Personality and Social Psychology, 70*, 1037–1051.

Kassin, S.M. (1997). The psychology of confession evidence. *American Psychologist, 52*, 221–233.

Kassin, S.M. (1998). More on the psychology of false confessions. *American Psychologist, 52*, 221–233.

Kassin, S.M. & Fong, C.T. (1999). "I'm innocent!": Effects of training on judgments of truth and deception in the interrogation room. *Law and Human Behaviour, 23*, 499–516.

Kassin, S.M. & Kiechel, K.L. (1996). The social psychology of false confessions, compliance, internalization and confabulation. *Psychological Science, 7*, 125–128.

Kassin, S.M. & McNall, K. (1991). Police interrogations and confessions: Communicating promises and threats by pragmatic implication. *Law and Human Behavior, 15*, 233–251.

Kassin, S.M. & Neumann, K. (1997). On the power of confession evidence: An experimental test of the fundamental difference hypothesis. *Law and Human Behavior, 21*, 469–484.

Kassin, S.M. & Studebaker, C.A. (1998). Instructions to disregard and the jury: Curative and paradoxical effects. In J. Golding & C. Macleod (eds), *Intentional forgetting: Interdisciplinary approaches* (pp. 413–433). Mahweh, NJ: Erlbaum.

Kassin, S.M. & Sukel, H. (1997). Coerced confessions and the jury: An experimental test of the "harmless error" rule. *Law and Human Behavior, 21*, 27–46.

Kassin, S.M. & Wrightsman, L.S. (1980). Prior confessions and mock juror verdicts. *Journal of Applied Social Psychology, 10*, 133–146.

Kassin, S.M. & Wrightsman, L.S. (1981). Coerced confessions, judicial instruction, and mock juror verdicts. *Journal of Applied Social Psychology, 11*, 489–506.

Kassin, S.M. & Wrightsman, L.S. (1985). Confession evidence. In S.M. Kassin & L.S. Wrightsman (eds), *The psychology of evidence and trial procedure* (pp. 67–94). London: Sage.

Kassin, S.M., Ellsworth, P.C. & Smith, V.L. (1994). Déjà vu all over again: Elliot's critique of eyewitness experts. *Law and Human Behavior, 18*, 203–210.

Kassin, S.M., Tubb, V.A., Hosch, H.M. & Memon, A. (2001). On the "general acceptance" of eyewitness testimony research: A new survey of the experts. *American Psychologist, 56*, 405–416.

Kebbell, M. & Hatton, C. (1999). People with mental retardation as witnesses in court. *Mental Retardation, 3*, 179–187.

Kebbel, M.R. & Wagstaff, G.F. (1999). *Face value? Evaluating the accuracy of eyewitness information*. Police Research Series Paper No. 102. London: Home Office, Policing and Reducing Crime Unit.

Kebbell, M. & Wagstaff, G. (1998). Hypnotic interviewing: The best way to interview eyewitnesses? *Behavioral Sciences and the Law, 16*, 115–129.

Kelley, H.H. (1972). Attribution in social interaction. In E.E. Jones, D.E. Kanouse, H.H. Kelley, R.E. Nisbett, S. Valins & B. Weiner (eds), *Attribution: perceiving the causes of behavior* (pp. 1–26). Morristown, NJ: General Learning Press.

Kerr, N.L., Davis, J.H., Meek, D. & Rissman, A. (1975). Group position as a function of member attitudes: Choice shift effects from the perspective of social decision scheme theory. *Journal of Personality and Social Psychology, 35*, 574–593.

Kerr, N.L., Hymes, R.W., Anderson, A.B. & Weathers, J.E. (1995). Defendant–juror similarity and mock-juror judgements. *Law and Human Behavior, 19*, 545–568.

Kerwin, J. & Shaffer, D. (1994). Mock jurors versus mock juries: the role of deliberations in reaction to inadmissible testimony. *Personality and Social Psychology Bulletin, 20*, 153–162.

Kiesler, C. (1971). *The psychology of commitment*. New York: Academic Press.

Kihlstrom, J.F., Glisky, M.L. & Angiulo, M.J. (1994). Dissociative tendencies and dissociative disorders. *Journal of Abnormal Psychology, 103*, 117–124.

Klaven, H. & Zeisel, H. (1966). *The American jury*. Chicago: University of Chicago Press.

Kleinmuntz, B. & Szucko, J.J. (1982). On the fallibility of lie detection. *Law and Society Review, 17*, 85–104.

Kleinmuntz, B. & Szucko, J.J. (1984). Lie detection in ancient and modern times: A call for contemporary scientific study. *American Psychologist, 39*, 766–776.

Köhnken, G. (1987). Training police officers to detect deceptive eyewitness statements. Does it work? *Social Behaviour, 2*, 1–17.

Köhnken, G. (1995). Interviewing adults. In R. Bull & D. Carson (eds), *Handbook of psychology in legal contexts* (pp. 216–233). Chichester: Wiley.

Köhnken, G. (1999, July). Statement validity assessment. Paper presented at the pre-conference programme of applied courses "Assessing credibility", organised by the European Association of Psychology and Law, Dublin, Ireland.

Köhnken, G. (2002). A German perspective on children's testimony. In H.L. Westcott, G.M. Davies & R.H.C. Bull (eds), *Children's testimony: A handbook of psychological research and forensic practice* (pp. 233–244). Chichester: Wiley.

Köhnken, G. & Steller, M. (1988). The evaluation of the credibility of child witness statements in German procedural system. In G. Davies & J. Drinkwater (eds), *The child witness: Do the courts abuse children?* (pp. 37–45). Issues in Criminological and Legal Psychology, No. 13. Leicester: British Psychological Society.

Köhnken, G., Malpass, R.S. & Wogalter, M.S. (1996). Forensic applications of lineup research. In S.L. Sporer, R.S. Malpass & G. Köhnken (eds), *Psychological issues in eyewitness identification* (pp. 205–232). Mahwah, NJ: Erlbaum.

Köhnken, G., Schimossek, E., Aschermann, E. & Höfer, E. (1995). The cognitive interview and the assessment of the credibility of adults' statements. *Journal of Applied Psychology, 80*, 671–684.

Kovera, M. (2002). The effects of general pretrial publicity on juror decision: An examination of moderators and mediating mechanisms. *Law and Human Behavior, 26*, 43–72.

Kovera, M., Borgida, E. & Gresham, A. (1996). The impact of child witness preparation and expert testimony on juror decision making. Paper presented at the biennial meeting of the American Psychology-Law Society, Hilton Head, 1 March, 1996.

Kovera, M., Borgida, E., Gresham, A., Swim, J. & Gray, E. (1993). Do child sexual abuse experts hold pro-child beliefs? A survey of the international society for traumatic stress studies. *Journal of Traumatic Stress, 6*, 383–403.

Kozeny, E. (1962). Experimental investigation of physiognomy utilizing a photographic-statistical method. *Archiv für die Gesamte Psychologie, 114*, 55–71.

Kramer, G.P., Kerr, N.L. & Carroll, J.S. (1990). Pretrial publicity: Judicial remedies and jury bias. *Law and Human Behavior, 14*, 409–438.

Krauss, R.M. (1981). Impression formation, impression management, and nonverbal behaviors. In E.T. Higgins, C.P. Herman & M.P. Zanna (eds), *Social cognition: The Ontario Symposium* (vol. 1, pp. 323–341). Hillsdale, NJ: Erlbaum.

Kunda, Z. & Thagard, P. (1996). Forming impressions from stereotypes, traits and behaviors: A parallel-constraint-satisfaction theory. *Psychological Review, 103*, 284–308.

Kurtzberg, R., Safar, H. & Cavior, N. (1968). Surgical and social rehabilitation of adult offenders. *Proceedings of the 76th Annual Convention of the American Psychological Association, 3*, 649–650.

LaFrance, M. & Mayo, C. (1976). Racial differences in gaze behaviour during conversations: Two systematic observational studies. *Journal of Personality and Social Psychology, 33*, 547–552.

Lamb, M. & Sternberg, K. (1995). Making children into competent witnesses: Reactions to the Amichs Brief in Michaels. *Psychology, Public Policy, and Law, 1*, 438–449.

Lamb, M., Orbach, Y., Sternberg, K., Esplin, P. & Hershkowitz, I. (2002). The effects of forensic interview practices on the quality of information provided by alleged victims of child abuse. In H. Westcott, G. Davies & R. Bull (eds), *Children's testimony: A handbook of psychology research and forensic practice*. Chichester: Wiley.

Lamers-Winkelman, F. & Buffing, F. (1996). Children's testimony in the Netherlands: A study of statement validity analysis. In B.L. Bottoms & G.S. Goodman (1996), *International perspectives on child abuse and children's testimony* (pp. 45–62). Thousand Oaks, CA: Sage.

Lampinen, J. & Smith, V. (1995). The incredible (and sometimes incredulous) child witness: Child eyewitnesses' sensitivity to source credibility cues. *Journal of Applied Psychology, 80*, 621–627.

Lampinen, J.M., Neuschatz, J.S. & Payne, D.G. (1998). Memory illusions and consciousness: Examining the phenomenology of true and false memories. *Current Psychology: Developmental, Learning, Personality, Social, 16*, 181–224.

Lane, J.D. & DePaulo, B.M. (1999). Completing Coyne's cycle: Dysphorics' ability to detect deception. *Journal of Research in Personality, 33*, 311–329.

Langlois, J., Kalakanis, L., Rubenstein, A., Larson, A., Hallam, M. & Smoot, M. (2000). Maxims or myths of beauty? A meta-analytic and theoretical review. *Psychological Bulletin, 126*, 390-423.

Lassiter, G.D. & Irvine, A.A. (1986). Videotaped confessions: The impact of camera point of view on judgments of coercion. *Journal of Applied Social Psychology, 16*, 268–276.

Latané, B. (1981). The psychology of social impact. *American Psychologist, 36*, 343–356.

Lavrakas, P.J., Buri, J.R. & Mayzner, M.S. (1976). A perspective on the recognition of other-race faces. *Perception and Psychophysics, 20*, 475–481.

Leichtman, M.D. & Ceci, S.J. (1995). The effects of stereotypes and suggestions on preschoolers' reports. *Developmental Psychology, 31*, 568–578.

Leippe, M., Wells, G. & Ostrom, T. (1978). Crime seriousness as a determinant of accuracy in eyewitness identification. *Journal of Applied Psychology, 63*, 345–351.

Leippe, M.R. (1985). The influence of eyewitness nonidentifications on mock jurors' judgements of a court case. *Journal of Applied Social Psychology, 15*, 656–672.

Leippe, M.R. (1995). The case for expert testimony about eyewitness memory. *Psychology, Public Policy, and Law, 1*, 909–959.

Leo, R.A. (1992). From coercion to deception: The changing nature of police interrogation in America. *Crime, Law, and Social Change, 18*, 33–59.

Leo, R.A. (1996a). Inside the interrogation room. *Journal of Criminal Law and Criminology, 86*, 266–303.

Leo, R.A. (1996b). *Miranda's* revenge: Police interrogation as a confidence game. *Law and Society Review, 30*, 259–288.

Leo, R.A. & Ofshe, R.J. (1998). The consequences of false confessions: Deprivations of liberty and miscarriages of justice in the age of psychological interrogation. *Journal of Criminal Law and Criminology, 88*, 429–496.

Levine, L.J. (1997). Reconstructing memory for emotions. *Journal of Experimental Psychology: General, 126*, 165–177.

Levy, R.J. (1989). Using scientific testimony to prove child abuse: The Dorsey and Whitney professorship procedure. *Family Law Quarterly, 23*, 383–409.

Lewison, E. (1974). Twenty years of prison surgery: An evaluation. *Canadian Journal of Otolaryngology, 3*, 42–50.

Lindholm, T. & Christianson, S. (1998). Intergroup biases and eyewitness testimony. *Journal of Social Psychology, 138*, 710–723.

Lindsay, D.S. & Read, J.D. (1994). Psychotherapy and memories of childhood sexual abuse: A cognitive perspective. *Applied Cognitive Psychology, 8*, 281–338.

Lindsay, D.S., Read, J.D. & Sharma, K. (1998). Accuracy and confidence in person identification: The relationship is strong when witnessing conditions vary widely. *Psychological Science, 9*, 215–218.

Lindsay, R.C.L. (1994a). Biased lineups: Where do they come from? In D.F. Ross, J.D. Read & M.P. Toglia (eds), *Adult eyewitness testimony: Current trends and developments* (pp. 182–200). New York: Cambridge University Press.

Lindsay, R.C.L. (1994b). Expectations of eyewitness performance: Jurors' verdicts do not follow from their beliefs. In D.F. Ross, J.D. Read & M.P. Toglia (eds), *Adult eyewitness testimony: Current trends and developments* (pp. 362–384). New York: Cambridge University Press.

Lindsay, R.C.L. & Wells, G.L. (1985). Improving eyewitness identifications from lineups: Simultaneous versus sequential lineup presentations. *Journal of Applied Psychology, 70*, 556–564.

Lindsay, R.C.L., Martin, R. & Webber, L. (1994). Default values in eyewitness descriptions. *Law and Human Behavior, 18*, 527–541.

Lindsay, R.C.L., Wallbridge, H. & Drennan, D. (1987). Do the clothes make the man? An exploration of the effect of lineup attire on eyewitness identification accuracy. *Canadian Journal of Behavioral Science, 19*, 463–477.

Lindsay, R.C.L., Wells, G.L. & Rumpel, C.H. (1981). Can people detect eyewitness-identification accuracy within and across situations? *Journal of Applied Psychology, 66*, 77–89.

Lippard, P.V. (1988). "Ask me no questions, I'll tell you no lies": Situational exigencies for interpersonal deception. *Western Journal of Speech Communication, 52*, 91–103.

Littmann, E. & Szewczyk, H. (1983). Zu einigen Kriterien und Ergebnissen forensisch psychologischer Glaubwürdigkeitsbegutachtungen von sexuell misbrauchten Kindern und Jugendlichen. *Forensia, 4*, 55–72.

Lloyd-Bostock, S. (2000). The effects on juries of hearing about the defendant's previous criminal record: A simulation study. *Criminal Law Review, 62*, 734–755.

Lloyd-Bostock, S. & Thomas, C. (1999). Decline of the 'little jury parliament': Juries and jury reform in England and Wales. *Law and Contemporary Problems, 62*, 7–40.

Lockart v. *McCree* (1986). 106 S.Ct. 1758.

Loftus, E. & Davies, G. (1984). Distortions in the memory of children. *Journal of Social Issues, 40*, 51–67.

Loftus, E. & Ketcham, K. (1994). *The myth of repressed memory*. New York: St Martin's Press.

Loftus, E.F. (1976). Unconscious transference in eyewitness identification. *Law and Psychology Review, 2*, 93–98.

Loftus, E.F. (1986). Experimental psychologist as advocate or impartial educator. *Law and Human Behavior, 10,* 63–78.

Loftus, E.F. & Palmer, J.C. (1974). Reconstructions of automobile destruction: An example of the interaction between language and memory. *Journal of Verbal Learning and Verbal Behavior, 13,* 585–589.

Loftus, E.F. & Pickrell, J. (1995). The formation of false memories. *Psychiatric Annals, 25,* 720–725.

Loftus, E.F., Loftus, G.R. & Messo, J. (1987). Some facts about "weapon focus". *Law and Human Behavior, 11,* 55–62.

Loftus, E.F., Miller, D.G. & Burns, H.J. (1978). Semantic integration of verbal information into a visual memory. *Journal of Experimental Psychology: Human Learning and Memory, 4,* 19–31.

Loftus, E.F., Weingardt, K.R. & Hoffman, H.G. (1993). Sleeping memories on trial: Reactions to memories that were previously repressed. *Expert Evidence: The International Digest of Human Behaviour, Science and the Law, 2,* 51–60.

London, K. & Nunez, N. (2000). The effect of jury deliberation on jurors' propensity to disregard inadmissible evidence. *Journal of Applied Psychology, 85,* 932–39.

Lowenstein, L.F. (1999). Aspects of confessions: What the legal profession should know. *Justice of the Peace, 163,* 586–591.

Luus, C.A.E. & Wells, G.L. (1994a). Eyewitness identification performance. In D.F. Ross, J.D. Read & M.P. Toglia (eds), *Adult eyewitness testimony: Current trends and developments* (pp. 348–361). New York: Cambridge University Press.

Luus, C.A.E. & Wells, G.L. (1994b). The malleability of eyewitness confidence: Co-witness and perseverance effects. *Journal of Applied Psychology, 66,* 482–489.

Lykken, D.T. (1959). The GSR in the detection of guilt. *Journal of Applied Psychology, 43,* 385–388.

Lykken, D.T. (1960). The validity of the guilty knowledge technique: The effects of faking. *Journal of Applied Psychology, 44,* 258–262.

Lykken, D.T. (1988). The case against polygraph testing. In A. Gale (ed.), *The polygraph test: Lies, truth, and science* (pp. 111–126). London: Sage.

Lykken, D.T. (1991). Why (some) Americans believe in the lie detector while others believe in the Guilty Knowledge Test. *Integrative Physiological and Behavioral Science, 126,* 214–222.

Lykken, D.T. (1998). *A tremor in the blood: Uses and abuses of the lie detector.* New York: Plenum.

Maass, A. & Köhnken, G. (1989). Eyewitness identification: Simulating the "weapon effect". *Law and Human Behavior, 13,* 397–408.

Maass, A. & Brigham, J. (1982). Eyewitness identifications—the role of attention and encoding specificity. *Personality and Social Psychology Bulletin, 8,* 44–59.

MacCoun, R. (1990). The emergence of extralegal bias during jury deliberation. *Criminal Justice and Behavior, 17,* 303–314.

Mack, J. (1994). *Abduction: Human encounters with aliens.* New York: Scribners.

MacLaren, V.C. (2001). A quantitative review of the Guilty Knowledge Test. *Journal of Applied Psychology, 86,* 674–683.

Maclean, H. (1993). *Once upon a time.* New York: HarperCollins.

Macoubrie, J. (2002). *On stories in jury deliberation.* Submitted.

Macrae, C.N. & Shepherd, J. (1989a). Do criminal stereotypes mediate juridic judgements? *British Journal of Social Psychology, 28,* 189–191.

Macrae, C.N. & Shepherd, J. (1989b). The good, the bad, and the ugly: Facial stereotyping and juridic judgements. *Police Journal, 2,* 194–199.

Macrae, C.N., Bodenhausen, G.V., Milne, A.B. & Castelli, L. (2001). On disregarding deviants: Exemplar typicality and person perception. In H.D. Ellis & C.N. Macrae (eds), *Validation in psychology.* New Brunswick, NJ: Transaction.

Maguire, M. (1994). The wrong message at the wrong time? The present state of investigative practice. In D. Morgan & G.M. Stephenson (eds), *Suspicions and silence: The right to silence in criminal investigations* (pp. 39–49). London: Blackstone.

Malpass, R.S. (1996). Enhancing eyewitness memory. In S.L. Sporer, R.S. Malpass & G. Köhnken (eds), *Psychological issues in eyewitness identification* (pp. 177–204). Mahwah, NJ: Erlbaum.

Malpass, R.S. & Devine, P.G. (1981). Eyewitness identification: Lineup instructions and the absence of the offender. *Journal of Applied Psychology, 66,* 482–489.

Malpass, R.S. & Devine, P.G. (1984). Research on suggestion in lineups and photo-spreads. In G.L. Wells & E.F. Loftus (eds), *Eyewitness testimony: Psychological perspectives* (pp. 64–91). New York: Cambridge University Press.

Mandler, G. (1980). Recognizing: The judgment of previous occurrence. *Psychological Review, 75,* 421–441.

Mann, S. (2001). Suspects, lies and videotape: An investigation into telling and detecting lies in police/suspect interviews. Unpublished Ph.D. thesis, University of Portsmouth, Psychology Department.

Mann, S., Vrij, A. & Bull, R. (2002). Suspects, lies and videotape: An analysis of authentic high-stake liars. *Law and Human Behaviour, 26,* 365–376.

Marche, T. (1999). Memory strength affects reporting of misinformation. *Journal of Experimental Child Psychology, 73,* 45–71.

Marques, J.M. (1990). The black sheep effect: outgroup homogeneity in social comparison settings. In D. Abrams & M. Hogg (eds), *Social identity theory: Constructive and critical advances* (pp. 131–151). London: Harvester Wheatsheaf.

Martin, A.M., Kaplan, M.F. & Alamo, J. (2003, in press). Discussion content and perception of deliberation in Western European vs. American juries. *Psychology, Crime and Law.*

Masters, F. & Greaves, D. (1967). The Quasimodo complex. *British Journal of Plastic Surgery, 20,* 204–210.

Mattika, L. & Vesala, H. (1997). Acquiescence in quality of life interviews with adults who have mental retardation. *Mental Retardation, 35,* 75–82.

Mazzella, R. & Feingold, A. (1994). The effects of physical attractiveness, race, socioeconomic status, and gender of defendants and victims on judgements of mock jurors: A meta-analysis. *Journal of Applied Social Psychology, 24,* 1315–1344.

Mazzoni, G. & Memon, A. (2003). The effect of imagination on autobiographical beliefs and memories. *Psychological Science, 14,* 186–188.

Mazzoni, G.A.L. & Kirsch, I. (2003). Autobiographical memories and beliefs: A preliminary metacognitive model. In T. Perfect & B. Schwartz (eds), *Applied metacognition* (pp. 121–145). Cambridge: Cambridge University Press.

Mazzoni, G.A.L., Loftus, E.F. & Kirsch, I. (2001). Changing beliefs about implausible autobiographical events: A little plausibility goes a long way. *Journal of Experimental Psychology: Applied, 7,* 51–59.

Mazzoni, G.A.L., Loftus, E.F., Seitz, A. & Lynn, S.J. (1999). Changing beliefs and memories through dream interpretation. *Applied Cognitive Psychology, 13,* 125–144.

McCann, J.T. (1998a). A conceptual framework for identifying various types of confessions. *Behavioral Sciences and the Law, 16,* 441–453.

McCann, J.T. (1998b). Broadening the typology of false confessions. *American Psychologist, 53,* 319–320.

McClelland, J.L. & Chappell, M. (1998). Familiarity breeds differentiation: A subjective likelihood approach to the effects of experience in recognition memory. *Psychological Review, 105,* 724–760.

McCloskey, M. & Egeth, H. (1983). Eyewitness identification: What can a psychologist tell a jury? *American Psychologist, 38,* 550–563.

McCloskey, M. & Zaragoza, M. (1985). Misleading postevent information and memory for events: Arguments and evidence against memory impairment hypotheses. *Journal of Experimental Psychology, 114,* 3–18.

McConville, M. (1992). Videotaping interrogations. *New Law Journal, 10,* 960–962.

McConville, M. & Hodgson, J. (1993). *Custodial legal advice and the right to silence.* Royal Commission on Criminal Justice Research, Research Study No. 16. London: HMSO.

McEwan, J. (1998). *Evidence and the adversarial process: The modern law.* Oxford: Hart.

McGuire, M. & Bermant, G. (1977). Individual and group decisions in response to a mock trial: A methodological note. *Journal of Applied Social Psychology, 3,* 200–226.

McGurk, B., Carr, J. & McGurk, D. (1993). *Investigative interviewing courses for police officers: An evaluation.* Police Research Series: Paper No. 4. London: Home Office.

McKelvie, S. & Coley, J. (1993). Effects of crime seriousness and offender facial attractiveness on recommended treatment. *Social Behavior and Personality, 21,* 265–277.

McKenzie, I.K. (1994). Regulating custodial interviews: A comparative study. *International Journal of the Sociology of Law, 22,* 239–259.

Meissner, C.A. & Brigham, J.C. (2001a). A meta-analysis of the verbal overshadowing effect in face identification. *Applied Cognitive Psychology, 15,* 603–616.

Meissner, C.A. & Brigham, J.C. (2001b). Thirty years of investigating the own-race bias in memory for faces: A meta-analytic review. *Psychology, Public Policy, and Law, 7,* 3–35.

Meissner, C.A., Brigham, J.C. & Kelley, C.M. (2001). The influence of retrieval processes in verbal overshadowing. *Memory and Cognition, 29,* 176–186.

Melinder, A. (2001). Interviewers' perception of children's recall: What is helpful? In M. Korsenes, A. Raftopoulos & A. Demetrion (eds), *Studies of the mind: Proceedings of the first Norwegian–Cypriot meeting on cognitive psychology and neuropsychology.* Nicosia, Cyprus: Cassoulides.

Memon, A. & Bartlett, J.C. (2002). The effects of verbalisation on face recognition. *Applied Cognitive Psychology, 16,* 635–650.

Memon, A. & Bull, R. (1999). *Handbook of the psychology of interviewing.* Chichester: Wiley.

Memon, A. & Gabbert, F. (in press). Unravelling the effects of a sequential lineup. *Applied Cognitive Psychology.*

Memon, A. & Gabbert, F. (in press). Improving the identification accuracy of senior witnesses: Do pre-lineup questions and sequential testing help? *Journal of Applied Psychology.*

Memon, A. & Rose, R. (2002). Identification abilities of children: Does verbalisation impair face and dog recognition? *Psychology, Crime, and Law, 8,* 229–242.

Memon, A. & Wright, D. (2000). Eyewitness testimony: Theoretical and practical issues. In J. McGuire, T. Mason & A. O'Kane (eds), *Behaviour, crime, and legal process* (pp. 65–82). Wiley: Chichester.

Memon, A. & Young, M. (1997). Desperately seeking evidence: The recovered memory debate. *Legal and Criminological Psychology, 2,* 131–154.

Memon, A., Bartlett, J. & Rose, R. (2002). *Ageing and eyewitness identification: Moderators of false choosing.* Submitted.

Memon, A., Holley, A., Wark, L., Bull, R. & Köehnken, G. (1996). Reducing suggestibility in child witness interviews. *Applied Cognitive Psychology, 10,* 503–518.

Memon, A., Hope, L. & Bull, R.H.C. (in press). Exposure duration: Effects on eyewitness accuracy and confidence. *British Journal of Psychology.*

Memon, A., Hope, L., Bartlett, J. & Bull, R. (2002). Eyewitness recognition errors: The effects of mugshot viewing and choosing in young and old adults. *Memory and Cognition, 30,* 1219–1227.

Memon, A., Hope, L. & Gabbert, F. (2002). "Gut feeling": Eyewitness expectations and identifications. Paper presented at the American Psychology-Law Society Meeting, Austin, Texas.

Memon, A., Wark, L., Bull, R. & Köehnken, G. (1997). Isolating the effects of the cognitive interview. *British Journal of Psychology, 88*, 179–197.

Metts, S. (1989). An exploratory investigation of deception in close relationships. *Journal of Social and Personal Relationships, 6*, 159–179.

Meyer, J. & Jesilow, P. (1996). Obedience to authority: Possible effects on children's testimony. *Psychology, Crime, and Law, 3*, 81–95.

Milgram, S. (1974). *Obedience to authority: An experimental view.* New York: Harper and Row.

Miller, G.R. & Stiff, J.B. (1993). *Deceptive communication.* Newbury Park, CA: Sage.

Mills, C.J. & Bohannon, W.E. (1980). Juror characteristics: To what extent are they related to jury verdicts? *Judicature, 64*, 23–31.

Milne, R. & Bull, R. (1996). Interviewing children with mild learning disability with the cognitive interview. In N.K. Clarke & G.M. Stephenson (eds), *Investigative and forensic decision making: Issues in Criminological Psychology, No. 26.* Leicester: British Psychological Society.

Milne, R. & Bull, R. (1999). *Investigative interviewing: Psychology and practice.* Chichester: Wiley.

Milne, R. & Bull, R. (2002). Back to basics: A componential analysis of the original cognitive interview mnemonics with three age groups. *Applied Cognitive Psychology, 16*, 743–753.

Milne, R. & Bull, R. (2003). Interviewing by the police. In D. Carson & R. Bull (eds), *Handbook of psychology in legal contexts*, 2nd edn. Chichester: Wiley.

Milne, R. & Bull, R. (in press). Does the cognitive interview help children to resist the effects of suggestive questioning? *Legal and Criminological Psychology.*

Milne, R., Clare, I. & Bull, R. (1999). Interviewing adults with learning disability with the cognitive interview. *Psychology, Crime, and Law, 5*, 81–100.

Milne, R., Clare, I. & Bull, R. (2002). Interrogative suggestibility among witnesses with mild intellectual disabilities: The use of an adaptation of the GSS. *Journal of Applied Research in Intellectual Disabilities, 15*, 8–17.

Mitchell, K. & Johnson, M.K. (2000). Source monitoring: Attributing mental experiences. In E. Tulving & F.I.M. Craik (eds), *The Oxford handbook of memory* (pp. 179–196). Oxford: Oxford University Press.

Montero-Aroca, J. & Gomez-Colomer, J.J. (eds) (1999). *Comentarios a la ley del jurado.* Pamplona: Aranzadi.

Moran, G. & Comfort, J.C. (1982). Scientific jury selection: Sex as a moderator of demographic and personality predictors of impaneled felony jury behaviour. *Journal of Personality and Social Psychology, 47*, 1052–1063.

Mortimer, A. (1994). Cognitive processes underlying police investigative interviewing behaviour. Unpublished Ph.D. thesis. University of Portsmouth, Psychology Department.

Mortimer, A. & Shepherd, E. (1999). Frames of mind: Schemata guiding cognition and conduct in the interviewing of suspected offenders. In A. Memon & R. Bull (eds), *Handbook of the psychology of interviewing* (pp. 293–315). Chichester: Wiley.

Moscovici, S. (1985). Social influence and conformity. In G. Lindzey & E. Aronson (eds), *The handbook of social psychology* (pp. 347–412). New York: Random House.

Moston, S. (1996). From denial to admission in police questioning of suspects. In G. Davies, S. Lloyd-Bostock, M. McMurran & C. Wilson (eds), *Psychology, law, and criminal justice: International developments in research and practice* (pp. 91–99). Berlin: de Gruyter.

Moston, S. (1987). The suggestibility of children in interview studies. *Child Language, 7*, 67–78.

Moston, S.J. & Stephenson, G.M. (1994). Helping the police with their enquiries outside the police station. In D. Morgan & G.M. Stephenson (eds), *Suspicion and silence: The right to silence in criminal investigations* (pp. 50–65). London: Blackstone.

Moston, S.J. & Engelberg, T. (1993). Police questioning techniques in tape-recorded interviews with criminal suspects. *Policing and Society, 3*, 223–237.

Moston, S. & Stephenson, G.M. (1992). Predictors of suspect and interviewer behaviour during police questioning. In F. Lösel, D. Bender & T. Bliesener (eds), *Psychology and law: International perspectives* (pp. 212–219). Berlin: de Gruyter.

Moston, S. & Stephenson, G.M. (1993a). The changing face of police interrogation. *Journal of Community and Applied Social Psychology, 3*, 101–115.

Moston, S. & Stephenson, G.M. (1993b). *The questioning and interviewing of suspects outside the police station*. Royal Commission on Criminal Justice, Research Study No. 23. London: HMSO.

Moston, S., Stephenson, G.M. & Williamson, T.M. (1992). The effects of case characteristics on suspect behaviour during police questioning. *British Journal of Criminology, 32*, 23–40.

Moston, S.J., Stephenson, G.M. & Williamson, T.M. (1993). The incidence, antecedents and consequences of the use of the right to silence during police questioning. *Criminal Behaviour and Mental Health, 3*, 30–47.

Mullin, C. (1989). *Error of judgment: The truth about the Birmingham bombers*. Dublin: Poolberg.

Myers, J.E.B. (1993). Expert testimony regarding child sexual abuse. *Child Abuse and Neglect, 17*, 175–185.

Myklebust, T. & Alison, L. (2000). The current state of police interviews with children in Norway: How discrepant are they from models based on current issues in memory and communication? *Psychology, Crime, and Law, 6*, 331–351.

Narby, D.J., Cutler, B.L. & Penrod, S.D. (1996). The effects of witness, target and situational factors on eyewitness identifications. In S.L. Sporer, R.S. Malpass & G. Köhnken (eds), *Psychological issues in eyewitness identification* (pp. 53–86). Mahwah, NJ: Erlbaum.

NCF (1998). *A practical guide to investigative interviewing*. Bramshill: National Crime Faculty and National Police Training.

Newby, I.R. & Ross, M. (1996). Beyond the correspondence metaphor: When accuracy cannot be assessed. *Brain and Behavioral Sciences, 19*, 205–206.

Nijboer, H. (1995). Expert evidence. In Bull, R. & Carson, D. (eds), *Handbook of psychology in legal contexts*. Chichester: Wiley.

O'Barr, W. (1982). *Linguistic evidence: Language, power and strategy in the courtroom*. New York: Academic Press.

O'Connor, M., Sales, B. & Shuman, D.W. (1996). Mental health professional expertise in the courtroom, In B. Sales & D. Shuman (eds), *Law, mental health and mental disorder* (pp. 40–59). New York: Brooks Cole.

O'Donnell, C. & Bruce, V. (2000). The Batman effect: Selective enhancement of facial features during familiarisation. *Perception, 29*, 76–76.

Ofshe, R. (1989). Coerced confessions: The logic of seemingly irrational action. *Cultic Studies Journal, 6*, 1–15.

Ofshe, R.J. & Leo, R.A. (1997a). The decision to confess falsely: Rational choice and irrational action. *Denver University Law Review, 74*, 979–1112.

Ofshe, R.J. & Leo, R.A. (1997b). The social psychology of police interrogation: The theory and classification of true and false confessions. *Studies in Law, Politics, and Society, 16*, 189–251.

Olio, K.A. & Cornell, W.F. (1998). The facade of scientific documentation: A case study of Richard Ofshe's analysis of the Paul Ingram case. *Psychology, Public Policy, and Law, 4*, 1182–1197.

Ord, B. & Shaw, G. (1999). *Investigative interviewing explained.* Woking: New Police Bookshop.

Ornstein, P., Baker-Ward, L., Myers, J., Principe, G. & Gordon, B. (1995). Young children's long-term retention of medical experiences: Implications for testimony. In F. Weinert & W. Schneider (eds), *Memory performance and competencies: Issues in growth and development.* Hillsdale, NJ: Erlbaum.

Ost, J., Vrij, A., Costall, A. & Bull, R. (2002). Crashing memories and reality monitoring: Distinguishing between perceptions, imagings, and false memories. *Applied Cognitive Psychology, 16,* 125–134.

Otte, M. (1998). Het onderzoek ter terechtzitting. *Justitiële Verkenningen, 24,* 26–36.

Paterson, B. & Bull, R. (1999). Young children's recall after long delays. Paper presented at the Annual Conference of the European Association of Psychology and Law, Dublin.

Paterson, B., Bull, R. & Vrij, A. (2000). Children's individual cognitive abilities in relation to event recall and suggestibility. Paper presented at the Annual Conference of the European Association of Psychology and Law, Limassol, Cyprus.

Paterson, B., Bull, R. & Vrij, A. (2001). Individual differences in children's event recall. Paper presented at the Annual Conference of the European Association of Psychology and Law, Lisbon, Portugal.

Paterson, B., Bull, R. & Vrij, A. (2002). The effects of interviewer style on children's recall. Paper presented at the 25th International Congress of Applied Psychology, Singapore.

Patrick, C.J. & Iacono, W.G. (1991). Validity of the control question polygraph test: The problem of sampling bias. *Journal of Applied Psychology, 76,* 229–238.

Pavlidis, J., Eberhardt, N.L. & Levine, J.A. (2002). Seeing through the face of deception. *Nature, 415,* 35.

Payne, D.G. (1987). Hypermnesia and reminiscence in recall: A historical and empirical review. *Psychological Bulletin, 101,* 5–27.

Payne, D.G., Elie, C.J., Blackwell, J.M. & Neuschatz, J.S. (1996). Memory illusions: Recalling, recognising, and recollecting events that never occurred. *Journal of Memory and Language, 35,* 261–285.

Payne, D.G., Neuschatz, J.S., Lampinen, J.M. & Lynn, S.J. (1997). Compelling memory illusions: The qualitative characteristics of false memories. *Current Directions in Psychological Sciences, 6,* 56–60.

Pearse, J. (1995). Police interviewing: The identification of vulnerabilities. *Journal of Community and Applied Social Psychology, 5,* 147–159.

Pearse, J. & Gudjonsson, G.H. (1996a). A review of the role of the legal advisers in police stations. *Criminal Behaviour and Mental Health, 6,* 241–249.

Pearse, J. & Gudjonsson, G.H. (1996b). How appropriate are appropriate adults? *Journal of Forensic Psychiatry, 7,* 570–580.

Pearse, J. & Gudjonsson, G.H. (1996c). Police interviewing techniques at two south London police stations. *Psychology, Crime and Law, 3,* 63–74.

Pearse, J. & Gudjonsson, G.H. (1996d). Understanding the problems of the appropriate adult. *Expert Evidence, 4,* 101–104.

Pearse, J. & Gudjonsson, G.H. (1997a). Police interviewing and legal representation: A field study. *Journal of Forensic Psychiatry, 8,* 200–208.

Pearse, J. & Gudjonsson, G.H. (1997b). Police interviewing and mentally disordered offenders: Changing the role of the legal adviser. *Expert Evidence, 5,* 49–53.

Pearse, J. & Gudjonsson, G.H. (1999). Measuring influential police interviewing tactics: A factor analytic approach. *Legal and Criminological Psychology, 4,* 221–238.

Pearse, J., Gudjonsson, G.H., Clare, I.C.H. & Rutter, S. (1998). Police interviewing and psychological vulnerabilities: Predicting the likelihood of a confession. *Journal of Community and Applied Social Psychology, 8,* 1–21.

Pennebaker, J.W. & Memon, A. (1996). Recovered memories in context: Thoughts and elaborations on Bowers and Farvolden. *Psychological Bulletin, 119*, 381–385.

Pennington, N. & Hastie, R. (1986). Evidence evaluation in complex decision making. *Journal of Personality and Social Psychology, 51*, 242–258.

Penrod, S. & Heuer, L. (1998). Improving group performance: The case of the jury. In R.S. Tindale (ed.), *Theory and research on small groups* (pp. 127–151). New York: Plenum.

Penrod, S.D., Fulero, S.M. & Cutler, B.L. (1995). Expert psychological testimony on eyewitness reliability before and after Daubert: The state of the law and the science. *Behavioral Sciences and the Law, 13*, 229–259.

Perr, I.N. (1990). "False confessions" and identification with the aggressor: Another forensic misuse of a psychiatric concept. *Bulletin of the American Academy of Psychiatry and Law, 18*, 143–151.

Perske, R. (1994). Johnny Lee Wilson did not kill anybody. *Mental Retardation, 32*, 157–159.

Perske, R. (1994). Thoughts on police interrogation of individuals with mental retardation. *Mental Retardation, 32*, 377–380.

Peterson, C. (1999). Children's memory for medical emergencies: 2 years later. *Developmental Psychology, 35*, 1493–1506.

Petty, R. & Cacioppo, J. (2000). *Communication and persuasion: Central and peripheral routes to attitude change.* New York: Springer-Verlag.

Pezdek, K., Finger, K. & Hodge, D. (1997). Planting false childhood memories: The role of event plausibility. *Psychological Science, 8*, 437–441.

Phillips, M., McAuliff, B., Kovera, M. & Cutler, B. (1999). Double-blind photoarray administration as a safeguard against investigator bias. *Journal of Applied Psychology, 84*, 940–951.

Pick, J. (1948). Ten years of plastic surgery in a penal institution: Preliminary report. *Journal of the International College of Surgeons, 11*, 315–319.

Pickel, K. (1999). The influence of "context" on the weapon focus effect. *Law and Human Behavior, 23*, 299–313.

Pipe, M. & Salmon, K. (2002). What children bring to the interview context: Individual differences in children's event reports. In M. Eisen, J. Quas & G. Goodman (eds), *Memory and suggestibility in the forensic interview* (pp. 235–261). Hillsdale, NJ: Erlbaum.

Platt, R.D., Lacey, S.C., Iobst, A.D. & Finkleman, D. (1998). Absorption, dissociation, and fantasy-proneness as predictors of memory distortion in autobiographical and laboratory-generated memories. *Applied Cognitive Psychology, 12*, 77–89.

Plimmer, J. (1997). Confession rate. *Police Review, 7 February*, 16–18.

Podlesney, J.A. (1995). *A lack of operable case facts restricts applicability of the guilty knowledge deception detection method in FBI criminal investigations.* FBI Technical Report, Quantico, VA.

Police and Criminal Evidence Act 1984 (Codes of Practice) Order 1988, HMSO.

Poole, D. & Lamb, M. (1998). *Investigative interviews with children: A guide for helping professionals.* Washington, DC: American Psychological Association.

Poole, D. & Lindsay, D.S. (1998). Assessing the accuracy of young children's reports: Lessons from the investigation of child sexual abuse. *Applied and Preventative Psychology, 7*, 1–26.

Poole, D. & Lindsay, D.S. (2001). Children's eyewitness reports after exposure to misinformation from parents. *Journal of Experimental Psychology: Applied, 7*, 27–50.

Poole, D.A. & White, L.T. (1991). Effects of question repetition and retention interval on the eyewitness testimony of children and adults. *Developmental Psychology, 27*, 975–986.

Poole, D.A., Lindsay, D.S., Memon, A. & Bull, R. (1995). Psychotherapy and the recovery of memories of childhood sexual abuse: U.S. and British practitioners' opinions, practices and experiences. *Journal of Consulting and Clinical Psychology, 63*, 426–437.

Porter, S. & Birt, A. (2001). Is traumatic memory special? A comparison of traumatic memory characteristics with memory for other emotional life experiences. *Applied Cognitive Psychology, 15,* 101–118.

Porter, S. & Yuille, J.C. (1996). The language of deceit: An investigation of the verbal clues to deception in the interrogation context. *Law and Human Behavior, 20,* 443–459.

Porter, S., Birt, A., Yuille, J.C. & Lehman, D. (2000). Negotiating false memories: Interviewer and rememberer characteristics relate to memory distortion. *Psychological Science, 11,* 507–510.

Porter, S., Woodworth, M. & Birt, A.R. (2000). Truth, lies, and videotape: An investigation of the ability of federal parole officers to detect deception. *Law and Human Behaviour, 24,* 643–658.

Porter, S., Yuille, J. & Bent, A. (1995). A comparison of the eyewitness accounts of deaf and hearing children. *Child Abuse and Neglect, 19,* 51–61.

Pozzulo, J.D. & Lindsay, R.C.L. (1998). Identification accuracy of children versus adults: A meta-analysis. *Law and Human Behavior, 22,* 549–570.

Pozzulo, J. & Lindsay, R. (1999). Elimination line-ups: An improved identification procedure for child eyewitnesses. *Journal of Applied Psychology, 84,* 167–176.

Price, E. (1996). Stereotyping of criminality by children of different ages: Are facially attractive people perceived as less criminal? Unpublished B.Sc. Psychology final year research project report. Department of Psychology, University of Portsmouth.

Pritchard, M.E. & Kennan, J.N. (2002). Does jury deliberation really improve jurors' memories? *Applied Cognitive Psychology, 16,* 589–601.

Quas, J., Eisen, M. & Rivers, V. (2000). The influence of interviewer-provided social support on maltreated children's memory and suggestibility. Paper presented at the Biennial Convention of the American Psychology-Law Society, New Orleans.

Quas, J., Goodman, G., Bidrose, S., Pipe, M-E., Craw, S. & Ablin, D. (1999). Emotion and memory: Children's long-term remembering, forgetting and suggestibility. *Journal of Experimental Child Psychology, 72,* 235–270.

R v. *Maxwell* (1990) High Court of England (unreported).

Rahaim, G.L. & Brodsky, S.L. (1982). Empirical evidence versus common sense: Juror and lawyer knowledge of eyewitness accuracy. *Law and Psychology Review, 7,* 1–15.

Raskin, D.C. (1979). Orienting and defensive reflexes in the detection of deception. In H.D. Kimmel, E. H. Van Olst & J. F. Orlebeke (eds), *The orienting reflex in humans* (pp. 587–605). Hillsdale, NJ: Erlbaum.

Raskin, D.C. (1982). The scientific basis of polygraph techniques and their uses in the judicial process. In A. Trankell (eds), *Reconstructing the past* (pp. 317–371). Stockholm: Norsted & Soners.

Raskin, D.C. (1986). The polygraph in 1986: Scientific, professional, and legal issues surrounding acceptance of polygraph evidence. *Utah Law Review, 29,* 29–74.

Raskin, D.C. (1988). Does science support polygraph testing? In A. Gale (ed.), *The polygraph test: Lies, truth and science* (pp. 96–110). London: Sage.

Raskin, D.C. (1989). Polygraph techniques for the detection of deception. In D.C. Raskin (ed.), *Psychological methods in criminal investigation and evidence* (pp. 247–296). New York: Springer-Verlag.

Raskin, D.C. & Esplin, P.W. (1991). Statement validity assessment: Interview procedures and content analysis of children's statements of sexual abuse. *Behavioral Assessment, 13,* 265–291.

Raskin, D.C. & Steller, M. (1989). Assessing the credibility of allegations of child sexual abuse: Polygraph examinations and statement analysis. In H. Wegener, F. Losel & J. Haisch (eds), *Criminal behavior and the justice system* (pp. 290–302). New York: Springer.

Raskin, D.C. & Yuille, J.C. (1989). Problems in evaluating interviews of children in sexual abuse cases. In S.J. Ceci, D.F. Ross & M.P. Toglia (eds), *Perspectives on children's testimony* (pp. 184–207). New York: Springer.

Ratneshwar, S. & Chaiken, S. (1991). Comprehension's role in persuasion: The case of its moderating effect on the persuasive impact of source cues. *Journal of Consumer Research, 18*, 52–62.

Read, J.D. (1995). The availability heuristic in person identification—the sometimes misleading consequences of enhanced contextual information. *Applied Cognitive Psychology, 9*, 91–121.

Read, J.D. (1997). Memory issues in the diagnosis of unreported trauma. In J.D. Read & D.S. Lindsay (eds), *Recollections of trauma: Scientific evidence and clinical practice*. New York: Plenum.

Read, J.D. (2000). The recovered/false memory debate: Three steps forward and two steps back. *Expert Evidence, 7*, 1–24.

Read, J.D. (2001). Introduction to the special issue: Trauma, stress and autobiographical memory. *Applied Cognitive Psychology, 15*, 1–7.

Read, J.D. & Lindsay, D.S. (2000). Amnesia for summer camps and high school graduation: memory work increases reports of prior periods of remembering less. *Journal of Traumatic Stress, 13*, 129–147.

Read, J.D., Lindsay, D.S. & Nichols, T. (1998). The relationship between confidence and accuracy in eyewitness identification studies: Is the conclusion changing? In C.P. Thompson, D.J. Hermann, D.J. Read, D. Bruce, D. Payne & M. Toglia (eds), *Eyewitness memory: Theoretical and applied perspectives* (pp. 107–130), Hillsdale, NJ: Erlbaum.

Reid, J.E. & Inbau, F.E. (1977). *Truth and deception: The polygraph (lie detector) technique*. Baltimore, MD: Williams & Wilkins.

Reifman, A., Gusick, S.M. & Ellsworth, P.C. (1992). Real jurors' understanding of law in real cases. *Law and Human Behavior, 16*, 539–554.

Reis, H.T., Senchak, M. & Solomon, B. (1985). Sex differences in the intimacy of social interaction: Further examination of potential explanations. *Journal of Personality and Social Psychology, 48*, 1204–1217.

Reisberg, D., Heuer, F. & Laney, C. (2000). Memory and emotion: Comparing memory for visually arousing and thematic events. Paper presented at the Annual Meeting of the Psychonomic Society, New Orleans, November 2000.

Reverie, S.L. & Bakeman, R. (2001). The effects of early trauma on autobiographical memory and schematic self-representation. *Applied Cognitive Psychology, 15*, 89–100.

Reyna, V., Holliday, R. & Marche, T. (2002). Explaining the development of false memories. *Developmental Review, 22*, 436–489.

Ricci, C., Beal, B. & Dekle, D. (1996). The effect of parent versus unfamiliar interviewers on children's eyewitness memory. *Law and Human Behavior, 20*, 483–500.

Ricci, C., Pacifico, J. & Katz, S. (1997). Effect of interview setting and questioning techniques on children's eyewitness memory and identification accuracy. Poster presented at the Biennial Meeting of the Society for Research in Child Development, Washington, DC.

Roberts, K. (2002). Children's ability to distinguish between memories from multiple sources: Implications for the quality and accuracy of eyewitness statements. *Developmental Review, 22*, 403–435.

Roberts, K.P. & Blades, M. (1998). The effects of interacting with events on children's eyewitness memory and source monitoring. *Applied Cognitive Psychology, 12*, 489–503.

Robertson, G., Pearson, R. & Gibb, R. (1996). Police interviewing and the use of appropriate adults. *Journal of Forensic Psychiatry, 2*, 297–309.

Robinson, W.P., Shepherd, A. & Heywood, J. (1998). Truth, equivocation/concealment, and lies in job applications and doctor–patient communication. *Journal of Language and Social Psychology, 17,* 149–164.

Robson, C. (2002). *Real world research* (2nd edn). Oxford: Blackwell.

Rosenthal, R. (1976). *Experimenter effects in behavioral research.* New York: Irvington.

Rosenthal, R. (2002). Suggestibility, reliability and the legal process. *Developmental Review, 22,* 334–369.

Ross, D.F., Read, J.D. & Toglia, M.P. (1994). *Adult eyewitness testimony: Current trends and developments.* Cambridge: Cambridge University Press.

Ross, L. (1977). The intuitive psychologist and his shortcomings: Distributions in the attribution process. In L. Berkowitz (ed.), *Advances in experimental social psychology,* vol. 10 (pp. 174–221). New York: Academic Press.

Ross, M. (1997). Validating memories. In N.L. Stein, P.A. Ornstein, B. Tversky & C. Brainerd (eds), *Memory for everyday and emotional events* (pp. 49–82). Hillsdale, NJ: Erlbaum.

Ross, M. (1989). Relation of implicit theories to the construction of personal histories. *Psychological Review, 96,* 341–357.

Rowatt, W.C., Cunningham, M.R. & Druen, P.B. (1998). Deception to get a date. *Personality and Social Psychology Bulletin, 24,* 1228–1242.

Ruby, C.L. & Brigham, J.C. (1997). The usefulness of the criteria-based content analysis technique in distinguishing between truthful and fabricated allegations. *Psychology, Public Policy, and Law, 3,* 705–737.

Ruby, C.L. & Brigham, J.C. (1998). Can criteria-based content analysis distinguish between true and false statements of African-American speakers? *Law and Human Behavior, 22,* 369–388.

Rudy, L. & Goodman, G. (1991). Effects of participation on children's reports: Implications for children's testimony. *Developmental Psychology, 27,* 527–538.

Ruva, C. & Bryant, B. (submitted). *The impact of age, speech style, and questions form on perceptions of witness credibility and trial outcome.*

Saladin, M., Saper, Z. & Breen, L. (1988). Perceived attractiveness and attributions of criminality: What is beautiful is not criminal. *Canadian Journal of Criminology, 30,* 251–259.

Salmon, K. & Irvine, P. (2002). Photograph reminders and young children's event reports: The influence of timing. *Legal and Criminological Psychology, 1,* 173–186.

Salmon, K. & Pipe, M.-E. (1997). Props and children's event reports: The impact of a 1-year delay. *Journal of Experimental Child Psychology, 65,* 261–292.

Santtila, P., Alkiora, P., Ekholm, M. & Niemi, P. (1999). False confession to robbery: The roles of suggestibility, anxiety, memory disturbance and withdrawal symptoms. *Journal of Forensic Psychiatry, 10,* 399–415.

Santtila, P., Roppola, H., Runtti, M. & Niemi, P. (2000). Assessment of child witness statements using criteria-based content analysis (CBCA): The effects of age, verbal ability, and interviewer's emotional style. *Psychology, Crime, and Law, 6,* 159–179.

Saunders, J. & MacLeod, M.D. (2002). New evidence on the suggestibility of memory: The role of retrieval-induced forgetting in misinformation effects. *Journal of Experimental Psychology: Applied, 2,* 127–142.

Saxe, L. (1991). Science and the GKT polygraph: A theoretical critique. *Integrative Physiological and Behavioral Science, 26,* 223–231.

Saxe, L., Dougherty, D. & Cross, T. (1985). The validity of polygraph testing: Scientific analysis and public controversy. *American Psychologist, 40,* 355–366.

Saywitz, K. & Snyder, L. (1993). *Preparing children for the investigative and judicial process: Improving communication, memory and emotional resiliency.* Final report to the National Center on Child Abuse and Neglect.

Saywitz, K., Goodman, G., Nicolas, G. & Moan, S. (1989). Children's memories for a genital exam: Implications for child sexual abuse. Symposium presented at the Biennial Meeting of the Society for Research in Child Development, Kansas City, MO.

Saywitz, K., Snyder, L. & Nathanson, R. (1999). Facilitating the communicative competence of the child witness. *Applied Developmental Science, 3*, 58–68.

Schaaf, J., Alexander, K., Goodman, G., Ghetti, S., Edelstein, R. & Castelli, P. (2002). Children's eyewitness memory. In B. Bottoms, M. Kovera & B. McAuliff (eds), *Children, social science, and the law.* New York: Cambridge University Press.

Schacter, D.L. (1996). *Searching for memory: The brain, the mind and the past.* New York: Basic Books.

Schacter, D.L. & Scarry, E. (2000). *Memory, brain and belief.* Cambridge: Harvard University Press.

Scheck, B., Neufeld, P. & Dwyer, J. (2000). *Actual innocence: Five days to execution and other dispatches from the wrongly convicted.* New York: Doubleday.

Schooler, J. (1994). Cutting towards the core: the issues and evidence surrounding recovered accounts of sexual trauma. *Consciousness and Cognition, 3*, 452–469.

Schooler, J. & Eich, E. (2000). Memory for emotional events. In E. Tulving & F.I.M. Craik (eds), *The Oxford handbook of memory.* New York: Oxford University Press.

Schooler, J.W. & Engstler-Schooler, T.Y. (1990). Verbal overshadowing of visual memories: Some things are better left unsaid. *Cognitive Psychology, 22*, 36–71.

Schooler, J., Ambadar, Z. & Bendiksen, M.A. (1997). A cognitive corroborative case study approach for investigating discovered memories of sexual abuse. In J.D. Read & D.S. Lindsay (eds), *Recollections of trauma: Scientific research and clinical practice* (pp. 379–388). New York: Plenum.

Schooler, J.W., Gerhard, D. & Loftus, E.F. (1986). Qualities of the unreal. *Journal of Experimental Psychology: Learning, Memory and Cognition, 12*, 171–181.

Schuller, R.A. (1992). The impact of battered woman syndrome evidence on jury decision process. *Law and Human Behaviour, 16*, 597–620.

Schwartz-Kenny, B., Bottoms, B. & Goodman, S. (1996). Improving children's person identification. *Child Maltreatment, 1*, 121–133.

Scullin, M.H. & Ceci, S.J. (2001). A suggestibility scale for children. *Personality and Individual Differences, 30*, 843–856.

Scullin, M.H. & Hembrooke, H. (1998). Development and validation of a suggestibility scale for children. Paper presented at the meeting of the American Psychology-Law Society, Redondo Beach, California.

Sealy, A.P. & Cornish, W. (1973). Jurors and their verdicts. *Modern Law Review, 36*, 496–508.

Sear, L. & Stephenson, G.M. (1997). Interviewing skills and individual characteristics of police interrogations. In G.M. Stephenson & N.K. Clark (eds), *Procedures in criminal justice: Contemporary psychological issues* (pp. 27–34). Leicester: The British Psychological Society.

Sear, L. & Williamson, T. (1999). British and American interrogation strategies. In D. Canter & L. Alison (eds), *Interviewing and deception* (pp. 67–81). Dartmouth: Ashgate.

Searcy, J.H., Bartlett, J.C. & Memon, A. (1999). Age differences in accuracy and choosing in eyewitness identification and face recognition. *Memory and Cognition, 27*, 538–552.

Searcy, J., Bartlett, J.C. & Seipel, A. (2000). *Crime characteristics and lineup identification decisions.* Unpublished Manuscript.

Searcy, J.H., Bartlett, J.C. & Memon, A. (2000). Relationship of availability, lineup conditions and individual differences to false identification by young and older eyewitnesses. *Legal and Criminological Psychology, 5*, 219–236.

Searcy, J.H., Bartlett, J.C., Memon, A. & Swanson, K. (2001). Aging and lineup performance at long retention intervals: Effects of metamemory and context reinstatement. *Journal of Applied Psychology, 86*, 207–214.

Serketich, W. & Dumas, J. (1997). Adults' perceptions of the behaviour of competent and dysfunctional children based on the children's appearance. *Behaviour Modification, 21,* 457–469.

Shaffer, R.E. & Cozolino, L.J. (1992). Adults who report childhood ritualistic abuse. *Journal of Personality and Theology, 20,* 188–193.

Shanab, M. & Yahya, K. (1977). A behavioural study of obedience in children. *Journal of Personality and Social Psychology, 35,* 530–536.

Shapiro, P.N. & Penrod, S. (1986). Meta-analysis of facial identification studies. *Psychological Bulletin, 100,* 139–156.

Shaver, K. (1970). Defensive attribution: Effects of severity and relevance on the responsibility assigned for an accident. *Journal of Personality and Social Psychology, 14,* 101–113.

Shaw, J.S. & McClure, K.A. (1996). Repeated postevent questioning can lead to elevated levels of eyewitness confidence. *Law and Human Behavior, 20,* 629–654.

Shaw, J.S., III, Woythaler, K.A. & Zerr, T.K. (in press). Courtroom pressures can alter eyewitness confidence. *Psychology in the Courts: International Advances in Knowledge.*

Shepherd, E. (1996). *Becoming skilled.* London: Law Society.

Shepherd, J.W. & Ellis, H.D. (1996). Face recall: Methods and problems. In S.L. Sporer, R.S. Malpass & G. Köhnken (eds), *Psychological issues in eyewitness identification* (pp. 87–116). Mahwah, NJ: Erlbaum.

Shepherd, J.W., Ellis, H.D. & Davies, G.M. (1982). *Identification evidence.* Aberdeen: Aberdeen University Press.

Shepherd, J., Ellis, H., McMurran, M. & Davies, G. (1978). Effect of character attribution on photofit construction of a face. *European Journal of Social Psychology, 8,* 263–268.

Sherif, M. (1936). *The psychology of social norms.* New York: Harper & Row.

Shuy, R.W. (1998). *The language of confession, interrogation, and deception.* Thousand Oaks, CA: Sage.

Sigall, H. & Ostrove, N. (1975). Beautiful but dangerous: Effects of offender attractiveness and nature of crime on juridic judgement. *Journal of Personality and Social Psychology, 31,* 410-414.

Sigelman, C.K., Budd, E.C., Spanhel, C.L. & Schoenrock, C.J. (1981). When in doubt say yes: Acquiescence in interviews with mentally retarded persons. *Mental Retardation, 19,* 53–58.

Sigurdsson, J.F. & Gudjonsson, G.H. (1994). Alcohol and drug intoxication during police interrogation and the reasons why suspects confess to the police. *Addiction, 89,* 985–997.

Sigurdsson, J.F. & Gudjonsson, G.H. (1996). The relationship between types of claimed false confessions and the reasons why suspects confess to the police according to the Gudjonsson Confession Questionnaire (GCQ). *Legal and Criminological Psychology, 1,* 259–269.

Singh, K.K. & Gudjonsson, G.H. (1984). Interrogative suggestibility, delayed memory and self-concept. *Personality and Individual Differences, 20,* 321–329.

Skolnick, J.H. & Leo, R.A. (1992). Ethics of deceptive interrogation. In J.W. Bizzack (ed.), *Issues in policing: New perspectives* (pp. 75–95). Lexington, KY: Autumn House.

Slobogin, C. (2003). An empirically based comparison of American and European police investigative techniques. In P.J. van Koppen & S.D. Penrod (eds), *Adversarial versus inquisitorial justice: Psychological perspectives on criminal justice systems* (pp. 28–52). New York: Plenum.

Smith, S., McIntosh, W. & Bazzini, D. (1999). Are the beautiful good in Hollywood? An investigation of the beauty-and-goodness stereotype on film. *Basic and Applied Social Psychology, 21,* 69–80.

Smith, V.L. (1991). Prototypes in the courtroom: Lay representations of legal concepts. *Journal of Personality and Social Psychology, 61,* 857–872.

Smith, V.L. & Studebaker, C.A. (1996). What do you expect? The influence of people's prior knowledge of crime categories on fact-finding. *Law and Human Behavior, 20*, 517–532.

Softley, P. (1980). *Police interrogation: An observational study in four police stations*. London: HMSO.

Sommers, S. & Kassin, S. (2001). On the many impacts of inadmissible testimony: Selective compliance, need for cognition and the overcorrection bias. *Personality and Social Psychology Bulletin, 27*, 1368–1377.

Soukara, S., Bull, R. & Vrij, A. (2002). Police detectives' aims regarding their interviews with suspects: Any change at the turn of the millennium? *International Journal of Police Science and Management, 4*, 101–114.

Spanos, N.P. (1996). *Multiple identities and false memories: A sociocognitive perspective*. Washington, DC: American Psychological Association.

Spanos, N.P., Burgess, C.A., Burgess, M.F., Samuels, C. & Blois, W.O. (1999). Creating false memories of infancy with hypnotic and non-hypnotic procedures. *Applied Cognitive Psychology, 13*, 201–218.

Spiegel, D. & Cardena E. (1990). Dissociative mechanisms in posttraumatic stress disorder. In M.E. Wolf & A.D. Mosnaim (eds), *Posttraumatic stress disorder: Etiology, phenomenology, and treatment* (pp. 44–46), Washington, DC: American Psychiatric Press.

Spira, M., Chizen, J., Gerow, F. & Hardy, S. (1966). Plastic surgery in the Texas prison system. *British Journal of Plastic Surgery, 19*, 364–371.

Sporer, S.L. (1996). Describing others: Psychological issues. In S.L. Sporer, R.S. Malpass & G. Köhnken (eds), *Psychological issues in eyewitness identification* (pp. 53–86). Mahwah, NJ: Erlbaum.

Sporer, S.L., Köhnken, G. & Malpass, R.S. (1996). Introduction: 2000 years of mistaken identification. In S.L. Sporer, R.S. Malpass & G. Köhnken (eds), *Psychological issues in eyewitness identification* (pp. 1–6). Mahwah, NJ: Erlbaum.

Sporer, S.L., Malpass, R.S. & Köhnken, G. (1996). *Psychological issues in eyewitness identification*. Mahwah, NJ: Erlbaum.

Sporer, S.L., Penrod, S.D, Read, D. & Cutler, B.L. (1995). Choosing, confidence, and accuracy: A meta-analysis of the confidence–accuracy relation in eyewitness identification studies. *Psychological Bulletin, 118*, 315–327.

Steblay, N.M. (1992). A meta-analytic review of the weapon focus effect. *Law and Human Behavior, 16*, 413–424.

Steblay, N., Besirevic, J., Fulero, S. & Jiminez-Lorente, B. (1999). The effects of pre-trial publicity on juror verdicts: A meta-analytic review. *Law and Human Behavior, 23*, 219–235.

Steblay, N., Dysart, J., Fulero, S. & Lindsay, R.C.L. (2001). Eyewitness accuracy rates in sequential and simultaneous lineup presentations: A meta-analytic comparison. *Law and Human Behavior, 25*, 459–473.

Steller, M. (1989). Recent developments in statement analysis. In J.C. Yuille (ed.), *Credibility assessment* (pp. 135–154). Deventer, the Netherlands: Kluwer.

Steller, M. & Boychuk, T. (1992). Children as witnesses in sexual abuse cases: Investigative interview and assessment techniques. In H. Dent & R. Flin (eds), *Children as witnesses* (pp.47–73). New York: Wiley.

Steller, M. & Köhnken, G. (1989). Criteria-based content analysis. In D.C. Raskin (ed.), *Psychological methods in criminal investigation and evidence* (pp. 217–245). New York: Springer-Verlag.

Steller, M. & Wellershaus, P. (1996). Information enhancement and credibility assessment of child statements: The impact of the cognitive interview on criteria-based content analysis. In G. Davies, S. Lloyd-Bostock, M. McMurran & C. Wilson (eds), *Psychology, law, and criminal justice: International developments in research and practice* (pp. 118–127). Berlin: de Gruyter.

Stephens, M. & Becker, S. (1994). *Police force, police service: Care and control in Britain.* Basingstoke: Macmillan.

Stephenson, G.M. (1992). *The psychology of criminal justice.* Oxford: Blackwell.

Stephenson, G.M. & Moston, S. (1994). Police interrogation. *Psychology, Crime and Law, 1,* 151–157.

Stephenson, G.M., Clark, N.K. & Wade, G.S. (1986). Meetings make evidence: An experimental study of collaborative and individual recall of a simulated police investigation. *Journal of Personality and Social Psychology, 50,* 1113–1122.

Stewart, J. (1980). Defendant's attractiveness as a factor in the outcome of criminal trials: An observational study. *Journal of Applied Social Psychology, 10,* 348–361.

Stewart, J. (1985). Appearance and punishment: The attraction-leniency effect in the courtroom. *Journal of Social Psychology, 125,* 373–378.

Stinson, V., Devenport, J.L., Cutler, B.L. & Kravitz, D.A. (1996). How effective is the presence-of-counsel safeguard? Attorney perceptions of suggestiveness, fairness, and correctability of biased lineup procedures. *Journal of Applied Psychology, 81,* 64–75.

Stobbs, G. & Kebbell, R. (in press). Jurors' perceptions of witnesses with intellectual disabilities and the influence of expert evidence. *Journal of Applied Research in Intellectual Disabilities.*

Stockdale, J. (1993). *Management and supervision of police interviews.* Police Research Series, Paper No. 5. London: Home Office.

Strömwall, L.A. & Granhag, P.A. (2003). How to detect deception? Arresting the beliefs of police officers, prosecutors and judges. *Psychology, Crime, and Law, 9,* 9–36.

Studebaker, C.A., Robbennolt, J., Penrod, S., Pathak-Sharma, M., Groscup, J. & Devenport, J. (2002). Studying pretrial publicity effects: New methods for improving ecological validity and testing external validity. *Law and Human Behavior, 26,* 19–41.

Sutherland, R. & Hayne, H. (2001). Age-related changes in the misinformation effect. *Journal of Experimental Child Psychology, 79,* 388–404.

Tajfel, H. & Turner, J.C. (1986). The social identity theory of intergroup behaviour. In S. Worchel & W. Austin (eds), *Psychology of intergroup relations* (pp. 7–24). Chicago, IL: Nelson-Hall.

Taylor, R. & Vrij, A. (2000). The effects of varying stake and cognitive complexity on beliefs about the cues to deception. *International Journal of Police Science and Management, 3,* 111–124.

Taylor, T. & Hosch, H.M. (2002). *Jury decisions: An examination of jury verdicts for evidence of a similarity-leniency effect: An out-group punitiveness or a black-sheep effect.* Submitted.

Technical Working Group for Eyewitness Evidence (1999). *Eyewitness evidence: A guide for law enforcement.* Washington, DC: US Department of Justice, Office of Justice Programs.

Templeton, V. & Hunt, V. (1997). The effects of misleading information and level of authority of interviewer on children's witness memory. Poster presented at the Biennial Meeting of the Society for Research in Child Development, Washington, DC.

Thaman, S. (2000). Europe's new jury systems: The cases of Spain and Russia. In N. Vidmar (ed.), *World jury systems* (pp. 319–351). Oxford: Oxford University Press.

Thierry, K., Spence, M. & Memon, A. (2001). Before misinformation is encountered: Source monitoring decreases child witness suggestibility. *Journal of Cognition and Development, 2,* 1–26.

Thomas, G.C. (1996). Plain talk about the *Miranda* empirical debate: A "steady-state" theory of confessions. *UCLA Law Review, 43,* 939–959.

Thompson, C.P., Herrmann, D.J., Read, J.D., Bruce, D., Payne, D.G. & Toglia, M.P. (1998). *Eyewitness memory: Theoretical and applied perspectives.* Mahwah, NJ: Erlbaum.

Thompson, K. (1990). Refacing inmates: A critical appraisal of plastic surgery programs in prisons. *Criminal Justice and Behavior, 17,* 448–466.

Thorley, R. (1996). Criminality with respect to facial appearance. Unpublished B.Sc. Psychology final year research project report, Department of Psychology, University of Portsmouth.

Thornton, B. & Ryckman, R. (1983). The influence of a rape victim's physical attractiveness on observers' attributions of responsibility. *Human Relations, 36,* 549–562.

Thornton, G. (1939). The ability to judge crimes from photographs of criminals. *Journal of Abnormal and Social Psychology, 34,* 378–383.

Tobey, A. & Goodman, G. (1992). Children's eyewitness memory: Effect of participation and forensic context. *Child Abuse and Neglect, 16,* 807–821.

Tooke, W. & Camire, L. (1991). Patterns of deception in intersexual and intrasexual mating strategies. *Ethology and Sociobiology, 12,* 345–364.

Tulving, E. & Thomson, D.M. (1973). Encoding specificity and retrieval processes in episodic memory. *Psychological Review, 80,* 353–370.

Udry, R. & Eckland, B. (1984). Benefits of being attractive: Differential payoffs for men and women. *Psychological Reports, 54,* 47–56.

Ugwuegbu, D. (1979). Racial and evidential factors in juror attribution of legal responsibility. *Journal of Experimental Social Psychology, 15,* 133–146.

Underwager, R. & Wakefield, H. (1992). False confessions and police deception. *American Journal of Forensic Psychology, 10,* 49–66.

Undeutsch, U. (1984). Courtroom evaluation of eyewitness testimony. *International Review of Applied Psychology, 33,* 51–67.

United States v. *Sokolow* 109 S. Ct. 1581 (1989).

U.S. v. *Allsup,* 566 F 2d 68 9th Cir. (1997).

U.S. v. *McVeigh* , 918 F. Supp. 1467 (1996).

Van den Adel, H.M. (1997). *Handleiding verdachtenverhoor.* Den Haag: VUGA.

Van Knippenberg, A., Dijksterhuis, A. & Vermeulen, D. (1999). Judgement and memory of a criminal act: The effects of stereotypes and cognitive load. *European Journal of Social Psychology, 29,* 191–201.

Vidmar, N. (2002). Case studies of pre- and midtrial prejudice in criminal and civil litigation. *Law and Human Behavior, 26,* 73–105.

Vine, M., and Bull, R. (2003). Does facial attractiveness affect judgements of deception? Poster presented at the Annual Conference of the European Association of Psychology and Law, Edinburgh.

Vornik, L., Sharman, S.J. & Garry, M. (in press). The influence of accent on the misinformation effect. *Memory.*

Vrij, A. (1991). *Misverstanden tussen politie en allochtonen: Soci-aal-psychologische aspecten van verdacht zijn.* Amsterdam, the Netherlands: VU Uitge-verij.

Vrij, A. (1993). Credibility judgments of detectives: The impact of nonverbal behavior, social skills and physical characteristics on impression formation. *Journal of Social Psychology, 133,* 601–611.

Vrij, A. (1994). The impact of information and setting on detection of deception by police detectives. *Journal of Nonverbal Behavior, 18,* 117–137.

Vrij, A. (1995a). Behavioral correlates of deception in a simulated police interview. *Journal of Psychology: Interdisciplinary and Applied, 129,* 15–29.

Vrij, A. (1995b). The psychology of interrogations, confessions and testimony [book review]. *Criminal Justice Review, 20,* 99–101.

Vrij, A. (2000a). *Detecting lies and deceit: The psychology of lying and its implications for professional practice.* Chichester: Wiley.

Vrij, A. (2000b). Telling and detecting lies as a function of raising the stakes. In C.M. Breur, M.M. Kommer, J.F. Nijboer & J.M. Reintjes (eds), *New trends in criminal investigation and evidence II* (pp. 699–709). Antwerp: Intersentia.

Vrij, A. (2001). Implicit lie detection. *The Psychologist, 14,* 58–60.

Vrij, A. (2002). Telling and detecting lies. In N. Brace & H.L. Westcott (eds), *Applying Psychology* (pp. 179–241). Milton Keynes: Open University.

Vrij, A. (2003). "We will protect your wife and child, but only if you confess": Police interrogations in England and the Netherlands. In P.J. van Koppen & S.D. Penrod (eds), *Adversarial versus inquisitorial justice: Psychological perspectives on criminal justice systems* (pp. 57–79). New York: Plenum.

Vrij, A. & Bush, N. (2000). Differences in suggestibility between 5–6 and 10–11-year-olds: The relationship with self-confidence. *Psychology, Crime and Law, 6,* 127–138.

Vrij, A. & Firmin, H. (2001). Beautiful thus innocent? The impact of defendants' and victims' physical attractiveness and participants' rape beliefs on impressions formation in alleged rape cases. *International Review of Victimology, 8,* 245–255.

Vrij, A. & Graham, S. (1997). Individual differences between liars and the ability to detect lies. *Expert Evidence: The International Digest of Human Behaviour Science and Law, 5,* 144–148.

Vrij, A. & Lochun, S.K. (1997). Neuro-linguistic programming and the police: Worthwhile or not? *Journal of Police and Criminal Psychology, 12,* 25–31.

Vrij, A. & Mann, S. (2001a). Lying when the stakes are high: Deceptive behavior of a murderer during his police interview. *Applied Cognitive Psychology, 15,* 187–203.

Vrij, A. & Mann, S. (2001b). Who killed my relative? Police officers' ability to detect real-life high-stake lies. *Psychology, Crime, and Law, 7,* 119–132.

Vrij, A. & Semin, G.R. (1996). Lie experts' beliefs about nonverbal indicators of deception. *Journal of Nonverbal Behavior, 20,* 65–80.

Vrij, A. & Taylor, R. (2003). Police officers' and students' beliefs about telling and detecting little and serious lies. *International Journal of Police Science and Management, 5,* 1–9.

Vrij, A. & Winkel, F.W. (1991). Cultural patterns in Dutch and Surinam nonverbal behavior: An analysis of simulated police/citizen encounters. *Journal of Nonverbal Behavior, 15,* 169–184.

Vrij, A. & Winkel, F.W. (1992). Crosscultural police–citizen interactions: The influence of race, beliefs and nonverbal communication on impression formation. *Journal of Applied Social Psychology, 22,* 1546–1559.

Vrij, A. & Winkel, F.W. (1994). Perceptual distortions in cross-cultural interrogations: The impact of skin color, accent, speech style and spoken fluency on impression formation. *Journal of Cross-Cultural Psychology, 25,* 284–296.

Vrij, A., Akehurst, L., Soukara, S. & Bull, R. (2002). Will the truth come out? The effect of deception, age, status, coaching, and social skills on CBCA scores. *Law and Human Behavior, 26,* 261–283.

Vrij, A., Akehurst, L., Soukara, R. & Bull, R. (in press). Detecting deceit via analyses of verbal and nonverbal behavior in adults and children. *Human Communication Research.*

Vrij, A., Dragt, A.W. & Koppelaar, L. (1992). Interviews with ethnic interviewees: Nonverbal communication errors in impression formation. *Journal of Community and Applied Social Psychology, 2,* 199–209.

Vrij, A., Edward, K. & Bull, R. (2001a). People's insight into their own behaviour and speech content while lying. *British Journal of Psychology, 92,* 373–389.

Vrij, A., Edward, K. & Bull, R. (2001b). Police officers' ability to detect deceit: The benefit of indirect deception measures. *Legal and Criminological Psychology, 6,* 185–196.

Vrij, A., Edward, K. & Bull, R. (2001c). Stereotypical verbal and nonverbal responses while deceiving others. *Personality and Social Psychology Bulletin, 27,* 899–909.

Vrij, A., Edward, K., Roberts, K.P. & Bull, R. (2000). Detecting deceit via analysis of verbal and nonverbal behavior. *Journal of Nonverbal Behavior, 24,* 239–263.

Vrij, A., Harden, F., Terry, J., Edward, K. & Bull, R. (2001). The influence of personal characteristics, stakes and lie complexity on the accuracy and confidence to detect deceit. In R. Roesch, R.R. Corrado & R.J. Dempster (eds), *Psychology in the courts: International advances in knowledge* (pp. 289–304). London: Routledge.

Vrij, A., Kneller, W. & Mann, S. (2000). The effect of informing liars about criteria-based content analysis on their ability to deceive CBCA-raters. *Legal and Criminological Psychology*, 5, 57–70.

Vrij, A., Nunkoosing, K., Paterson, B., Oosterwegel, A. & Soukara, R. (2002). Characteristics of secrets and the frequency, reasons and effects of secrets keeping and disclosure. *Journal of Community and Applied Social Psychology*, 12, 56–70.

Vrij, A., Semin, G.R. & Bull, R. (1996). Insight in behavior displayed during deception. *Human Communication Research*, 22, 544–562.

Vrij, A., Winkel, F.W. & Koppelaar, L. (1991). Interactie tussen politiefunctionarissen en allochtone burgers: twee studies naar de frequentie en het effect van aan en wegkijken op de impressie-formatie. *Nederlands Tijdschrift voor de Psychologie*, 46, 8–20.

Wade, K.A., Garry, A., Read, J.D. & Lindsay, D.S. (2002). A picture is worth a thousand lies: Using false photographs to create false childhood memories. *Psychonomic Bulletin and Review*, 9, 597–603.

Wagenaar, W.A. (1988). *Identifying Ivan*. Cambridge, MA: Harvard University Press.

Wagenaar, W.A. & Loftus, E.F. (1991). Tien identificaties door ooggetuigen: Logische en procedurele problemen. In P.J. van Koppen & H.F.M. Crombag (eds), *Psychologie voor Juristen* (pp. 175–208). Arnhem, the Netherlands: Gouda Quint.

Wagenaar, W.A., van Koppen, P.J. & Crombag, H.F.M. (1993). *Anchored narratives: The psychology of criminal evidence*. London: Harvester Wheatsheaf.

Wakefield, H. & Underwager, R. (1998). Coerced or nonvoluntary confessions. *Behavioral Sciences and the Law*, 16, 423–440.

Walkley, J. (1987). *Police interrogation: A handbook for investigators*. London: Police Review Publication.

Wallbott, H.G. & Scherer, K.R. (1991). Stress specifics: Differential effects of coping style, gender, and type of stressor on automatic arousal, facial expression, and subjective feeling. *Journal of Personality and Social Psychology*, 61, 147–156.

Warren, A., Hulse-Trotter, K. & Tubbs, E. (1991). Inducing resistance to suggestibility in children. *Law and Human Behavior*, 15, 273–285.

Warren, A., Woodall, C., Thomas, M., et al. (1999). Assessing the effectiveness of a training program for interviewing child witnesses. *Applied Developmental Science*, 3, 128–135.

Wartna, B., Beijers, G. & Essers, A. (1999). Ontkennende verdachten: Hoe vaak komt het voor? *Tijdschrift voor de Politie*, 61, 20–23.

Weber, N. & Brewer, N. (in press). The effect of judgment type and confidence scale on confidence–accuracy calibration. *Journal of Applied Psychology*.

Wegner, D.M. & Erber, R. (1992). The hyperaccessibility of suppressed thoughts. *Journal of Personality and Social Psychology*, 63, 903–912.

Wegner, D.M., Schneider, D.J., Carter, S., III & White, L. (1987). Paradoxical effects of thought suppression. *Journal of Personality and Social Psychology*, 58, 409–418.

Wells, G.L. (1978). Applied eyewitness-testimony research: System variables and estimator variables. *Journal of Personality and Social Psychology*, 36, 1546–1557.

Wells, G.L. (1993). What do we know about eyewitness identification? *American Psychologist*, 48, 553–571.

Wells, G.L. & Bradfield, A.L. (1998). "Good, you identified the suspect": Feedback to eyewitnesses distorts their reports of the witnessing experience. *Journal of Applied Psychology*, 83, 360–376.

Wells, G.L. & Luus, C.E. (1990). Police lineups as experiments: Social methodology as a framework for properly conducted lineups. *Personality and Social Psychology Bulletin, 16*, 106–117.

Wells, G.L. & Seelau, E.P. (1995). Eyewitness identification: Psychological research and legal policy on lineups. *Psychology, Public Policy and Law, 1*, 765–791.

Wells, G.L., Ferguson, T.J. & Lindsay, R.C.L. (1981). The tractability of eyewitness confidence and its implications for triers of fact. *Journal of Applied Psychology, 66*, 688–696.

Wells, G.L., Malpass, R.S., Lindsay, R.C.L., Fisher, R.P., Turtle, J.W. & Fulero, S.M. (2000). From the lab to the station: A successful application of eyewitness research. *American Psychologist, 55*, 581–598.

Wells, G.L., Seelau, E.P., Rydell, S.M. & Luus, C.A.E. (1994). Recommendations for properly conduced lineup identification tasks. In D.F. Ross, J.D. Read & M.P. Toglia (eds), *Adult eyewitness testimony: Current trends and developments* (pp. 223–244). New York: Cambridge University Press.

Wells, G.L., Small, L., Penrod, S., Malpass, R.S., Fulero, S.M. & Brimacombe, C.A.E. (1998). Eyewitness identification procedures: Recommendations for lineups and photospreads. *Law and Human Behavior, 22*, 603–647.

Westcott, H. & Brace, N. (2002). Psychological factors in witness evidence and identification. In N. Brace & H. Westcott (eds), *Applying Psychology* (pp. 117–178). Milton Keynes: Open University.

Westcott, H. & Jones, D. (1999). Annotation: The abuse of disabled children. *Journal of Child Psychology and Psychiatry, 40*, 497–506.

Westcott, H., Davies, G. & Bull, R. (2002). *Children's testimony: A Handbook of psychological research and forensic practice*. Chichester: Wiley.

Whalen, J.E. & Nash, M.R. (1996). Hypnosis and dissociation: Theoretical, empirical, and clinical perspectives. In L. Michelson & W. Ray (eds), *Handbook of dissociation: Theoretical, empirical, and clinical perspectives* (pp. 191–206). New York: Plenum.

Widom, C. (1997). Accuracy of adult recollections of early childhood abuse. In J.D. Read & D.S. Lindsay (eds), *Recollections of trauma: Scientific evidence and clinical practice* (pp. 49–78). New York: Plenum.

Wiener, R.L., Hurt, L., Thomas, S., Sadler, M., Bauer, C. & Sargent, T. (1998). The role of declarative and procedural and declarative knowledge in capital murder sentencing. *Journal of Applied Social Psychology, 28*, 124–144.

Wiener, R.L., Richmond, T.L., Hope, M., Shannon, M., Rauch, M. & Hackney, A. (2002). The psychology of telling murder stories: Do we think in scripts, exemplars or prototypes? *Behavioral Sciences and the Law, 20*, 119–139.

Wilcox, D.T. & Sosnowski, D. & Middleton, D. (2000). Polygraphy and sex offenders. *Forensic Update, 61*, 20–25.

Williams, L. (1994). Recall of childhood trauma: A prospective study of women's memories of child sexual abuse. *Journal of Consulting and Clinical Psychology, 62*, 1167–1176.

Williamson, T. (1993). From interrogation to investigative interviewing: Strategic trends in police questioning. *Journal of Community and Applied Social Psychology, 3*, 89–99.

Williamson, T. (1994). Reflections on current police practice. In D. Morgan & G.M. Stephenson (eds), *Suspicion and silence: The right to silence in criminal investigations*. London: Blackstone.

Wilson, D. & Donnerstein, E. (1977). Guilty or not guilty? A look at the "simulated" jury paradigm. *Journal of Applied Social Psychology, 7*, 175–190.

Wilson, T.D., Lindsey, S. & Schooler, T.Y. (2000). A model of dual attitudes. *Psychological Review, 107*, 101–126.

Winkel, F.W., Vrij, A., Koppelaar, L. & Van der Steen, J. (1991). Reducing secondary victimisation risks and skilled police intervention: Enhancing the quality of police–rape victim encounters through training programmes. *Journal of Police and Criminal Psychology, 7,* 2–11.

Winograd, E. & Killinger, W.A. Jr. (1983). Relating age at encoding in early childhood to adult recall: Development of flashbulb memories. *Journal of Experimental Psychology: General, 112,* 413–422.

Wiseman, R. (1995). The megalab truth test. *Nature, 373,* 391.

Woodhead, M.M., Baddeley, A.D. & Simmonds, D.C. (1979). On training people to recognize faces. *Ergonomics, 22,* 333–343.

Wright, D.B. & Livingston-Raper, D. (2001). Memory distortion and dissociation: Exploring the relationship in a non-clinical sample. *Journal of Trauma and Dissociation, 3,* 97–109.

Wright, D.B. & Loftus, E.F. (1998). How misinformation alters memories. *Journal of Experimental Child Psychology, 71,* 155–164.

Wright, D.B. & Loftus, E.F. (1999). Measuring dissociation: Comparison of alternative forms of the dissociative experiences scale. *American Journal of Psychology, 112,* 497–519.

Wright, D.B. & Stroud, J.N. (2002). Age differences in lineup identification accuracy: People are better with their own age. *Law and Human Behavior, 26,* 641–654.

Wright, D.B., Boyd, C.E. & Tredoux, C.G. (2001). A field study of own-race bias in South Africa and England. *Psychology, Public Policy, and Law, 7,* 119–133.

Wright, D.B., Loftus, E.F. & Hall, M. (2001). Now you see it; now you don't: Inhibiting recall and recognition of scenes. *Applied Cognitive Psychology, 15,* 471–482.

Wright, L. (1994). *Remembering Satan.* New York: Knopf.

Wrightsman, L., Nietzel, M. & Fortune, W. (1998). *Psychology and the legal system.* Pacific Grove, CA: Brooks/Cole.

Wuensch, K., Castellow, W. & Moore, C. (1991). Effects of defendant attractiveness and type of crime on juridic judgement. *Social Behaviour and Personality, 6,* 713–724.

Yarmey, A.D. (1982). Eyewitness identification and stereotypes of criminals. In A. Trankell (ed.), *Reconstructing the past: The role of psychologists in criminal trials* (pp. 205–225). Stockholm: Norstedt.

Yarmey, A.D. (1993a). Adult age and gender differences in eyewitness recall in field settings. *Journal of Applied Social Psychology, 23,* 1921–1932.

Yarmey, A.D. (1993b). Stereotypes and recognition memory for faces and voices of good guys and bad guys. *Applied Cognitive Psychology, 7,* 419–431.

Yarmey, A.D. & Kruschenske, S. (1995). Facial stereotypes of battered women and battered women who kill. *Journal of Applied Social Psychology, 25,* 338–352.

Yarmey, A.D., Yarmey, M.J. & Yarmey, A.L. (1996). Accuracy of eyewitness identifications in showups and lineups. *Law and Human Behavior, 20,* 459–477.

Ybarra, O. (2002). Naïve causal understanding of valenced behaviors and its implications for social information processing. *Psychological Bulletin, 128,* 421–441.

Young, K., Powell, M. & Dudgeon, P. (2003, in press). Individual differences in children's suggestibility: A comparison between intellectually disabled and mainstream samples. *Personality and Individual Differences.*

Young, W., Cameron, N. & Tinsley, Y. (1999). *Juries in criminal trials,* Law Commission, Preliminary Paper no. 37. New Zealand.

Yuille, J.C. (1988). The systematic assessment of children's testimony. *Canadian Psychology, 29,* 247–262.

Yuille, J.C. (1993). We must study forensic eyewitnesses to know about them. *American Psychologist, 48,* 572–573.

Zajac, R. & Hayne, H. (2000). Questioning children in court. Poster presented at the Biennial Convention of the American Psychology-Law Society, New Orleans.

Zebrowitz, L. & McDonald, S. (1991). The impact of litigants' baby-facedness and attractiveness on adjudications in small claims courts. *Law and Human Behavior, 15,* 603–623.

Zebrowitz, L., Andreoletti, C., Collins, M., Lee, S. and Blumenthal, J. (1998a). Bright, bad, babyfaced boys: Appearance stereotypes do not always yield self-fulfilling prophecy effects. *Journal of Personality and Social Psychology, 75,* 1300–1320.

Zebrowitz, L., Collins, M. & Dutta, R. (1998). The relationship between appearance and personality across the lifespan. *Personality and Social Psychology Bulletin, 24,* 736–749.

Zuckerman, M., DePaulo, B.M. & Rosenthal, R. (1981). Verbal and nonverbal communication of deception. In L. Berkowitz (ed.), *Advances in experimental social psychology,* vol. 14 (pp. 1–57). New York: Academic Press.

INDEX

Lightning Source UK Ltd.
Milton Keynes UK
21 August 2010

158752UK00001B/14/P